Dying to be One

David Butler

Dying to be One

English Ecumenism: History, Theology and the Future

SCM PRESS LTD

0 334 02654 7

First published in Britain 1996
by SCM Press Ltd
9–17 St Albans Place, London N 1 0NX

Typeset at The Spartan Press Ltd
Lymington, Hants
and printed in Great Britain by
Biddles Ltd, Guildford and King's Lynn

Contents

Preface

The debts that I owe to so many people for their contributions to this book will be obvious from the introduction, but my thanks go especially to those who were concerned in the process of its immediate preparation. First my thanks go to Fionna, Michael and Jonathan, who did not complain while I spent a sabbatical term last summer reading and writing at home. Secondly I owe a large debt to Joanna Vials who typed the chapters from some very badly written originals with many corrections on the pages. The dedication is to the staffs and students of the two ministerial training colleges in Birmingham, St Mary's Oscott and The Queen's College. Without their encouragement and dialogue this book would not have been written.

David Butler

Introduction

This book has come about because of a consuming interest in the ecumenical movement in England over a period of years. The interest began in Coventry where I was brought up and where ecumenism was high on the agenda of the Methodist Central Hall of which I was a member. I recall many occasions when we had preachers from other churches in our pulpit. I think it was on Tuesdays that a group of us from school, from several different churches, used to go to lunchtime ecumenical services in the Chapel of the Cross in the newly constructed crypt of Basil Spence's cathedral. The Methodist Society at Hinde Street in London in the early sixties provided a context which had university students like myself thinking in widely ecumenical terms. We had regular conversations with both Anglican and Roman Catholic students during my years there, and these contacts were increased at the Leicester ecumenical youth conference in 1962. Three years followed for me in Sierra Leone where I taught and experienced a context where denominational labels mattered little. Where Christians were a minority, even if a significant minority, Christians had to do a lot more things together than they did in England. There was for example a Roman Catholic ordination at which ministers of other churches were asked to lay on hands.

Two years of theology at Wesley House in Cambridge gave me a fuller idea of why the churches differed from one another. But it was a year of study in Rome that enabled me to see another church close up and perhaps to see that church at its best and at its worst. Gibbon's remark about the church clearly being of divine origin because of the corruption in it once or twice seemed close to the truth. But so too did C. S. Lewis' remark that while Protestants had got a lot of people to an 'O' level grade in the spiritual life, the

Catholics seemed to have got a lot more to 'A' level.

When I began to minister to the Methodist people, it was not long before I recognized that 'we' were 'chapel' people, while 'they' were 'church' people. The Anglicans were different from Methodists not primarily because of their beliefs but because they came from a different social group. That was an old-fashioned view but it still existed in 1969. At the school where I was the chaplain most of the girls were not Methodists but were Anglicans and each year we had a joint confirmation for both sets of candidates at which the diocesan bishop and the Methodist chairman both laid on hands. It was during this first ministry that I felt the inadequacy of my preaching during the Week of Prayer for Christian Unity. It seemed to me then that to base all on John 17.21, Jesus' prayer that they may all be one, while extremely relevant, was a little thin. So chapter 3 of this book probably began with my first anxiety about John 17.21 but it also owes a great deal to the friendly atmosphere created in our village by the local incumbent, Edmund Haviland. He always tried to make me see that the unity movement demanded prayer, persistence and humility.

My next appointment was in a large suburb of London where I had two churches. When the local Council of Churches failed to get a door-to-door mission off the ground, a group of local churches came together to create a Local Ecumenical Project. Initially we were the Anglicans, Methodists and URCs, but later another Anglican church and the Roman Catholics joined the project. We learned a great deal about local ecumenism in our life together, particularly how to do it when all the churches were comparatively successful and were not in the state, as a colleague put it, of being like two drunks who have to remain standing to support each other. Ecumenism looks different from a position of strength. During this period in South London I became the Methodist District ecumenical secretary and discovered a great deal about local ecumenism, its successes and failures. Twice I had the task of inspecting LEPs along with an Anglican colleague. One of these was a village cause where Anglicans and Methodists had recognized that the sharing of a building was the most obvious way forward. The other situation was where a new housing development had made the Anglicans sit down with the Methodists from day one and plan two joint church centres. This period as an ecumenical secretary saw the beginning of a new way of working in our district by means of a sponsoring body of church representatives. This body is now called an ecumenical council and deals with far more than local ecumenical partnerships, but at the time of its birth it gave the opportunity for us to see local ecumenism as a whole, and one remembers it to have been a very encouraging period.

After South London the opportunity came for the family to move to Kenya where I had the responsibility of teaching church history to East Africans who were training for the ministries of the Anglican, Presbyterian, Methodist and Reformed churches. It was gratifying that, after I had spent a year teaching mainly European history, the new syllabus demanded a great deal more African church history. This meant that early Christianity in North Africa as well as in Ethiopia, Egypt and Nubia had to be looked at. The themes of Donatism and Monophysitism, as well as the insights of African traditions, had quite an impact on my eurocentric view of the church. When we had to look at the missionary movements in the nineteenth and twentieth centuries, the comity agreements between various missionary societies clearly indicated that unity was seen as a need rather earlier in Africa than it was in Europe. The later stories of the unity attempts in both East Africa and in Nigeria showed why the Church of South India union in 1947 would be the exception rather than the rule, but the attempts in Africa showed that unity would never be a simple process.

After Kenya we returned to a suburban church in South West London that was shared with the local Anglicans. Suddenly the ecumenical agenda was about the implications of the Sharing of Church Buildings Act that had been passed by Parliament in 1969. Would Anglicans be able to do in a Methodist building what they had done in their own building? The Act seemed to imply that fish and chip suppers with beer had to be possible even in premises where alcohol had been forbidden under a Model Trust Deed. On my return to England I was made the chairman of the British Methodist Ecumenical Committee of which Jennifer Carpenter was the indefatigable secretary. Jenny taught me a great deal about practical ecumenism and I shall always be grateful for what she gave me of her expertise and experience. During this time I also served on the

British Council of Churches and was able to take a part in the events that led up to Swanwick 1987. These were heady times to be involved in ecumenism. Part of my ecumenical work since 1984 had been to convene the British Roman Catholic-Methodist Committee, and this has taken a large slice of my time ever since. The colleagueship of my co-conveners on the Roman Catholic side, first Dennis Corbishley, then Michael Jackson and now Sean Healy, has been of the highest order and they have each in turn shown a wonderful commitment to the ecumenical task. We have been graced with a wonderful committee and have been very ably chaired, first by Bishop Charles Henderson and Revd Raymond George, and now by Bishop Leo McCartie and Revd Dr Richard Jones. From 1987 till 1991 I also took part in the international Roman Catholic-Methodist dialogue that produced the Singapore Report, *The Apostolic Tradition.*[1]

Since 1987 I have taught at The Queen's College, Birmingham, still the only fully ecumenical theological college in Britain. Sharing the worship tradition of three denominations, Anglican, Methodist and United Reformed, week by week has not always been easy and occasionally one still finds students that want to slip back into 'our' way of doing things. But one has to remember that there is no longer an 'our' way of doing things but a rich cross-section of traditions even within each denomination. When we share our life with Roman Catholic students from St Mary's Oscott, the spectrum of traditions becomes even wider and we are able to see what a true catholicity of expression could mean. When my wife, Fionna, herself became a Roman Catholic in 1993 we suddenly found ourselves an inter-church family. Within a few weeks Martin and Ruth Reardon had us enrolled as members of the Association of Interchurch Families and at the next annual general meeting of the Association I became the Free Church chairperson, alongside Martin Reardon (Church of England) and John Coventry (Roman Catholic).

The reader will notice that a lot of this book is autobiographical and will understand why. Perhaps one can only be committed to the ecumenical process in England if one is deeply involved in it. During my ministry it has affected almost every level of my involvement with the churches; pastoral work, preaching, marriage, the eucharist, evangelism, ministerial training, spirituality, and even church buildings. In his recent encyclical on ecumenism, *Ut Unum Sint*, Pope John Paul II asks all of us to see that ecumenism is not some sort of optional extra for the church, a sort of add-on to her traditional activity. 'Rather, ecumenism is an organic part of her life and work, and consequently must pervade all that she is and does . . .' (20). That which unites us is indeed far greater than that which divides us. This book is a plea that the ecumenical task should remain part of the agenda of all the English churches, a hope that we may be 'dying to be one'.

Was the Church United in New Testament Times?

The minister of a large suburban church decided that it would be good for his congregation to have a series on what the early church was really like. By this means he hoped to give the church members some energy that at times seemed to be lacking. He chose to picture the early church from the Acts of the Apostles. It was a church where converts were made, where all were faithful to the teaching of the apostles, kept the fellowship and continued to pray and break bread together. Signs and miracles were frequent and the early Christians even shared things in common so that nobody was ever in need (Acts 2.41–45). This was the picture the minister wanted to convey as the general picture of the early church. But as he read more carefully in the Acts and New Testament generally he began to realize that the rosy picture just would not do.

The early community included Ananias and Sapphira who proved to be fraudulent (Acts 5.1–11); it managed to make a distinction between Jewish widows and Greek widows to the disadvantage of the Greeks (Acts 6.1); Simon, the converted magician in Samaria, after baptism tried to buy himself the power of the Holy Spirit and gave the name simony thereafter to all who attempted to buy offices in the church (Acts 8.9–24). Controversy raged over the admission of the Gentiles to the church and even Peter was carried back to the Jewish camp despite his experience with the centurion Cornelius (Acts 10; Acts 15; Gal. 2.11–14). Compromise also appears to have been often used in a way not all might feel now to be appropriate: Gentiles have to keep Jewish food regulations despite the freedom brought to them by Christ (Acts 15.29); Paul feels it necessary to have Timothy circumcised, despite his being a Greek (Acts 16.3); Paul agrees to

observe the Law while he is in Jerusalem, despite his letters where
freedom from the Law is the primary theme (Acts 21.21–26). The
leaders of this exemplary community thus look less than exemplary
in their behaviour and two of the leaders, Paul and Barnabas, have a
controversy over John Mark in Acts 15.36–39. The communities
themselves sometimes look less like the ideal when individuals
cannot listen to sermons without literally dropping off (Acts 20.9). A
deficient theology of baptism is seen elsewhere where converts have
received only John's baptism (Acts 19.1–11) and the horror of
syncretism or the mixing of faiths arises when Christians combine
their belief with magical practices (Acts 19.18–19). While the more
catholic-minded of modern believers may find helpful both the
healing power of Peter's shadow (Acts 5.15) and the curative
properties of handkerchiefs that had touched Paul (Acts 19.12),
others will see the shadow of superstition polluting the purity of the
early church.

> So remarkable were the miracles worked by God at Paul's hands
> that handkerchiefs or aprons which had touched him were taken
> to the sick, and they were cured of their illnesses, and the evil
> spirits came out of them (Acts 19.11–12).

Thus the minister of the suburban church was forced to recognize
that the early church was not quite as united in faith, moral life and
church strategy as he had wanted to believe. That didn't mean that
he couldn't preach the intended sermon, but he was a little more
careful than he might have been.

Modern New Testament scholarship has recognized that the
documents that the first-century church has left us are something of
a mixture. The Gospels, for example, so long regarded as bio-
graphies of Jesus, written by those nearest to the apostles and
sometimes claimed to be totally historical, are now seen very
differently. In the earliest period, say for the first thirty years of
Christianity, all that circulated were oral traditions about Jesus so
that Jesus was known in the preaching, teaching and experience of
the early church but not in any documents. Possibly the deaths of the
two great apostles, Peter and Paul, in Rome in the Neronian
persecution of AD 64, gave some incentive to the early Christians to
put down in writing some of the traditions about Jesus which came

from the apostles. Many give Mark's Gospel the setting of Rome and its writing around AD65 for this reason. The other Gospels of Matthew and Luke almost certainly used Mark and interspersed extra material within the framework of Mark; in Matthew's case some five blocks of teaching, perhaps a parallel to the five books of the Jewish Law; in Luke's case Jesus' teaching in parables and other special emphases.

John's Gospel is so different that it seems to belong to a different style of writing. John is cavalier with the order of events as given in the other three Gospels (he puts the cleansing of the Temple at the beginning of Jesus' ministry for example; he also offers a different perspective and date for the crucifixion) and seems to have an entirely different perspective from the other three. All four Gospels indicate in their texts that their aim is to make new disciples of Jesus:

Go, therefore, and make disciples of all nations . . . (Matt. 28.19).

The beginning of the gospel about Jesus Christ, the Son of God (Mark 1.1).

I in my turn, after carefully going over the whole story from the beginning, have decided to make an ordered account for you, Theophilus, so that your Excellency may learn how well founded the teaching is that you have received (Luke 1.3–4).

These are recorded so that you may believe that Jesus is the Christ, the Son of God, and that believing this you may have life through his name (John 20.31).

Thus they are written from the viewpoint of the faith of the early Christians, even though that faith looks to be differently described for its different readers. Matthew seems to want to prove Jesus in some sense the fulfilment of the Jewish Law and so he makes his readers see the role of Jesus as the teacher of the new law by the use of his five teaching blocks (Matt. 5–7; 10; 13; 18; 23–25). Mark wants his readers to see in Jesus the Son of God and so emphasizes the nature miracles such as the feeding of the five thousand and the stilling of the storm (Mark 6.30–44; 8.1–10; 4.35–41). At the pivot point of the Gospel Simon Peter recognizes Jesus as the Christ of

God (Mark 8.27–30) and at the end of the Gospel the centurion at
the cross recognizes the Son of God (Mark 15.39). Luke shows
Jesus as the one who had compassion on the poor and the outcast,
showing too a special interest in women (Luke 1; 10.29–37; 13.10–
13; etc.). The Gospel comes as good news to very diverse people
(Luke 7.1–10; 7.36–50; 15.11–32; 16.19–31; 18.9–14; 19.1–10).
John's Gospel is written in such simple Greek that some believe that
it was done as a deliberately evangelical work. It opens with the idea
of the Logos, the Greek principle of reason, who became man (John
1.1–14). Simple words and concepts such as light, life, water, food
and bread, are packed with significance by the one who as Word
came among us. Thus the Gospels are very diverse documents
although they have their unity in Christ whom they proclaim from
their different standpoints. There is thus a Matthaean theology, a
Marcan theology, a Lucan theology and a Johannine theology to be
found in the first four books of the New Testament. Although some
writers, such as Tatian in the second century, have tried to
harmonize the four accounts, they still remain with all their
differences even though they each point to Christ.

The New Testament has always been regarded in every generation as the very bastion of Christian orthodoxy. Yet strangely it
contains competing theologies and enormous diversity in, for
example, its interpretation of Jesus, the ministry of the church, ways
of worship and even moral teaching. Christians have always
regarded the New Testament as being a whole and have lived quite
happily with it without really being concerned about its diversity.
Because the official books have been confirmed by the church (the
canon of scripture as it is called was probably finally confirmed at the
Council of Carthage in AD 397) then we are happy to live with the
diversity, without perhaps even noticing it.

The text from the Council of Carthage in 397 comes from Canon
39 of the acts of the Council. It is offered in Latin since its meaning
will be clear. The books of the New Testament are:

Evangeliorum libri quattor.
Actuum Apostolorum liber unus.
Epistulae Pauli Apostoli xiii.
Eiusdem ad Hebreos una.

Petri apostoli duae.

Iohannis tres.

Iacobi i.

Iudae i.

Apocalypsis Iohannis liber unus.

All twenty seven of the books we know as the New Testament are here listed, though in a slightly different order. The placing of Hebrews after the thirteen of Paul indicates doubt in North Africa concerning Pauline authorship.

Since the time C. H. Dodd wrote a book called *The Apostolic Preaching and its Developments* in 1936 a core of orthodox Christian proclamation or *kerygma* has been noticed which is common to all the strata of the New Testament:

1. *The proclamation of Christ as risen.* This is expressed differently in different places; for some authors it means one thing, for others quite another. For example, in John the Easter belief sheds its light over the whole of John's work, while in Paul Easter means that Christ's lordship extends over all of creation. But, however stated, the Jesus who was once crucified has been raised and is now alive.

2. *Call for human beings to put their faith in Jesus Christ.* While this call is not part of the original message of Jesus whose proclamation was of the Kingdom of God, it is clear that even the gospel writers make this plea for faith in their works as was indicated above. The original ending of the Gospel of John puts it: 'These are recorded so that you may believe that Jesus is the Christ, the Son of God, and that believing this you may have life through his name' (John 20.31). It is perhaps worth mentioning that faith is at stake and not mere orthodoxy; right belief alone is not called for but a commitment to a personal relationship with Jesus Christ.

3. *The promise of the future offered to humanity in Christ*, sometimes expressed as forgiveness or salvation, life, or union with Christ. Sometimes this is drawn out to include the believer in the community of salvation, the church, where he or she is responsible for continuing the life of love and service within and outside the community.

Not one of these three aspects of the proclamation as indicated above will be found in any of the books of the New Testament. But these are the core elements of the *kerygma*. The impression is that the early church was able to accept that although authors might disagree on the details of the *kerygma*, nevertheless they would have agreed that the differences were acceptable and valid understandings of the Christian faith. If the good news worked then it was true.

It might help at this point to offer one or two examples from the New Testament of these differences in order to illustrate the point being made. The first Christians believed that the Jesus who had been born and had lived as a Jew was now an exalted being at the right hand of God. For Jewish readers it was important that Jesus was the Christ, the Messiah of Jewish expectation (see Acts 2.36; Matt. 6.16; John 1.14). For Jews brought up in a Hellenistic environment the discovery of Jesus as Son of God seems to have been the crucial point (see Matt. 14.43; Acts 9.20; Heb. 4.14). Gentiles would have resonated to the theme of Jesus as Lord, indeed Paul who was the great apostle of the Gentiles uses this term nearly 230 times in his letters (II Cor. 4.5; Col. 2.6; Rom. 10.9 are good examples).

That the New Testament has a diversity of concepts of ministry has been the source of problems at least since the time of the Reformation. Before that the usual tradition was to espouse the threefold order of bishop, presbyter and deacon first found together in the Letters of Ignatius of Antioch from the early second century, *c*.AD115. The Reformation sent some Christians back to the New Testament to see if the threefold order could in fact be found there. Calvin and Bucer found a different understanding in Eph. 4.11 where apostles and prophets are listed along with evangelists, pastors and teachers, no mention being made of bishops, presbyters or deacons. In the pages of the New Testament the ministry of James in Jerusalem seems to have been one of dominance with a body of elders gathered around him after the pattern of synagogue government (see Acts 15.2; 15.13–22; 21.18). This pattern presumably arose because James had the authority of being the brother of Jesus, was one of the first witnesses of the resurrection (I Cor. 15.7), and was known for the blamelessness of his life. The Pauline churches on the other hand were more charismatic in their understanding of ministry. The gifts of the Spirit had been given out to each person and church members were to have different functions within the body of Christ (see Rom. 12; I Cor. 12; Eph. 4). Ministry belonged to all Christians and not just to a special few and each person depended for his or her Christian life on the diversity of ministries within each church community. When we turn to the Pastoral Letters, I and II Timothy, and Titus, we clearly move beyond the time of Paul, despite their ascription to Paul in some Bibles. Elders appear for the first time in 'Paul' (I Tim. 5.17–19; Titus 1.5) while overseers or 'bishops' (I Tim. 3.1–7; Titus 1.7–9) and deacons (I Tim. 3.8–13) look as if they have the status of office holders in the church. Some time in the early second century the church took the decision to go in the direction of the Pastoral Letters and Ignatius in establishing the threefold order as the future of ministry in the church. That the New Testament period was one of some diversity should not however be forgotten when ecumenical dialogues take place.

It would be tedious to list all the possible examples of diversity in the New Testament, but two final ones may be helpful. First, there is the diversity in the descriptions of Jesus. It is clear from what was said above that the early Christians believed Jesus to be Messiah (especially if they were of Jewish origin), to be Son of God (this was held in the Hellenistic Jewish context) and to be the Lord (Gentiles seem to have preferred to use this title). This shows that differing understandings of the person of Christ, different christologies, were abroad in the earliest churches. The role of Christ as the miracle worker, the 'divine man' concept, was important to some Hellenistic Christians (see for example Mark 4.35–5.43; Mark 6.31–56). For others the idea of Christ's pre-existence with the Father before time was important (see Heb. 1.14; John 1.1–14; Phil. 2.6–11). The dominant role of Christ as the one who sits at the right hand of God in heaven with ultimate authority dominated the christology of others (see especially the Letter to the Hebrews).

Second, there is a great deal of difference in New Testament worship. The diversity of worship styles in the early church might alarm later Christians who hopefully see their way of worship as being the norm that goes back to New Testament times. In the environs of Jerusalem the traditions of Temple worship at first remained (see Acts 2.46; 3.1; etc.) with commitment to the hours of prayer. Meetings in private houses were certainly also early, perhaps taking either the forms of synagogue worship or of fellowship meal (see Acts 2.46). After the death of Stephen some broke with the Temple, no doubt the Hellenists and not the Jews (Acts 7). Paul gives us a hint of the charismatic worship of the Gentile house churches, though he is anxious to ensure that speaking in tongues should not totally dominate worship (I Cor. 12.4–11; 14.1–25). In this century scholars have increasingly recognized the presence of hymns in the New Testament, some of which must certainly have been sung in the gatherings for Christian worship. Principal among these would have been the ones which probably belonged to the early Palestinian Christians and have been known for generations as the Magnificat, the Benedictus, and the Nunc Dimittis (Luke 1.46–55; 1.68–79; 2.29–32). Revelation also contains shouts of praise and doxologies to God and to the Lamb of God which perhaps derive from the Hellenistic Jewish-Christian groups (Rev. 4.8; 5.9–10; etc.) Early Christian hymns are also thought to be preserved in the famous passage in Phil. 2.6–11 where Christ's obedient servant role is celebrated, and in Col. 1.15–20 where Christ is hailed as the image of the invisible God, agent of creation and head of the church. Other passages said to be parts of Christian hymns are John 1.1–16, I Tim. 3.16 and Eph. 5.14. The diversity of interpretation in these early hymns shows that no one theology was felt to be 'orthodox' in its understanding of Jesus Christ. In so far as it is possible to be precise there seems to have been no established liturgical forms apart from the words of Jesus over the bread and wine at the Last Supper which are enshrined in I Cor. 11.23–25 and in the Gospels at Matt. 26.26–29, Mark 14.22–25 and Luke 22.17–20.

That the New Testament documents as they have come down to us show a massive diversity could be a surprise to many who might have preferred more cohesion and a more 'authoritative' New Testament. For those who are concerned with the unity of the church the model evidenced by the New Testament of 'unity in diversity' gives a sign of what a future model of organic unity would have to be.

> The New Testament canon does not, as such, constitute the foundation of the unity of the Church. On the contrary, as such . . ., it provides the basis for the multiplicity of the confessions.[1]

The question for the church after the new Testament period would very quickly become, 'What diversity is legitimate and what diversity is illegitimate?' To go too far along the path of diversity might be dangerous to the faith. Not all explanations of the Christian faith could be held. Some would make Jesus less than he was for Christian faith, others might deny his humanity. Heresies which arose would make diversity seem a lot less important than uniformity. The fact of heresy would make legitimate ministry vital and apostolic succession an important doctrine. Eventually church councils would have to make decisions about matters of faith. But the 'orthodoxy' of the New Testament looks a lot less rigid than later orthodoxy became.

2

What's Worth Keeping from the Early Church?

Everyone must have had an experience of going to a place where the twentieth century seems not yet to have arrived. For some it can be a wonderful experience – no noise, no radios, no television, no newspapers, no cars, no pneumatic drills. Probably such experiences are only now possible in places like monasteries where silence and contemplation are of importance. Yet sometimes such experiences are found in churches that don't seem to have moved for a long time. 'We've always done it this way,' they say. Of course it depends on what 'always' means. In the Church of England, 'we've always used the Book of Common Prayer' is really only since 1662; before that the Prayer Book was not permitted by the Commonwealth. In the Methodist Church, 'we've always used the Methodist Hymn Book' only dates from 1933 when that year the formerly disunited parts of Methodism began to use a new hymn book. In the Roman Catholic Church, 'we've always worshipped in Latin' is more nearly true, Latin having been the main language of the European church and national leaders but before the Liturgy of Trent was approved in 1563, there were several regional variations. When the Baptist Church claims 'we've always baptized believers and by full immersion', history actually shows that the original Baptists were baptized by sprinkling and that believer's baptism of those who had been 'baptized' in infancy began in the sixteenth century.

'Always' then is a relative term. What has the church 'always' had in its now nearly two thousand years? As far as we can be absolutely sure of anything, the following seem to have been 'always' there:

1. The scriptures of the Old and New Testaments, although initially there was some difference of opinion about what constitutes

scripture. Some argued (eg Marcion) that the Old Testament was not Christian, others that certain books did not deserve a place in the New Testament (chief among these were James, II and III John, Jude and Revelation).

2. A statement of the main points of the faith, sometimes called the 'canon of truth' or 'rule of faith'. Later these statements were the formulated official creeds of the church such as the Nicene and Apostles' Creeds.

3. An authorized ministry, usually claimed to have been left in place by the apostles themselves. By the middle of the second century this had become a threefold ministry of bishop or overseer, presbyter or priest, and deacon. Other more informal ministries seem to have died out by this period.

4. Places of worship owned by the Christians themselves in which worship and instruction took place. At first these would have been the houses of church members, house churches.

5. A sacramental life, specifically baptism as the means of entry into the church, and the eucharist as the regular celebration of the Last Supper of Christ. Baptism often took place on the evening of Easter at a solemn ceremony while the eucharist seems to have been celebrated at least weekly on Sunday, the Lord's Day.

6. A disciplined life. It was assumed that Christians would be those who aimed at the holiness without which no one would see the Lord (Heb. 12.14). Initially many avoided baptism until their death beds on the grounds that their baptism could be of no effect if they sinned after it was performed. Slowly a disciplined system of public repentance came into the life of the church so that sinners could be reconciled to the church.

'What can we keep from the early church?' thus became a question about which of these elements needs to be reaffirmed for the twentieth century. The first one, the place of the scriptures, is not a contentious issue although the interpretation of the scriptures will be given some space below.

The place of the official statements of the Christian faith is clearly an important one. We have now the Nicene Creed (formulated in 381 at Constantinople) and the Apostles' Creed (originally an early baptismal creed which reached its present form only in the eighth century). These creeds offer the bald outline of the Christian faith and theologians have in all centuries, including our own, given their own comments upon them.

A major task of the Faith and Order Commission of the World Council of Churches has been the exposition of the Nicene-Constantinople Creed of 381 'Confessing One Faith'. It is hoped that all churches will accept this Creed as an ecumenical explication of the Apostolic faith.[1]

Alongside these creeds go the work of the foremost theologies of the early church, usually called 'the Fathers'. Though there is no official list of these orthodox Fathers, nor is it absolutely clear when the period of the Fathers ends, there are several whose authority is head and shoulders above the others. These include Athanasius and John Chrysostom from the East and Ambrose and Augustine from the West. These four are represented in a sculpture of bronze by Bernini at St Peter's in Rome; surrounding the throne of St Peter as they do they obviously represent the true faith of the church in all ages.

. . . the term 'Fathers of the Church' itself stems from the sphere of dogma and originated in the needs of Catholic apologetics. Patristics originated in the urge to assemble witnesses to the 'authentic' orthodox tradition, that it might add its weight of authority to valid or disputed doctrines. To this end efforts were made as early as the fourth century to establish the views of authoritative theologians who were expressly described as 'Fathers of the Church'. Their authority was accepted as valid in the present and was added to the earlier and more evident authority of the Bible.[2]

Perhaps it is understandable why new formulations of the faith, if not to be found in the scriptures, in the creeds and councils of the church, nor in the Fathers, could be denounced as heretical.

The place of authorized ministry in the church has occupied those concerned with the ecumenical task for many years. There is no one pattern of ministry to be found in the New Testament, for example. Calvin believed that his fourfold Genevan ministry of pastor, elder, teacher and deacon had a rightful claim to be the New Testament pattern as in Eph. 4.11.

To begin with there are four sorts of offices that our Lord instituted for the government of his Church.

That is to say, first pastors, then teachers, after which elders and, in the fourth place, deacons . . .

With respect to the pastors, whom the Scriptures variously designate supervisors, elders and ministers, it is their duty to proclaim the Word of God so as to indoctrinate, admonish, exhort and reprimand both publicly and privately; to administer the sacraments and exercise fraternal discipline with the elders and commissioners . . .

The examination (of ministerial candidates) should consist of two parts, the first of these dealing with doctrine, to see if the candidate possesses a good and sound knowledge of the Scriptures. And then, whether he can fittingly and properly communicate the same to the people unto edification.

Moreover, to make certain that the candidate does not hold to any harmful opinions, it will be well to have him swear that he accepts and follows the doctrines approved by the Church . . . [3]

Others have found the offices of overseer, elder and deacon (bishops, priests and deacons) in the pages of the New Testament (see Phil. 1.1 and Acts 20.17 for example). The early church opted for this threefold order early in the second century (Ignatius of Antioch describes it in his letters *c.*AD115) and it seems to have become general by the mid-second century.

Avoid divisions, as the beginning of evil. Follow, all of you, the bishop, as Jesus Christ followed the Father; and follow the presbytery as the Apostles. Moreover, reverence the deacons as the commandment of God. Let no man do aught pertaining to the Church apart from the bishop. Let that eucharist be considered valid which is under the bishop or him to whom he commits it. Wheresoever the bishop appears, there let the people be, even as wheresoever Christ Jesus is, there is the Catholic Church. It is not lawful apart from the bishop either to baptize, or to hold a love-feast. But whatsoever he approves, that also is well-pleasing to God, that everything which you do may be secure and valid. [4]

The three orders were usually described as having respectively the functions of oversight (*espicopē*), presidency of the eucharist, and service of the community. Clearly the first function could be performed by a conference or Christian assembly as well as by an individual and this is why churches which do not have bishops nevertheless still describe themselves as offering oversight to the church as a whole. The one who presides over the eucharist is normally the local minister in most churches, though authorized lay presidency is well known in many free churches; the theological justification offered for the latter is that of the priesthood of all believers as opposed to the priesthood of one individual.

The Model Deed of the Methodist Church in Great Britain offers the following paragraphs:

> The Methodist Church holds the doctrine of the priesthood of all believers and consequently believes that no priesthood exists which belongs exclusively to a particular order or class of men but in the exercise of its corporate life and worship special qualification for the discharge of special duties are required and thus the principle of representative selection is recognized.

> The preachers itinerant and lay are examined tested and approved before they are authorized to minister in holy things. For the sake of the church order and not because of any priestly virtue inherent in the office the ministers of the Methodist Church are set apart by ordination to the ministry of the word and sacraments.[5]

The function of service or the diaconal role is receiving increasing attention at the present time. While in some churches, e.g. the Roman Catholic Church and the Church of England, the diaconate was once regarded as a stepping stone to the presbyteral role, now the diaconate has been recognized as a proper, full-time order of ministry in several churches. In the Roman Catholic Church married men have been ordained to this office since the Second Vatican Council.

> . . . and the diaconate can in the future be restored as a proper and permanent rank of the hierarchy. It pertains to the competent territorial bodies of bishops, of one kind or another, to decide, with the approval of the Supreme Pontiff, whether and where it is opportune for such deacons to be appointed for the care of souls.

With the consent of the Roman Pontiff, this diaconate will be able to be conferred upon men of more mature age, even upon those living in the married state.[6]

Places of worship and for the assemblies of Christians are the best landmarks in both towns and villages. When during the Second World War The Queen's College in Birmingham had to decide on the shape of its new chapel, it was fortunate in having as its principal the Revd J. O. C. Cobham. Father Jock had been for many years a leader in the liturgical movement in England. His design was based on the shape of the early Christian basilicas of Rome such as are still to be seen in Santa Sabina, San Clemente and Santa Maria in Cosmedin. The basilican shape consisted of an oblong nave for the people with a sanctuary area in the form of an apse. At the centre of the apse was the holy table for the eucharistic celebration at which the minister faced the people. This particular shape meant that the words spoken by the celebrant were reflected off the back round wall and half dome and were clearly audible to the people. In the early

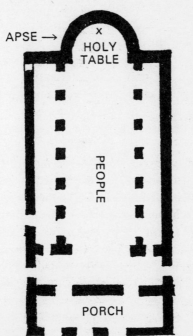

period it is likely that the minister sat behind the table in order to preach, as we know St Augustine did at Hippo in North Africa. The particular advantages of the basilican shape were the visibility, the audibility, and the comparative accessibility to the table for all people.

Over the centuries the sanctuary became elongated in order to allow space for a choir and people were removed further from the action which was done by the minister for them rather than with them. The position of the minister also changed from facing the people to one with his back to the people. This came about because holy objects such as relics of the saints increasingly were put on altars as were candles and other items; eventually the minister had to come in front of the altar and turn to face it or not be seen at all. The modern liturgical movement has helped many Christian Churches to return to the earlier shape of the churches for the celebration of the eucharist.

The first full account of the celebration of the eucharist comes from the writings of St Justin about AD 150. It is clear from this work that the eucharist was the regular Sunday worship of the church and that many of the ingredients that we regard as important were there from the beginning. Justin mentioned the readings from what we now call the epistles and the Gospels, the sermon of the minister, the kiss of peace, the prayers of intercession and the prayer of thanksgiving over the elements of bread and wine. He also mentioned the reservation of the bread and wine for distribution by the deacons to those who are absent on the Lord's Day.

At the end of the prayers, we salute one another with a kiss. There is then brought to the president of the brethren bread and a cup of wine mixed with water; and he taking them, offers up praise and glory to the Father of the universe, through the name of the Son and of the Holy Ghost, and gives thanks at considerable length for our being counted worthy to receive these things at His hands . . . And when the president has given thanks, and all the people have expressed their joyful assent, those who are called by us deacons give to each of those present to partake of the bread and wine mixed with water over which the thanksgiving was pronounced, and to those who are absent they carry away a portion.[7]

Justin's description of baptism is less full but clearly it is regarded as the form of entry into the church. Only the baptized members of the church qualify to receive the Lord's Supper. As far as we know there was no one official eucharistic prayer used at all times and in all places. An early Christian writing called the *Didache*, which probably comes from Syria, suggests that local prophets (the local church leaders?) should pray over the bread and wine as they are led by the Holy Spirit. In fact it gives us one of the earliest examples we have of a thanksgiving prayer for the eucharist. At the end of the prayer, it simply offers the statement, 'But allow the prophets to give thanks as much as they will.' Perhaps all this means is that charismatic leaders might have been able to do what they wanted while others used a fixed formula. Fixed words eventually became more usual, possibly an indication that not all leaders of worship had the ability or the theology to lead in an extempore style. One of the earliest liturgical prayers we have comes from Rome and was written by Hippolytus of Rome, *c.*AD220. It is important because it appears in a modified form in many recent prayer books and could perhaps claim to be a truly ecumenical eucharistic prayer. Here is the opening:

> We render thanks to you, O God, through your beloved child Jesus Christ, whom in the last times you sent to us as a saviour and redeemer and angel of your will;
> Who is your inseparable Word, through whom you made all things, and in whom you were well pleased.
> You sent him from heaven into the Virgin's womb; and, conceived in the womb, he was made flesh and was manifested as your Son, being born of the Holy Spirit and the Virgin.
> Fulfilling your will and gaining for you a holy people, he stretched out his hands when he should suffer, that he might release from suffering those who have believed in you.
> And when he was betrayed to voluntary suffering that he might destroy death, and break the bonds of the devil, and tread down hell, and shine upon the righteous, and fix the limit, and manifest the resurrection, he took bread . . .

The Alternative Service Book has this prayer as Eucharistic Prayer 3 and the Roman Catholic Church uses it as Eucharistic Prayer II, both in a modified form. The biblical references in the prayer of

Hippolytus will be obvious to those who know the scriptures. As such and as one of the earliest prayers of the eucharist that have come down to us, it has a claim to be a eucharistic prayer that could be used by all.

The final point concerns church discipline. The bringing back to the Christian fellowship of those who had sinned grievously was an early problem for the church. In AD250, after the first general persecution of the church by the state under the Emperor Decius, the question of reconciling those who had burned incense to the imperial gods was a critical one.

> However, according to what had been before determined, when the persecution was lulled, and opportunity given for meeting together, a large number of us bishops whom our own faith and the protection of the Lord had preserved uninjured and safe, met together and, the divine Scriptures being adduced on both sides, we balanced our resolution with wholesome moderation; so that neither should hope of communion and peace be altogether denied to the lapsed, lest through desperation they should fall away still further, and, because the Church was shut against them, following the world, should live as heathens; nor yet on the other hand should evangelical strictness be relaxed, so that they might rush in haste to communion; but that penance should be long protracted, and the Fatherly clemency entreated with mourning, and the cases and purposes and exigencies of each be examined . . . [8]

Many of the penitential practices of the church came about in response to the falling from grace of many who had once been loyal to Christ. Restoration was never regarded as an easy matter. In the end fixed tariffs of time and actions were introduced. Outside some churches there would be seen people on their knees pleading for the prayers of the faithful as they went inside. Many would have spent years outside before being re-admitted to the sacrament by the bishop. Modern leniency in the penitential practice of the churches was certainly not to be found in the early period. When at the time just after the English Reformation many English puritans insisted on discipline as an element in the Christian life, they were true to the insights of the early church.

A comprehensive list of the sins deserving ecclesiastical censures is given by Stephen Ford in his *A Gospel-Church: or, God's Holy Temple Opened*, published in the year 1675. The following sins, if persisted in and not repented of, are deserving of excommunication:

1. Strong and violent passions. 2. Apparent Wrath, Envy, Bitterness and Anger shewed, without great provocation. 3. Apparent Frowardness, Peevishness, Clamour and Strife. 4. Jangling, Disputing and Peace breakings, and all things that directly hinder the Edification and Peace of the Church. 5. Backbitings, and speaking evil against, or of one another. 6. Constant or frequent neglects of Family and Church-duties, and the Ordinances of God in them. 7. Needless Associating and holding Communion with profane and scandalous persons. 8. Defrauding any persons of their first dues any way, on any account whatsoever, when it might have been prevented. 9. Disobedience to the Lawful Commands and Rules of Parents, Masters, Magistrates, Elders, or any other that have Authority over them. 10. Publishing false Doctrines against the Fundamentals of the Gospel, Faith, and Worship. 11. False accusing any Persons, especially any of the Church. 12. Railing at, or reviling others to their face, or behind their backs. 13. Idleness, Tatling, and being Busie-bodies in other mens matters that concern them not.[9]

It is to be noted that the element of discipline, although not always appreciated in our generation, has always been important in the life of the church. Along with the other elements listed above, it is probably a constant in all ages and in all places.

These six 'constants' seem to have been there from the first period of the life of the church. For some churches all of the six are of equal importance; perhaps the Roman Catholic, Orthodox and Anglican communions might claim to take this position. Clearly in these three cases the appeal is often made to the early church, to Christian antiquity as the final court of appeal. Other churches might well argue that the acceptance of formulated creeds and a non-biblical form of ministry is to allow that the early church was in some way 'better' than any later period of the life of the church. In fact they would argue that the Reformation Church in fact put a more biblical and less traditional view of what the church ought to be. A return to the Bible as the fount of the Christian faith was needed in the sixteenth century to reform a church which had allowed itself to fall below the level of scriptural Christianity. It is of interest that such churches have in their dialogues with other more 'catholic' denominations increasingly seen that the church has never stood on the basis of 'scripture alone' and that the six headings seem to be needed in some sense to make every church effective in its witness and service to the world.

3

A Theology of Ecumenism

The Week of Prayer for Christian Unity runs each year from 18 January to the feast of the Conversion of St Paul on 25 January. Pulpits are exchanged and preachers in England and elsewhere try to do justice to the theme of Christian Unity. Unfortunately they find it extremely hard, mainly because most believe that they only have one text available, the one where Jesus prays to God for his disciples and asks:

> May they all be one, just as, Father, you are in me and I am in you, so that the world may believe it was you who sent me (John 17.21).

The hope that all Christians might be one is preached on and the reason offered is an evangelical one 'that the world may believe'. In fact the context in John's Gospel will not bear the weight of what preachers during the Week of Prayer want it to bear. The context of John 17.21 is of a Christian community of about AD 90 (most probably in Ephesus but possibly in Syria) which is faced with danger from false teachers from within and danger from without by the threat of persecution. John authentically reproduces the thinking of Jesus in terms of the future church and Jesus' prayer is that it may be one after the pattern of the relationship of the Father and the Son. Although John 17.21 has become almost an ecumenical slogan and has the implication of future organic unity there are commentators who believe that it implies just the opposite. They make the point that the Godhead is three, not one, and that this offers for the churches a model of separation rather than one of unity. John 17.21 is in fact a statement from the Christ who addresses the life situation of the local Christians and prays that the unity of the Father with the Son should be paralleled by the unity of his people, both now and in the future. The situation of the church in any other century, not least our own where churches are divided in their understanding of faith, worship and sacraments, is not the context of John 17.21.

If a theology of ecumenism is to be stated and firmly believed it has to be based on more than an isolated text, however important John 17.21 might appear to be. Christopher Ellis, a Baptist minister, in his important book *Together on the Way* outlines a theology of ecumenism that offers biblical reflections on unity. He states that classical texts such as John 17, I Corinthians 1 and Ephesians 4 have too frequently had to bear the whole weight of ecumenical preaching and theology. While these 'purple' passages are important, he says, we must see whether concern for unity is a substantial element in the New Testament. If it is, then a challenge which cannot be dismissed is offered to the churches.

He begins by looking at the theme of peace, in Hebrew *shalom* and in Greek *eirene*. The Old Testament *shalom* means more than the absence of war but has the positive meaning of well-being or wholeness. It does not denote a specifically inward peace but has a social meaning, concerned not with emotions but relationships. The Greek word *eirene* is used similarly in the New Testament although it has a wider range of meanings, from a greeting to the hope of salvation. The word is perhaps best translated as 'all the very best to you', so that today when the peace is offered in a Christian service of worship we are wishing every blessing of mind, body and soul to the people next to us. That 'peace' has to do with relationships is shown when Jesus challenges the person who is not at peace with their neighbour to sort the matter out before offering gifts to God at the altar (Matt. 5.23–24). Peace in the sense of the well-being and reconciliation of people is used at least eighty-five times in the New Testament, showing it to be an important concept both for theological study and for ecumenical theology.

Ellis then looks at the word *koinonia* which is translated roughly as 'fellowship'; both the horizontal fellowship between human beings on earth and the fellowship which Christians share vertically with the Father and the Son (I John 1.3). Material sharing of the goods of the earth is an expression of the concreteness of the fellowship (Acts 2.42, Rom. 15.26, II Cor. 8.4); to be part of the fellowship costs time and money as Christians in every age have discovered. The word is also translated as 'communion' when Christians gather for the

Lord's Supper; it is a communion with Christ and with each other (I Cor. 10.16–17). The use of *koinonia* has become very important in recent ecumenical dialogues. Both ARCIC I and ARCIC II have used it extensively and so has the Methodist–Roman Catholic dialogue. It would be better for a theology of ecumenism if it were more widely used in the New Testament, as it is used only about eighteen times there. Nevertheless, it has become a widely used ecumenical term. ARCIC II completed its statement on 'Church as Communion' in 1990. The term enables Christians to recognize the certain yet imperfect communion that they already share. ARCIC II looked first at how the term 'communion' was unfolded in many places in scripture, including words and expressions that pointed to its reality such as 'people of God', 'body of Christ', 'flock', 'temple' and 'vine'. It then explored the way in which the church as communion is the sacrament of the merciful grace of God for all humankind. The relationship of communion to the apostolicity, catholicity, and holiness of the church followed this with a consideration of the necessary elements needed for unity and ecclesial communion. The existing communion between Anglicans and Catholics was then affirmed with an outline of the remaining issues that still divided the two churches.

The word 'reconciliation' is well known in the writings of Paul. But the concept was current already in the ministry of Jesus in his concern for the sinners and outcasts of society, in his invitation to people to be reconciled to God and to recognize themselves as his children. Paul's use of 'reconciliation' centres on the idea of 'change', a changed relationship between God and humanity, as expressed in: 'For anyone united to Christ, there is a new creation; the old creation has gone; a new order has already begun' (II Cor. 5.17). The implications of the new humanity is that it is obligated to bring others into reconciliation with God and with each other. Reconciliation with each other is best seen as the content of the famous passage in Galatians: 'There can be neither Jew nor Greek, there can be neither slave nor free, there can be neither male nor female, for you are all one in Christ Jesus' (Gal. 3.28). While the words 'reconcile' and 'reconciliation' are only used some ten times (and only by Paul) it will be clear that the concept is a fundamental one in the New Testament.

The concept of unity is important in the New Testament as will be obvious. The church in Acts finds that the experience of the tower of Babel and the confusion of languages is symbolically overcome in the descent of the Holy Spirit upon the disciples and in the way that all hear the good news in their own languages (Acts 2.1ff.). Unity in Paul centres on his use of the body image; there are many parts of a single body so we who are united with Christ, though different in many ways, belong to the body of Christ as its limbs and organs (Rom. 12.4–5). When he uses the same image of the body in I Corinthians 12, he is writing to a young and enthusiastic church where the gifts of the Holy Spirit have caused people to take a pride in what they have received, the result being that factions have appeared in Corinth. Paul confronts the splits in Corinth with the thought that the diversity of gifts is for building up the church and making the one body image a reality:

> For as with the human body which is a unity although it has many parts – all the parts of the body, though many, still making up one single body – so it is with Christ. We were baptized into one body in a single Spirit, Jews as well as Greeks, slaves as well as free, and we were all given the same Spirit to drink (I Cor. 12.12–13).

The Pauline emphasis on 'a unity', 'one single body', 'one body', needs to be noted; the familiarity of such a passage should not blind us to the importance Paul set by the unity of the local church. Elsewhere Paul is anxious to make the unity of the church the prime consideration in how the Corinthian church celebrates the Lord's Supper; the people are one body because they eat from one loaf; factions must not appear when the Lord's Supper is eaten together; the body has to be recognized and this means that the Corinthians must not ignore the needs of their fellow Christians (see I Cor. 10.16–17 and I. Cor. 11.17–34).

The Letter to the Ephesians gives a picture of unity as that which is given by the Holy Spirit but which also needs the co-operation of the people in the church:

> Take every care to preserve the unity of the Spirit by the peace that binds you together. There is one Body, one Spirit, just as one hope is the goal of your calling by God. There is one Lord, one

faith, one baptism, and one God and Father of all, over all, through all and within all (Eph. 4.3–6).

The use of the words 'one' seven times and of 'all' four times is noteworthy. The faith proclaimed here does not allow divisions of any kind and is meant to be totally inclusive. Theologians have often pointed out that the Nicene Creed gives four 'notes' of the church:

We believe in one holy catholic and apostolic Church.

The four 'notes' then are unity, holiness, catholicity in the sense of inclusiveness, apostolicity in the sense that the faith proclaimed is the same as that handed down from the apostles. Ephesians 4.3–6 certainly centres on two notes of the church; its inclusiveness or catholicity ('one God and Father of all, who is over all and through all and in all'); its unity in the seven 'ones'. Those who want to be pedantic might argue that the other two notes of 'holiness' and 'apostolicity' are there too in the work of the Holy Spirit in the church and in the 'one faith' which is clearly the faith of the apostles. But perhaps even more important for a theology of ecumenism is the way in which the Father, the Son, and the Holy Spirit are used in the passage, some three centuries before the Trinity was recognized as an official doctrine of the church. Unity in the passage is related to the God who is Trinity and also One. Unity then becomes not an optional extra for ecumenical enthusiasts but something which belongs to the very nature of God and must therefore be reflected in the life of his church.

Oneness also appears in John's Gospel, usually linking the unity of Jesus with the Father, the relation between Jesus and his followers, and the relationships between the disciples of Jesus. We have already looked at John 17.21 as the main place where the unity of Father and Son is related to the unity between the disciples of Jesus, past and present. In the passage where Jesus calls himself the good shepherd we read: 'And there are other sheep I have that are not of this flock, and I must lead these too. They will listen to my voice, and there will be only one flock, one shepherd' (John 10.16). In the context of John's Gospel the 'other sheep' are clearly the Gentiles who are not part of Israel. The flock of Christ then will not be exclusively Jewish and will have all the racial and national groups within it. Jesus who lays down his life for the sheep also gathers the sheep together. The theme appears again when Caiaphas the high priest prophesies that Jesus will die for the nation: 'and not for the nation only, but also to gather together into one the scattered children of God' (John 11.52). Here Caiaphas predicts the unity that Christ's death will bring to his people, anticipating perhaps the words of the next chapter about Christ's death as drawing people to him: 'And when I am lifted up from the earth, I shall draw all people to myself' (John 12.32).

The antagonisms of the period after the Reformation which have sometimes lasted into our own day have made many people observe cynically, 'see how these Christians love one another'. The original quotation comes from Tertullian's late second-century *Apology* and was meant to contrast with pagan hatred. If pagan hatred had indeed drifted into Christianity in ecumenical encounters then the Christian theme of love needs reconsideration. Paul of course puts love as the primary thing about Christianity; 'the best way of all' is love (I Cor. 13). Jesus himself laid down the primacy of love; love of God, love of our neighbour, love even of our enemies (Mark 12.29–31; Matt. 5.43–48). In John's Gospel Jesus echoes the call to love one another: 'I give you a new commandment: love one another; you must love one another just as I have loved you' (John 13.34). The call to love each other is specific for the church:

> Let us love, then, because he first loved us. Anyone who says 'I love God', while at the same time hating his fellow-Christians is a liar. If we do not love the fellow-Christian whom we have seen, we are incapable of loving God whom we have not seen. We have this command from Christ himself: whoever loves God must love their fellow-Christians too (I John 4.19–21).

The gap between what should be and what actually occurs is never more important than here where Christian love is at stake. In the New Testament, while there are several passages where God's love for us asks to be recognized by an answering love for him, nevertheless the majority of the uses of the verb 'love' ask us as Christian believers to have love for our neighbours and particularly for those who are of the community of faith.

From the biblical basis for ecumenism we turn to its implications in the life of the churches.

If peace means that Christians must desire every good thing for other people, then we cannot be contented with anything less than this. The Pentecostal, for example, cannot be content with the way in which the Anglican neighbour sees her religious life. She will seek for her Anglican friend an experience of God the Holy Spirit that will be revitalizing for the faith. The Catholic will feel that his Baptist neighbour does not have the fullness of faith, without the intercession of the saints, the primacy of the Pope, devotion to the Blessed Virgin Mary, etc. He will seek to offer a fuller understanding on these matters. Such examples as these do not seem to offer 'peace' in any meaningful way but will be deemed to bring factional things to the fore, so much so that ecumenical dialogue becomes impossible. Perhaps then we need to take on the truth of a statement offered during the *Not Strangers But Pilgrims* process: 'I need your faith to make mine whole.' The implication of this is that in so far as I am not in full unity with my Christian neighbours I lack the fullness of Christianity, and this is true even if my denomination has a claim to have all the truth.

> If the churches really wanted to be one, they could be one within measurable time; what holds them apart is in large measure the deep-seated love of separate existence, and the sense of superiority enjoyed by those who feel themselves to have been endowed with a special portion of the truth.[1]

Fellowship, the English word which translates the Greek word *koinonia*, is an important theological concept. It means of course both a relationship with God and a relationship with fellow believers. Those who are closest to God are also closest to other Christians. This is one reason why at the heart of the quest for unity prayer is fundamental and why we have a Week of Prayer for Christian Unity. The horizontal relationship with other Christians becomes more important as we get to know other traditions.

> Theoretical ecumenism has little meaning, because it is speculation born of misunderstanding. It is only when we hear the account of another's faith from that other person that we begin to understand another's faith as something which is alive. It is in the personal encounter that prejudice and ignorance are surprised and persuaded to listen.[2]

A good example of this occurred some years ago when a Baptist church and a Roman Catholic church had a dialogue evening with each other. The Baptists were asked to tell the Roman Catholics what they (the Baptists) thought they (the Roman Catholics) believed and vice versa. The fellowship was very much enriched by the interchange and quite a few opinions were altered; the others really did believe in the same Christ and were (if not physically) of the same church. This is perhaps a local discovery of the 'imperfect but real communion' talked about in the ARCIC II document *Church as Communion.*

Reconciliation between human beings is a direct consequence of their reconciliation to God through the work of Jesus Christ. That there is now no longer 'Jew nor Greek, neither slave nor free, neither male nor female' (Gal. 3.28) should mean that 'there is no longer Baptist nor Roman Catholic, neither Methodist nor Anglican, neither United Reformed nor Orthodox'. But the process whereby this reconciliation comes about may be a long one. It demands first of all the mutual understanding that comes about through the fellowship of dialogue, then the ability to recognize the effectiveness of the worship and sacramental life of another group of Christians and, perhaps only finally, the recognition of the ministries exercised in the other churches. Just as for the early Christians in the New Testament period it took some time for Gentiles to be recognized as part of the community and that only after the 'conversion' of Peter and James to the validity of Gentile Christianity, so it may take something of a 'conversion' for some Christians to recognize valid Christianity in other churches than their own. If the Holy Spirit could do it for the church of the first century, no doubt he can still convert Christians in the twentieth. What the New Testament seems to suggest to us is an all-inclusive Christianity, a 'body' type where all the parts of the body have functions which go to form the whole. One sees churches where most people are wholly spectators, where the body seems to be only the head. Others seem to be only feet where scurry and hurry and social activity are the norm in which all the members are occupied. Some seem to be only heart where only the emotions are engaged and where study and the use of the mind are almost regarded as pointless. Needless to say, some other churches seem to be all brain where only people with university degrees are to be found. If 'body' Christianity is the model of the true church, then all of the above are deficient. Some theologians such as John Macquarrie have seen in this deficiency a key to the ecumenical future. In so far, he says, as the Pope is not in communion with, say, the Archbishop of Canterbury, his faith lacks an important element, namely the Anglican element. The wholeness of the body demands all the constituent bits. While we are separated from each other, we all lack the fullness of the body of Christ though we may claim to be that body.

> Each church has existed as though it were the only true church and thus is has been closed to the truth in others as well as the greater truth, which is only apprehended in the tension between truths.[3]

The truths which others have preserved even in a state of disunity may be essential for the building up of the body of Christ. To be reconciled demands recognition of other Christians.

Finally there are important clues in the Christian doctrine of God. Augustine suggested that love formed a sort of cement for the God who is Trinity; the bond of love unites the Father, the Son and the Holy Spirit. The model of God as Trinity is in at least one sense a model for the church. The model is of diversity in unity. God in his manifestations shows us different aspects of himself, in creation, in redemption and in sanctification. They all nevertheless stem from the God who is love. This is shown in many works of art where at the great moments of the life of Christ, such as the baptism, the transfiguration and the crucifixion, not only is Jesus depicted but the Father and the Holy Spirit. Perhaps just as all acts of God are the acts of the Trinity, so all ideas of unity in the Church should take their model from the unity in diversity which is at the heart of God.

Before turning to practical matters implied in a theology of ecumenism, there is an understanding of ecumenism that has often been put forward that needs to be questioned. This understanding assumes that 'spiritual unity' is the only real need for relationships between churches. The subject to be considered is really not the reunion of separated churches but unity and fellowship between Christians. For example the Lambeth Quadrilateral of 1888 was wrong in pointing to episcopacy as being essential in the ecumenical

future. A more scriptural understanding would speak of maintaining
the purity of the faith, drawing closer to one common Lord, giving
ourselves to prayer, and cultivating a spirit of love between
Christians. This will keep Christians heavenly-minded whereas
endeavours to bring churches together is a misapplication of what
Jesus taught. Jesus prayed for spiritual unity in the Upper Room and
not for denominational unity. But, as has often been stated:

> So-called 'spiritual unity' is not enough, for we are summoned to
> be disciples in *this* world. We must take the structures of the
> church seriously and we must take the notion of incarnation
> seriously.[4]

The 'spiritual unity' argument is held by many evangelical
Christians, and many others who would argue that in so far as we are
'in Christ' we already have as much unity as we need. The problem
with the argument is that it seems to imply a 'spiritual' church where
people are united in love of a common Lord. It also looks like an
'invisible' church of which the members are known only to God. It
seems too as if Christians have to make their own judgment about
who belongs to this 'spiritual' church. In order to belong do I have to
believe the same as you do about the interpretation of the Bible,
about the way sacraments can be administered, about intercessory
prayer, and so on? If I do, then you might turn out to be the only
member of the 'true' church, for it is guaranteed that two completely
like-minded people will not be found that easily. The 'spiritual' unity
argument also misses out because the church has always had a
'visible' aspect; there are churches called 'Roman Catholic', 'Anglican', 'URC', 'Methodist', 'Baptist', 'Pentecostal', and so on. In the
end I have to make a choice to belong somewhere where flesh and
blood people exist, in all their awkwardness and difference from me.
Visible 'organic' unity is demanded, not 'spiritual unity', however
enticing and easy the latter might seem.

The practical implications of the visible and organic theology of
ecumenism have to some degree been indicated above, but we have a
little room here to look at some other matters:

1. If an agreement on the essentials of faith is to be found, as is
suggested for example by the World Council of Churches *Confessing
the Faith Today* and using the Niceno-Constantinopolitan Creed as

its basis, at least one essential matter of agreement needs to follow. This is the recognition that the Holy Spirit has been active in separated churches and has not been active only in those churches that have not themselves become schismatic. Thus differences in sacrament, ministry and corporate decision-making within churches can be acknowledged as gifts preserved or given by the Spirit. For example, the Baptist insistence on the baptism of believers can be seen as the Spirit reminding Christians of the vital importance of personal conversion to the Christian way and its acknowledgment in a sacramental form. The insistence on the place of elders in the United Reformed Church can be seen as the work of the Spirit in breaking down the barriers often erected between lay and ordained who are equally parts of the people of God. Similar arguments would apply to John Wesley's ordination of his preachers in 1784 and so also the place of religious experience within the Pentecostal denominations.

> Recognition must be given to the continuing activity of the Holy Spirit over long periods of separation among churches . . . As various Christian churches sought to reform and renew themselves in fidelity to the gospel, the Holy Spirit granted certain valid insights and spiritual gifts proper to authentic Christian life. Subject to spiritual discernment, such gifts and insights may well be intended for the future life of a visibly united church.[5]

2. If reconciliation is about drawing Christians together, then there are implications. We need to forgive other Christians when they have belittled the contributions to the life of the churches that we have made. The Methodist has to forgive the High Anglican who said of the local Methodist chapel, 'that's not a church'. The Roman Catholic has to forgive the writer of the pamphlet *From Rome to Christ* for the implication in its title that Christ was unavailable in the Catholic tradition of faith. The Black Pentecostalist has to forgive the United Reformed member who accused his church of offering simple answers when he should have known that a holistic spirituality was at stake. We shall all need a period at some time in the future when we look to 'the healing of ecumenical memories'.

3. When important unity schemes have worked such as that of the Church of South India there has been loss as well as gain. In South

India the names Anglican, Methodist, and United Church went
although their essential contributions to the new church clearly
remained. When Methodist Union came about in Britain in 1932
there was a feeling that the old family homes had been demolished
and even now, over sixty years later, there are still those who identify
themselves as Wesleyan, Primitive or United. The old foundation
stones and the names on the chapels still exist in many places.
Stephen Neill has pointed to the difficulty of churches uniting unless
they are also willing to die for the future unity of the Church. The
pattern of death followed by resurrection is of course an important
Christian notion but it is not always one that is accepted in practice.

> The final and terrible difficulty is that churches cannot unite
> unless they are willing to die. In a truly united Church there would
> be no more Anglicans or Lutherans or Presbyterians or Meth-
> odists. But the very disappearance from the world of those great
> and honoured names is the very thing that many loyal churchmen
> are not prepared to face. Much has already been achieved. But
> until church union clearly takes shape as a better resurrection on
> the other side of death, the impulse towards it is likely to be weak
> and half-hearted; and such weak impulses are not strong enough
> to overcome the tremendous difficulties in the way.[6]

4. 'May they be one, that the world may believe' is often quoted,
even if out of context. The very important relationship of unity to
mission cannot be overstated.

> Unity and mission are inseparable because the church doesn't live
> for itself: it is a community which exists because it has been
> *called* ... The church's own understanding of its function is
> usually described in terms of *mission* ... *the gospel determines the
> church*. This means that the preaching of the gospel summons
> people to faith and at the same time this very gospel has at its heart
> the dynamics which push the church outside itself.[7]

A divided church cannot easily preach reconciliation to individuals nor to a divided society. The importance of a fully united church
to mission would mean that Christians could witness to the
comprehensiveness of the church. Some accepting the faith for the
first time might be taken with the order and solemnity of the Roman

Catholics or high Anglicans, others might prefer the spontaneity of the Pentecostal/Evangelical parts of the church. But converts would be joining the same church where diversity was consistent with the fullness of unity.

4

Past Problems in a Nutshell

Although the early church tried hard to maintain its unity and although there was a great deal of diversity in the early period, there were obviously going to be limits to the diversity. Could a person be a Christian and not believe in the humanity of Jesus Christ? Could a Christian believe that Jesus was human without believing that he was also divine? Were there different levels of Christianity so that you were more exalted if you had received the Holy Spirit and less exalted if you hadn't?

The word 'heresy' in Greek originally meant 'opinion'. Eventually it came to mean 'wrong opinions'. Among the early believers who held these wrong opinions chief among them were:

The Gnostics (from the period of the New Testament writings and onwards) whose heresies were many and various. Some refused to believe that Jesus had taken human flesh at all (Cerinthus, Cerdon). Others insisted that people had to be initiated into a body of knowledge (in Greek, *gnosis*, hence the name Gnostics) before being truly Christian (Valentinus, Basilides).

A certain Cerinthus also in Asia taught that the world was not made by the first God, but by a certain Virtue far separated and removed from the Principality which is above all things, a Virtue which knows not the God over all. He added that Jesus was not born of a virgin but was the son of Joseph and Mary, like other men, but superior to all others in justice, prudence and wisdom. And that after his baptism Christ descended upon him in the form of a dove, from that Principality which is above all things; and that then he revealed the Unknown Father and performed deeds of virtue, but that in the end Christ flew back, leaving Jesus, and Jesus suffered and rose again, but Christ remained impassible, being by nature spiritual.

Basilides, that he may seem to have found out something higher and more plausible, vastly extends the range of his teaching, declaring that Mind was first born of the Unborn Father, then Reason from Mind, from Reason, Prudence, from Prudence, Wisdom and Power, and from Wisdom and Power the Virtues, Princes and Angels, whom he also calls 'the First.' By them the First Heaven was made; afterwards others were made, derived from these, and they made another Heaven like to the former, and in like manner others . . . [in all, 365 Heavens].[1]

The Christian faith was not sufficiently complex for these early gnostics.

Marcion (*c.*AD 70–150) was the son of a Christian church leader. He believed that the creator God (or Demiurge in Greek) was not the God revealed in Jesus Christ. Hence the Old Testament was about a vengeful tyrant, whereas the New Testament was about a God of love. Because of this belief the Marcionites refused to regard the Old Testament as a Christian book and Marcion reduced the New Testament to Luke's Gospel (even that was abbreviated) and the major epistles of St Paul.

Irenaeus, in the late second century describes Marcion's work:

Besides this, he mutilates the Gospel which is according to Luke, removes all that is written respecting the generation of the Lord, and sets aside a great deal of the teaching of the Lord's discourses, in which the Lord is recorded as most clearly confessing that the Maker of this universe is His Father. He likewise persuaded his disciples that he himself was more worthy of credit than are those apostles who have handed down the gospel to us, delivering to them not the gospel, but merely a fragment of it. In like manner, too, he dismembered the epistles of Paul, removing all that is said by the apostle respecting that God who made the world, to the effect that He is the Father of our Lord Jesus Christ, and also those passages from the prophetical writings which the apostle quotes, in order to teach us that they announced beforehand the coming of the Lord.[2]

Montanus (*fl. c.*AD 156) was a native of Phrygia in Asia Minor. He and two prophetesses, Priscilla and Maximilla, believed that the last times had come and that the Holy Spirit had been poured out upon them.

The Christian writer Epiphanius, late fourth century, quotes some sayings of Maximilla in his *Panarion*:

> Hear not me, but hear Christ (48.12).
> After me shall be no prophetess any more, but the consummation . . . (48.2).
> The Lord sent me to be the party-leader, informer, interpreter of this task, profession, and covenant, constrained, whether he will or nill, to learn the knowledge of God (48.13).[3]

They seem to have believed that they were speaking the thoughts of God and were not afraid to add their own words to the revealed scriptures of the church. It was from this group that there came that listing of the gravest sins, that which we now know as the seven deadly sins.

Tertullian (*c.*AD 160–*c.*220) was the first great Latin theologian and was later converted to Montanism which had become very rigorous.

Tertullian during his Montanist period, sounds off against the new method in Rome applied by Bishop Callistus to the forgiveness of sinners:

> Christian modesty is being shaken to its foundations . . . I hear that there has even been an edict set forth, and a peremptory one too. The Sovereign Pontiff(!) – the Bishop of Bishops – issues an edict: 'I remit, to such as have discharged the requirements of repentance, the sins both of adultery and of fornication.' O edict, on which cannot be inscribed 'well done!' And where shall this liberality be posted up? On the very spot, I suppose, on the very gates of lust, beneath the very advertisement of lust. There is the place for such repentance to be published, where the delinquency itself shall haunt. There is the place to read the pardon, where entrance shall be made under the hope thereof. But it is in the Church that this edict is read, and in the Church that it is pronounced: and she is a virgin! Far, far from Christ's betrothed be such a proclamation![4]

Against these early heresies the church countered with its list of approved books (the earliest list of these dates from about AD 190, the 'Muratorian fragment') although the final list of approved books of the New Testament was not formulated until AD 397 at the Council of Carthage (this is usually called 'the canon', the rule). The church also formulated approved formulae of faith usually called 'The Rule of Faith' or 'The Canon of Truth'. These were not 'creeds' in the modern sense where every phrase has been carefully examined, but were informal statements offered by church leaders which summed up the faith of the local churches.

Irenaeus in the late second century offers this Rule of Faith:

> For the Church, though dispersed throughout the whole world, even to the ends of the earth, has received from the apostles and their disciples this faith: in one God, the Father Almighty, who made the heaven and the earth and the seas and all things that are in them; and in one Christ Jesus, the Son of God, who became incarnate for our salvation; and in the Holy Spirit, who proclaimed through the prophets the dispensations and the advents, and the birth from a virgin, and the passion, and the resurrection from the dead, and the incarnate ascension into heaven of the beloved Christ Jesus, our Lord, and His future manifestation from heaven in the glory of the Father *to sum up all things* and to raise up anew all flesh of the whole human race . . .[5]

Around the same time the understanding of 'apostolic succession' arose. This needs to be carefully explained as it has often been misunderstood. The Bishop Irenaeus of Lyons was the first to formulate it in detail around AD 180. If you want to know the faith of the church you need to go to those places where the faith of the church was first handed on from the apostles. The successors of the apostles, the local bishops in those places, will be able to offer the best account to those who come after. Even before the time of Irenaeus other writers had offered succession lists of bishops to show the continuity of the faith from apostolic times. Irenaeus suggests that the pre-eminent place where the apostolic faith can be found is at Rome because there the bishops received their understanding of Christianity from Peter and Paul.

Irenaeus offers a good example of the place where the apostolic teaching has been maintained:

Since, however, it would be very tedious, in such a volume as this, to reckon up the successions of all the churches, we do put to confusion all those who, in whatever manner, whether by an evil self-pleasing, by vainglory, or by blindness and perverse opinion, assemble in unauthorized meetings, by indicating that tradition derived from the apostles, of the very great, the very ancient, and universally known church founded and organized at Rome by the two most glorious apostles, Peter and Paul; and also by pointing out the faith preached to men, which comes down to our time by means of the successions of the bishops. For it is necessary that every church, that is, the faithful everywhere, should resort to (?agree with) this church, on account of its pre-eminent authority, in which the apostolic tradition has been preserved continuously by those who exist everywhere.[6]

Other heresies arose in the course of time before the first major council of the church at Nicaea in AD 325. These were mostly concerned with how Jesus could be truly called God and yet be man. The chief heretics at this time were Sabellius (early third century) and Paul of Samosata (late third century), both of whom were perceived to have erroneous ideas of God the Father and of Jesus' nature. The Council of Nicaea was called by the Emperor Constantine because of the controversy that surrounded the name of Arius, a presbyter of Alexandria. Arius claimed that Jesus Christ was a kind of demi-God, neither quite man nor quite God. He seemed to have scripture on his side ('The Father is greater than I', John 14.28). One of his main opponents was Athanasius, later to be Bishop of Alexandria, who objected that if Jesus were not God he could not save us, that if he were not man he could not understand our human condition.

St Athanasius writes on the incarnation and the work of Christ:

Now, if there were merely a misdemeanour in question, and not a consequent corruption, repentance were well enough. But if, when transgression had once gained a start, men became involved in that corruption which was their nature, and were deprived of the grace which they had, being in the Image of God, what further step was needed? or what was required for such grace and such recall, but the Word of God, which had also at the beginning made everything out of nought? For His it was once more both to bring the corruptible to incorruption, and to maintain intact the just claims of the Father upon all. For being Word of the Father and above all, He alone of natural fitness was both able to recreate everything, and worthy to suffer on behalf of all and to be ambassador for all with the Father.[7]

The Council of Nicaea decided that Jesus was 'of one substance' (in Greek, *homoousios*) with the Father, truly God.

Eusebius, the church historian and Bishop of Caesarea, offers an account of the teaching of the Council of Nicaea in 325 to his own church, although he was clearly not happy with the term 'consubstantial with the Father':

> We believe in One God, the Father, Almighty, Maker of all things visible and invisible:
> And in One Lord Jesus Christ, the Son of God, begotten of the Father, Only-begotten, that is, from the very substance of the Father; God from God, Light from Light, Very God from very God, begotten not made, Consubstantial with the Father, by Whom all things were made, both things in heaven and earth; Who for us men and for our salvation came down and was incarnate, was made man, suffered, and rose again the third day, ascended into heaven, and is coming to judge living and dead.
> And in the Holy Ghost.
> And those who say 'There was when he was not,' and 'Before his generation he was not,' and 'he came to be from nothing,' or those who pretend that the Son of Man is 'Of other *hypostasis* or substance,' or 'created,' or 'alterable,' or 'mutable,' the Catholic and Apostolic Church anathematizes.[8]

The next half century saw a great many disputes about this definition and the Christian church almost became entirely Arian for a while. In 381 at the next major council in Constantinople the doctrine of Nicaea was formulated in a creed (this is what we now describe as the Nicene Creed, but we should really call it the 'Niceno-Constantinopolitan' Creed). Also in 381 the co-equality of the Father, the Son and the Holy Spirit was finally clarified, the doctrine of the Trinity. The next major controversy was over the place of Mary in the Christian faith; was she Mother of God (*theotokos* in Greek) or only the Mother of the human Jesus. Nestorius, Bishop of Constantinople, objected to *theotokos* as over-exaltation of the mother of Jesus. After a long and complicated battle

at the Council of Ephesus in AD 431 the term *theotokos* was recognized as being the orthodox one and Nestorius was condemned.

This extract is from a letter of Cyril of Alexandria to John of Antioch in the year 433, two years after the Council of Ephesus:

> In accordance with this sense of the unconfused union, we confess the holy Virgin to be *Theotocos*, because God the Word became incarnate and was made man, and from the very conception united to himself the temple taken from her. And as to the expressions concerning the Lord in the Gospels and Epistles, we are aware that theologians understand some as common, as relating to one Person, and others they distinguish, as relating to two natures, explaining those that befit the divine nature according to the Godhead of Christ, and those of a humble sort according to his Manhood.[9]

A little time later an ancient theologian in Constantinople, Eutyches, claimed that the divine nature (*physis*) in Jesus was so dominant that it could be said that he had only one nature (hence the term '*monophysite*'). Other theologians objected at the loss of the human nature of Jesus. Leo the Bishop of Rome wrote a thesis that set the work of the human nature of Jesus alongside the work of his divine nature, using the Gospel accounts. Leo's stance was vindicated at the Council of Chalcedon in 451 but not all the bishops voted for the theology of Leo.

The following is an extract from the 'Tome of Leo' dated AD 449:

> The birth of the flesh is a manifestation of human nature; the childbearing of a virgin a token of divine power. The infancy of the babe is shown by its lowly cradle; the greatness of the Most High is declared by the voices of angels. He whom Herod wickedly strives to kill is like a human infant; but he is the Lord of all whom the Magi rejoice humbly to adore. Already when he came to the baptism of his forerunner, John, lest he should not be known

because his divinity was hidden by the veil of flesh, the Father's voice thundered from heaven *This is my beloved Son in whom I am well pleased.* He whom the craft of the Devil tempts as man, is the same that the Angels minister to as God. To hunger, to thirst, to be weary and to sleep, is obviously human; but with five loaves to satisfy five thousand people and to bestow on the woman of Samaria that living water, a draught of which will cause the drinker to thirst no more; to walk upon the surface of the sea with feet that do not sink, and to calm the rising waves by rebuking the tempest, is without question divine.[10]

A large number left Chalcedon without taking up the faith of Chalcedon and began the Monophysite Schism. This schism has still not been properly healed. As a result there are churches such as the Coptic Church of Alexandria, the Syrian Jacobites and the Armenians who do not hold to the definition of Jesus' two natures as formulated at Chalcedon. These churches do not like the term 'monophysite' (one nature). They claim that the divine nature in Jesus is dominant but not exclusive. It is as if a drop of oil (i.e. Jesus' humanity) were to be put into the ocean (Jesus' divinity); the oil would be there but the dominant impression would be of water.

During the next few centuries the churches of the East and West who had accepted Chalcedon began to drift apart. In the West the Bishop of Rome, Gregory the Great, was instrumental in the conversion of the Angles and Saxons in England when Gregory sent Augustine to the Kentish tribes and Ethelbert was baptized in AD 597. The general picture is of the papacy looking to the north and not to the east. By AD 800 the Bishop of Rome, Leo III, sought the protection of the Franks rather than that of the Emperor in Constantinople, and crowned Charlemagne as Holy Roman Emperor in St Peter's. By the early eleventh century the phrase concerning the Holy Spirit, 'who proceeds from the Father and the Son', was incorporated into the creed in the Roman liturgy. This was an importation from the north into Rome and, although it could be said to be orthodox, it was not in the creed of 381. This *filioque* clause (Latin for 'and the Son') was the cause of a major theological dispute between East and West.

Another cause of dispute was the increasing importance given to

the primacy of the Bishop of Rome in the West. Since the time of
Damasus (d. 384) the 'Petrine texts' in the Gospels had been used
increasingly to prove the doctrinal and legislative ascendancy of the
Bishop of Rome.

Damasus at a council in AD 382 made these claims for Rome:

> The Roman church possesses a primacy over all the other
> churches in virtue, not of conciliar decisions, but of the Dominical
> promise to St Peter, i.e. the *Tu es Petrus*, and for its foundation
> both he and St Paul were together responsible. It proceeds:
>
> 'The first see of Peter the Apostle belongs to the Roman
> church, "having no spot nor wrinkle nor any such thing". And the
> second see was consecrated at Alexandria in the name of blessed
> Peter by Mark his disciple and evangelist, and he after being sent
> forth by Peter the Apostle to Egypt, preached the work of truth
> and accomplished a glorious martyrdom. Moreover the third see
> of the most blessed Apostle Peter at Antioch is held in honour
> because he dwelt there before he came to Rome, and there first of
> all the name of the new-born race of Christians had its origin.'[11]

To the Eastern churches the papacy was first but only the first among
equals (*primus inter pares* in Latin). Added to these doctrinal and
legislative disputes was the fact that the churches looked so different
from the outside: the Eastern churches had never insisted on a
celibate clergy but this had become a norm in the Western church;
two differing types of eucharistic bread were used, unleavened in the
West and leavened in the East; the ministers of the church looked
different, bearded in the East, clean shaven in the West.

All of this need not have led to a schism, but in 1054 the papal
legate put a bull of excommunication on the altar of Hagia Sophia in
Constantinople. Cardinal Humbert's action is usually said to have
been the beginning of the Orthodox-Catholic schism.

Here is part of the letter of excommunication by Leo IX to
Michael Caerularius, Patriach of Constantinople, 1054:

> 5. . . . You are said to have publicly condemned the Apostolic
> and Latin Church, without either a hearing or a conviction. And
> the chief reason for this condemnation, which displays an
> unexampled presumption and an unbelievable effrontery, is that

the Latin Church dares to celebrate the commemoration of the Lord's passion with unleavened bread. What an unguarded accusation is this of yours, what an evil piece of arrogance! You 'place your mouth in heaven, while your tongue, going through the world,' strives with human arguments and conjectures to undermine and subvert the ancient faith . . .

11. . . . In prejudging the case of the highest See, the see on which no judgment may be passed by any man, you have received the anathema from all the Fathers of all the venerable Councils.

32. . . . As a hinge, remaining unmoved, opens and shuts a door, so Peter and his successors have an unfettered jurisdiction over the whole Church, since no one ought to interfere with their position, because the highest See is judged by none . . .[12]

Of course the schism was already there in all but name. There were several attempts to mend the schism, which were not helped when the Western Crusaders in 1204 sacked the city of Constantinople. Agreements were however put together in the next four centuries but came to nothing because they were not usually received in the East. When the Turks took Constantinople in 1453 further dialogue with the West was clearly out of the question, with the Eastern Christians eventually becoming a persecuted minority in a Muslim state. Similar plights overtook the other Orthodox and Monophysite churches in the East.

5

The Reformation Divides
and Subdivides

Around 1500 it would be fair to say that the Western church was united. There had been large schisms in the past, not least the splits in the papacy when at one time there had been three who claimed to be rightful pope, but these were resolved in 1417 and for the rest of the century there had been comparative quiet. Some criticized the Renaissance papacy for its excesses, not least Savonarola, the Dominican monk from Florence. The papacy indeed was not as exemplary as might have been expected. Alexander VI (1492–1503) had at least two illegitimate children and his surname Borgia was synonymous with corruption; Julius II (1503–1513) spent a lot of his time in armour fighting wars in the Italian peninsula and seems to have spent the rest of his time asking Michelangelo when he was going to finish the ceiling of the Sistine Chapel; Leo X (1513–1521) from contemporary portraits looks a gross man and he certainly did not have the theological wit to see what Luther was talking and writing about.

It is impossible to compress into a paragraph the history of Martin Luther. In the end it is about being sure of personal salvation. Theology at the time said that no one could do enough to be absolutely sure of salvation but that God had to intervene to make good what a human being could not do. The best description is this. The distance between God and humanity is vast and human beings can only go so far, even when they do their best: Because there is a gap between the best that humans can do and God, God fills it with his gracious act. All human beings have to do their best (doing 'what in them lay' as the theologians put it) and God supplies the rest by the merits of Christ. The analogy often used was of two coins, one of bronze the other of gold. God requests a golden coin from us but we can only offer him a bronze one. The deficiency is enormous, but God allows the bronze coin to be worth the same as the gold one he requires. It's a wonderful analogy, but suppose that persons cannot be sure that they have reached even the bronze standard? How can you be sure you have done what in you lies? Luther's dilemma even after becoming an Augustinian monk was clear; how could he be sure that he had done enough to ensure his salvation? The solution came to him while reading Paul's Letter to the Romans, and the doctrine of justification by faith could be said to be Luther's discovery. Human beings can do *nothing* towards their salvation; they get right with God (are justified) through faith in Christ.

> I had certainly been overcome with a great desire to understand St Paul in his letter to the Romans, but what had hindered me thus far was not any 'coldness of the blood' so much as that one phrase in the first chapter: 'The righteousness of God is revealed in it.' Although I lived an irreproachable life as a monk, I felt that I was a sinner with an uneasy conscience before God; nor was I able to believe that I had pleased him with my satisfaction. I did not love – in fact, I hated – that righteous God who punished sinners, if not with silent blasphemy, then certainly with great murmuring.
>
> At last, God being merciful, as I meditated day and night on the connection of the words 'the righteousness of God is revealed in it, as it is written: the righteous shall live by faith', I began to understand that 'righteousness of God' as that by which the righteous lives by the gift of God, namely by faith, and this sentence, 'the righteousness of God is revealed', to refer to a passive righteousness, by which the merciful God justifies us by faith, as it is written, 'The righteous lives by faith'. This immediately made me feel as though I had been born again, and as though I had entered through open gates into paradise itself. From that moment, the whole face of scripture appeared to me in a different light.[1]

Luther used the sale of indulgences, which were said to guarantee the release of souls in purgatory for a money payment, to publicize his discovery, and his act of attaching ninety-five theses to the door of the church in Wittenberg on 31 October 1517 was both a protest against indulgences and an invitation to debate the issue. This date is usually taken to be the start of the Reformation. Eventually Luther came to question not only the Catholic solution to human salvation and indulgences but also the authority of councils, popes and bishops, the number of sacraments instituted by Christ, and the place of the lay nobility in the church. Finally in 1521 he was outlawed by the authority of the imperial diet which took place at Worms in Germany. Luther claimed that the chief organ for deciding the doctrines of Christianity was not a pope or a council but scripture.

> To these words the imperial orator replied in tones of reproach that Luther's answer was not to the point; it was not for Luther to call in question things which had once been condemned or defined by Church councils. He therefore demanded a simple answer with no strings attached: would Luther revoke or would he not?
>
> Luther replied: 'Since your serene Majesty and your lordships request a simple answer, I shall give it, with no strings and no catches. Unless I am convicted by the testimony of scripture or plain reason (for I believe neither in Pope nor councils alone, since it is agreed that they have often erred and contradicted themselves), I am bound by the scriptures I have quoted, and my conscience is captive to the Word of God. I neither can nor will revoke anything, for it is neither safe nor honest to act against one's conscience. Amen.'[2]

Sometimes his attitude has been described as *sola scriptura* (scripture alone) but he was sensible enough to recognize that scripture alone could not solve every difficulty, e.g. why the church baptized infants and why the eucharist was celebrated in the way that it was.

Ulrich Zwingli claimed that he in Zurich had been preaching Reformation themes even before Luther. Certainly in this part of Switzerland the Reformation was more radical; two of the obvious differences were the way in which the churches were totally stripped of all ornaments and statues, and the new thinking on the eucharist which made it a bare memorial of the Last Supper. In July 1530, Zwingli made his final statement on the eucharist.

I believe that in the holy meal of the eucharist (that is, of giving thanks), the true body of Christ is present in the mind of the believer [*fidei contemplatione*]: that is to say that those who thank the Lord for the benefits conferred on us in his son acknowledge that he became true flesh, truly suffered therein and truly washed away our sins by his own blood. Thus everything done by Christ becomes as it were present to them in their believing minds. But that the body of Christ, that is his natural body in essence and reality, is either present in the supper or eaten with our mouth and teeth as the papists, and some who long for the flesh pots of Egypt [the Lutherans], assert, we not only deny but firmly maintain to be an error opposed to the word of God . . .

The natural body of Christ is not eaten with our mouth as he himself showed when he said to the Jews who were arguing about the corporeal eating of his flesh, 'The flesh is of no avail', that is, for eating naturally, but for eating spiritually it is very much so as it gives life . . .[3]

Later, in Geneva, John Calvin (1509–1565) gave the Reformation a strong support in his theological and biblical works, while offering a biblical basis for the church's ministry with his pastors, elders, doctors and deacons. The Presbyterian tradition (so called from the presbyters or elders of the church) became the largest and widest spread of the Reformation Churches and gained footholds not only in Switzerland but in France, Scotland, England, Hungary and in the Netherlands. The fourfold ministry of pastors, elders, doctors and deacons was held to be the main form of ministry in the New Testament (Eph. 4.11, etc.).

The English Reformation has to be seen partly in the light of the events on the continent but partly as a phenomenon all of its own. Reformation ideas were already around in England when Henry VIII made the breach with Rome in 1533 over his desire to divorce Katherine of Aragon, who had not been able to furnish a male heir. Everyone knows the story of the other five wives and the lone, somewhat sickly, boy born from Jane Seymour who became Edward VI. Henry's archbishop by 1533 was Thomas Cranmer who we know became increasingly Protestant in his thinking.

In the ordering of a reformed worship, his own interest came to the fore and he showed a real initiative. The litany in English was his own handiwork. Its euphony, economy of expression, and general charity make it without contemporary parallel. Equally, in the first Prayer Book of Edward VI, talent and aptitude combined to encourage his genius to rise to its fullest expression. His telescoping of the traditional monastic offices into Morning and Evening Prayer for the use of lay people has proved itself, over a period of nearly four centuries, peculiarly adapted to English temperament and religious feeling. The collects which he translated from the Sarum rite, together with those of his own composition, show uniformly the right 'touch': a 'touch', however, which was lacking in his verse as he himself was the first to admit.

It is by his contribution in this field that Cranmer deserves well of the Church of England. The political reformation, leading to the breach with Rome, was essentially the work of the King, aided by Cromwell. The religious Reformation begun, in spite of himself, by Henry, and advanced by Somerset and Northumberland in the reign of Edward VI, took its worshipful shape from the piety of Cranmer.[4]

Already by Henry's death in 1547 the monasteries had been dissolved (in 1536 and 1539), the English Bible had been put into each church for the use of the laity (1536) and a Litany in English produced (1544). After Henry's death the chantries were also dissolved (those places in churches, cathedrals and elsewhere where Mass was said for the souls of the dead in purgatory) and two English Prayer Books were produced in 1549 and 1552.

How Protestant England had become by the death of Edward in 1553 is debatable because the new services in English which were clearly Protestant in intention had not been in circulation long and some priests were interpreting them with Catholic eyes in any case. The reign of Mary (1553–1558) brought back a papal Catholicism to which the people of England had not been accustomed for some twenty years. Notable executions took place of some 282 Protestants, including Bishops Ridley and Latimer and Archbishop Thomas Cranmer. The Queen died without giving birth to any offspring, though it was clear that any of her successors would have been Catholic since she had married the King of Spain, Philip II.

Elizabeth (1558–1603) was the daughter not only of Henry VIII but of the convinced Protestant, Anne Boleyn. It was unlikely that she would want to move England in anything other than a Protestant direction. And so it proved, though there was constant conflict in her reign between the Church of England faction (sometimes called 'Anglican' though this word was only used later) and the Presbyterian faction. The Presbyterian faction was very quickly termed 'Puritan', since it wanted services to be held in accordance with the scriptures only, in the light of the 'pure' word of God. The other Church of England faction took its stand on the 1559 Book of Common Prayer, a minor revision of Cranmer's book of 1552. The other faction in Elizabeth's reign was of course the Roman Catholic. Increasingly Catholics were subject to more and more severe penalties during Elizabeth's reign and became known in this period as 'recusants' (from the Latin word *recusare*, to refuse) because of their refusal to attend the services of the Church of England.

In the 1580s Robert Browne and Robert Harrison in Middleburg, Holland, established the first Congregational church. First called Brownists, they believed in a 'gathered' church of believers, not in a church which was authorized or established, as was the Church of England under Elizabeth. This ideal of the gathered church of the chosen few who were holy Christians became an important facet of the new thinking about the church.

> Browne's views were set out in a series of books he published in 1582. For him the church was by definition 'planted or gathered', 'a company or number of Christians or believers which by a willing covenant made with their God are under the government of God and Christ'. Every member of the church should be a 'king, a priest, and a prophet under Christ': a king because he joined in pronouncing the church's censures, a priest because he shared in its ministry of prayer, a prophet because he should help to 'exhort, move, and stir up to the keeping' of Christ's laws.[5]

Critics of the new thinking argued that constant splits in such church groups would be inevitable, that no one could be sure who was truly a member of the elect, that children would have to be converted members in their turn, but the Congregationalist form of the church had come to stay.

A little later another group took the 'gathered' church concept a little further when they insisted in 1612 that believers' rather than infant baptism should be essential.

The new practice soon grew in favour, for the Particular Baptist Confession of Faith of 1644 says:

> The way and manner of the dispensing of this Ordinance the Scripture holds out to be dipping or plunging the whole body under water; it being a sign, must answer the things signified, which are these: first, the washing the whole soul in the blood of Christ; secondly, that interest the Saints have in the death, burial and resurrection; thirdly, together with a confirmation of our faith, that as certainly as the body is buried under water, so certainly shall the bodies of the saints be raised by the power of Christ, in the day of the resurrection, to reign with Christ.

Both the General and the Particular Baptists adopted the new practice, thus making baptism exactly what it was in the New Testament times, both as regards the mode and the recipient.[6]

Since members *chose* to become Baptists and to be part of the true church, they refused the idea of the Calvinists that people were predestined to become part of the true church. In 1633 a congregation in London of Calvinists took the opposite line and became 'Particular Baptists' because of their belief in predestination. The earlier and eventually smaller group of 1612 took the name of 'General Baptists'.

By the time of the English Civil War the Puritan party was mainly composed of Presbyterians (who wanted the church to be structured as at Geneva, and consequently without bishops) and Independents (at this time the Congregationalists were so called). For a while England and its churches were under a mainly Presbyterian structure until the return of Charles II in 1660. Charles at first offered liberty 'to tender consciences'. His Declaration of Breda, issued on 4 April 1660, contained the following words:

> And because the passion and uncharitableness of the times have produced several opinions in religion, by which men are engaged in parties and animosities against each other which, when they shall hereafter unite in a freedom of conversation, will be

composed or better understood; we do declare a liberty to tender consciences, and that no man shall be disquieted or called in question for differences of opinion in matters of religion, which do not disturb the peace of the kingdom; and that we shall be ready to consent to such an Act of Parliament, as upon mature deliberation shall be offered to us, for the full granting of such indulgence.[7]

But by 24 August 1662 all clergy had to accept the revised Book of Common Prayer or renounce their ministry in the church.

This awful edict enforcing the Book of Common Prayer which came into force on St Bartholomew's Day formally divided the English church into Anglicans and Dissenters. In all some 1,900 or so ministers were ejected from the established church out of a total of about 8,500. Some of these were the sort of people the established church could ill afford to lose such as Richard Baxter of Kidderminster, the writer of *The Reformed Pastor*, the great book that describes the pastoral office of the minister.

We must also have a special eye upon families, to see that they be well ordered, and the duties of each relation performed. The life of religion, and the welfare and glory of Church and state dependeth much on family government and duty. If we suffer the neglect of this, we undo all.

Get certain information how each family is ordered, and how God is worshipped in them, that you may know how to proceed in your carefulness for their further good. Go now and then among them when they are like to be most at leisure, and ask the master of the family whether he pray with them or read the Scriptures or what he doth?

. . . You are like to see no general reformation till you procure family reformation. Some little obscure religion there may be in here and there one; but while it sticks in single persons, and is not promoted by these societies, it doth not prosper, nor promise much for future increase.[8]

John Wesley, although himself a priest of the Church of England, was perhaps unique in having two dissenting grandfathers, who were ejected in 1662, John Westley (as the name was originally spelt) and Samuel Annesley, the great London pastor and preacher.

A few years after the ejection, in 1668, a new religious movement sprang up in England, the Society of Friends or Quakers, founded by George Fox. Fox believed that in every person was the divine light of Christ and that this inner-light was the best guide rather than the teachings and traditions of the churches which were on the whole all too human. This doctrine of the light Fox found later in the scriptures. Believers are more open to the Holy Spirit, even though he dwells in the hearts of all, so that in the silence of the Quaker worship the true believer would be open to the leading of God.

> All Friends everywhere, meet together, and in the measure of God's spirit wait, that with it all your minds may be guided up to God and to receive wisdom from God . . . And Friends, meet together; . . . and know one another in that which is eternal, in the Light which was, before the world was . . . And if ye turn from this Light, ye grow strange; and so neglecting your meetings, ye grow cold, and your minds run into the earth, and grow weary and slothful and careless, and heavy and sottish, and dull and dead.[9]

From this belief the Quakers, despite their small numbers and despite horrendous persecution in England, moved into their numerous practical activities which have given them an influence beyond their numbers. Thus little more than one hundred years after the Elizabethan settlement of religion of 1559 with the publication of the third Book of Common Prayer, the church in England was split along the denominational lines that have been familiar to us ever since.

The emergence of the Methodist movement is treated in more detail above. It is of interest that John Wesley found sources for his view of church and spirituality from all the sources mentioned above. He was a great exemplar of the 'catholic spirit', as it was then called, drawing from the continental Roman Catholics such as Fénelon and Juan d'Avila, from the Anglicans such as Jeremy Taylor and William Law, the Dissenters represented by Richard Baxter and John Bunyan, and from the continental pietists and mystics such as Johannes Arndt and Pierre Poiret.

Smaller groups of Christians in England remain to be described. The Brethren emerged from the establishment of a group in Plymouth by J. N. Darby in 1830 – hence the name Plymouth

Brethren, which is used by others and not by themselves. They combine elements from the puritan stream of Presbyterians, Congregationalists and Baptists, but also from the pietist stream represented by the Moravians and Methodists. Their initial emphasis was on the expected return of Christ to take up his people in the air (the rapture) and the need for holiness and entire consecration to Christ. They have usually been anti-denominational, believing that all churches, Protestant and Catholic, have lapsed from the purity of the New Testament church. As a gathered Christian community they 'break bread' every Sunday, although they had for a long time no approved ministry; many of their assemblies now have full-time ministers. Due to controversies over the human nature of Christ and church government they split into two groups in 1849, 'Open Brethren' and 'Exclusive Brethren'. Today the Open Brethren have about 1420 congregations with about 62,000 members. The stricter Exclusive Brethren have about 12,500 members in around 400 churches.

> The Christian fellowships known as Brethren owe their origins to a spontaneous movement of the Spirit in the early years of the nineteenth century, in a not dissimilar fashion to the Methodist societies of the eighteenth century. They began as liberating communities of believers who wished to meet with one another on the sole basis of their common faith in Christ and without denominational constraints on their unity.[10]

The early Methodists in England were joined in 1739 by Selina, the Countess of Huntingdon. When John Wesley agreed to differ with George Whitefield over his Calvinism and belief in predestination, Selina took Whitefield's side and opened Trevecca in Wales as a training college for Methodist itinerants, Calvinistic Methodists as they became known. Before her death in 1790 she formed her chapels into an association called 'The Countess of Huntingdon's Connexion', of which there existed some seven chapels, often containing wealthy congregations. Trevecca had supplied ministry to many other places before her death, Wales being the chief beneficiary of her bounty, and the Welsh Calvinistic Methodist Connexion became the strongest single denomination in Wales. In England the denomination has always been small, and at present numbers about a thousand members in twenty-four churches.

The Churches of Christ originated in the USA as a schism from Presbyterianism. The scriptures form the basis of their faith, creeds being rejected. They practise believers' baptism and celebrate the Lord's Supper every Sunday, while holding to a congregational polity. Although small in numbers they have exerted an influence on the ecumenical movement which is disproportionate to their numbers. One of their ministers, Philip Morgan, was for several years the General Secretary of the British Council of Churches. In 1981 the majority of the Reformed Association of Churches of Christ agreed to join the United Reformed Church, thus uniting two different doctrines and practices of baptism.

The Congregational Federation was re-formed in 1972 from those congregations who resisted the union of Presbyterians and Congregationalists in England to form the United Reformed Church. Their stance has been fiercely independent and they have in Revd Elsie Chamberlain a strong advocate of independency. Their numbers at 1980 were just over 10,000 in about 290 churches. Each local Church Meeting is autonomous and the members of the Federation refuse to be made as alike as 'fish fingers'.

> One of our ministers used the illustration of the huge variety of fish in the sea but whatever is made into fish fingers is reduced to uniformity. 'We don't want to be fish-fingers!' To quote the former Bishop of Taunton: 'Unity described by Paul is a harmony not a unison. Variety is not a problem to be overcome – it is a necessity. It is a glory, not a problem. Any approach to unity that neglects or overcomes that variety is a mistake!' And Edward Carpenter, Dean of Westminster, spoke of 'the cutting edge of the denominations'.[11]

Communities of Orthodox Christians in England tend to be in the areas where there are large cities and where small groups of Greeks, Cypriots, Russians and Serbians live. The attraction of the 'timeless' liturgy and the art of the icon have been significant in the conversion of many intellectuals to Orthodoxy, including John Tavener the composer. Tavener is a member of the Russian Orthodox Church which has about 1,500 members in five churches in Britain. The total Orthodox community is about 290,000 members in just over 200 churches.

However, it is also the case to quote tradition 'that we know where the Holy Spirit is, but we do not say where He is not.' The Orthodox Church does not own the Holy Spirit, and He 'bloweth where He listeth.' Consequently in our dealings with other churches we look for the marks of the Spirit: of love, of repentance, and seek to relate these to the 'right believing' of the apostolic faith as set forth in the Nicene Creed. Whilst we seek good relations with Christians everywhere, we feel particularly drawn to all those denominations that seek to preserve and promote the gospel of our Lord Jesus Christ untainted by modernist interpretations.[12]

When William Booth, a minister in the Methodist New Connexion in 1861, saw the need to become a travelling evangelist, his request was refused by the Conference. By 1868 Booth had some thirteen independent preaching stations and became general of a number of independent evangelists. The Salvation Army was inaugurated in 1878, Booth became General in 1879 and the *War Cry* was first published in the same year. Flags and uniforms quickly became the norm of the new group while brass bands were formed to blow down the opposition from hecklers. Tambourines followed in 1881 and helped the singing of revivalist songs. In 1890 Booth published his *In Darkest England and the Way Out*, showing that 10% of England lived below the level of normal human beings. The Army quickly showed itself able to reach those parts of the population that other denominations could not reach. It is still one of the best known and loved Christian groups in England and its social work has been extensive. Salvationists number about 65,000 in Great Britain worshipping in some 930 places. Since they insist that the reception of inward spiritual grace does not depend on outward observance, they do not celebrate sacraments.

WE BELIEVE that just as the true church universal comprises all who believe in the Lord Jesus Christ, so each denominational church comprises a community of true believers who have in common the way the Lord, who through His Holy Spirit has dealt with them as a community. In turn, each denominational church comprises local churches regularly meeting together for worship, fellowship and service in a relatively confined geographical location.

> WE DO NOT BELIEVE that the validity of a denomina-
> tion or its local churches depends upon any particular ecclesiasti-
> cal tradition, structure, hierarchy, form of worship, or ritual.
> Where even two or three gather in Christ's name there He is
> present (Matthew 18.20) with a presence no less real than that
> discerned in larger, more formal or ritualistic settings.[13]

Other splits from the early Methodists total about 6,000 members at
present, mainly the Wesleyan Reform Union and the Independent
Methodists.

Unitarianism in England was fathered by John Biddle around
1652 in London, although he had previously published several
pieces about the unipersonality of God against the doctrines of
Trinity and the divinity of Christ. Joseph Priestley (1733–1804) and
James Martineau (1805–1900) were famous Birmingham Unitarians, the former suffering the destruction of his house by fire for his
beliefs. Their belief in the fundamental goodness of human nature
makes them critical of the orthodox doctrines of the Fall of
humanity, the need for Atonement by Christ, and the punishment of
the damned in Hell. At present the Unitarian and Free Christian
Churches is an association of about 9,000 members in some 240
churches.

> To present and nurture the eternal truths as well as the latest
> scientific thinking, and in a critical but supportive atmosphere to
> venture, in as open a manner as possible without an unhealthy fear
> or sense of guilt, into the unknown future. Organized Unitaria-
> nism promotes and defends the free and disciplined search for
> truth and meaning wherever it may lead, believing that this is an
> imperative for the wholeness and vitality of the human spirit. It
> follows from this that churches do not limit the range or extent of
> enquiry. Thus creeds are rarely to be found, and all orthodoxies of
> thinking whether personal or collective are open to challenge.[14]

The Moravian Church in Great Britain and Ireland has about
3,700 members in some 43 churches, and claims descent from the
Unitas Fratrum (the Bohemian Brethren) which began in 1457, a
radical group of followers of John Hus. The group was renewed
through the leadership of Count Zinzendorf, on whose estate at

Herrnhut in Saxony the Czechs found shelter. Their special emphasis is on the church as a fellowship of believers. Though small in number they were very influential in the beginnings of the Methodist movement in both America and England, their emphasis upon the necessity of conversion with the fellowship group being particularly important.

> Those entering the Church . . . are not required to give formal assent to any creed or doctrinal statement beyond an acknowledgment of Jesus Christ as Saviour and Lord. Members of the Moravian Church are allowed a great deal of personal freedom in interpreting and understanding the Christian Faith. 'In essentials, unity; in non-essentials, liberty; in all things, charity' sums up the Moravian attitude both to doctrine and practice.[15]

Perhaps a comment by Richard Baxter from 1681 might be a useful way to end this chapter:

> I earnestly desire to see that Wall or Hedge pull'd down, that Christ's Flock among us may be one . . . Your thorn-hedge hath enclosed but one corner of Christ's Vineyard, and I have business in the rest.
>
> I will go sometime on both sides of the Hedge, though by so doing I be scratcht.[16]

6

Strange Ideas: Protestant

English Christianity has been mainly Protestant for over four hundred years and it is tempting to think when cut off by the Channel from mainland Europe that we are the norm. When it is remembered that most Christians in the world are Catholic and that the next largest groups are Orthodox, it is well to remind English Protestants that in world terms, they belong to a minority cause. To the majority of Christians in the world, then, Protestants have some strange emphases.

Scripture alone – a paper pope?

Exaggerated ideas of the extent of papal authority have often been put out both by Catholics and Protestants. That they are exaggerations is explained briefly in the next chapter. Catholics have sometimes accused Protestants of replacing papal authority with biblical authority. The flesh and blood Bishop of Rome is replaced with a paper pope, perhaps with greater authority for Protestants than the pope has for Catholics. A parody of this position was once put as, 'I always read my Bible, it tells me what to think.' Catholics would argue that the Bible is a first-century document and earlier and that contemporary problems cannot be solved by it except by the church's meditation and reflection on scripture. In other words, scripture needs the authority of the church to help Christians understand its implications for today. The Bible cannot then be used as the ultimate authority, as a paper pope.

Any understanding of the Bible in the Protestant churches has to be very carefully stated. There are those who are usually described as 'fundamentalists', but there are many problems with this view and we shall leave it to be examined in a later chapter. 'Scripture alone' was a very important understanding that derived from the Reformation period, although some even earlier writers had come close to holding it. It means in practice that all doctrinal understanding and all moral understanding has to be derived from scripture and to be consistent with scripture. But the Reformers were not so unintelligent as to believe that the full doctrine of the Trinity and the description of Jesus Christ as 'of one substance with the Father' were to be lifted straight from the texts of scripture. The Thirty-Nine Articles puts the point very well in Article Six: 'Holy Scripture containeth all things necessary to salvation: so that whatsoever is not read therein, nor may be proved thereby, is not to be required of any man, that it should be believed as an article of the Faith, or be thought requisite or necessary to salvation.' The Anglican Reformers probably thought that the full doctrine of the Trinity and 'one substance with the Father' could be read in scripture or proved by it. That there were enormous arguments in the early church about these and other matters perhaps indicates that the Reformers were a bit out of touch with the history of the early church. However, their point is clearly put – the scriptures contain all things necessary to salvation.

The problem that Protestants have to engage with here is how a first-century book, whose contents were probably only finally decided in the late fourth century, can be always the most important authority when the Holy Spirit has also been directing the church for some two thousand years. If revelation ended with the death of the last apostle, as it has usually been put, did Jesus not promise that the Holy Spirit would continue to guide the church into all the truth (John 14.26, 16.13)? Protestants would argue that the guidance of the Holy Spirit has not always been clear; it is hardly possible that the execution of More and Fisher, on the one side, and Cranmer, Ridley and Latimer, on the other, were due to the Holy Spirit inspiring the church to do opposite things in sixteenth-century England. Nor could the Thirty-Nine Articles of 1562 and the Council of Trent which began in 1545 and met until 1563 have both been expressing the mind of the Holy Spirit. See, for example, their contradictory statements about the sacrificial aspect of the Mass:

XXI Of the One Oblation of Christ finished upon the Cross
The Offering of Christ once made is that perfect redemption, propitiation, and satisfaction, for all the sins of the whole world,

both original and actual; but there is none other satisfaction for
sin, but that alone. Wherefore the sacrifices of Masses, in the
which it was commonly said, that the Priest did offer Christ for the
quick and the dead, to have remission of pain or guilt, were
blasphemous fables, and dangerous deceits.

If anyone says that the sacrifice of the Mass is merely an offering
of praise and thanksgiving, or that is a simple commemoration of
the sacrifice accomplished on the cross, but not a propitiatory
sacrifice, or that it benefits only those who communicate; and that
it should not be offered for the living and the dead, for sins,
punishments, satisfaction and other necessities, *anathema sit*.

If anyone says that the sacrifice of the Mass constitutes a
blasphemy against the most holy sacrifice which Christ accomplished on the Cross, or that it detracts from that sacrifice,
anathema sit (statements from the 1562 session of the Council).

Where there is doubt over these issues, there isn't a final
authority. Councils have erred (remember the Council of Constance
which in 1415 burned John Hus), popes have even been heretics
(history points to Vigilius in 553 and John XXII in 1333), bishops
have not always defended the faith (the episcopate in the pre-
Reformation period were canon lawyers rather than theologians),
and priests have not always preached the gospel to their flocks. Only
scripture can therefore claim to have the necessary authority to offer
to humankind the message of salvation. Therefore in modern times
the scriptures have been translated into most of the languages on
earth and have been distributed far and wide. The power of the
scriptures to convert people to the way of Christ has been proved
time after time, sometimes without any reference to any church or
ecclesiastical organization.

Thomas Bilney, the English Reformer, seems to have been
converted in this way; in his own words:

> . . . at last I heard speak of Jesus even when the New Testament
> was first set forth by Erasmus; which when I understood to be
> eloquently done by him, being allured rather by the Latin than by
> the word of God for at that time I knew not what it meant, I bought
> it even by the providence of God (as I do now well understand and

perceive): and at the first reading (as I well remember) I chanced upon this sentence of St Paul (O most sweet and comfortable sentence to my soul) in I Tim. i: 'It is a true saying and worthy of all men to be embraced that Christ Jesus came into the world to save sinners, of whom I am chief and principal.' This one sentence, through God's instruction and inward working, which I did not then perceive, did so exhilarate my heart, being before wounded with the guilt of sins, and being almost in despair, that even immediately I seemed unto myself inwardly to feel a marvellous comfort and quietness, insomuch that my bruised bones leaped for joy.[1]

The scriptures have been their own interpreter. As the Nazi leader said in Scandinavia in 1942, 'the Bible is much too topical'. Far from being a first-century document, the scriptures prove that Christ speaks to his people through them still and no official interpreter is needed bar the Holy Spirit who brings the truth of the Word to God's people. This is the sense in which Protestants believe in the idea of private judgment. It is not really private judgment of the scriptures so much as the Holy Spirit revealing what is necessary for the salvation of the individual.

Believers' baptism

Over the years many people will have taken part in debates about infant baptism. Usually the arguments for it look pretty thin when compared with the case for baptizing believers who are usually but not necessarily adults. When the New Testament is carefully read there are only explicit references to people being admitted to the Christian church as adult believers. The only reference which might include children is when Paul refers to the baptism of households (I Cor. 1.16). Evidence for infant baptism in the scriptures looks extremely thin. Even in the early church after the time of the New Testament one of the few bits of major evidence comes from Polycarp who was burned at the stake in 156 who stated 'six and eighty years have I served him'.

So he was brought before the Proconsul, who asked him if he were Polycarp? He said 'Yes,' and the Proconsul tried to persuade him to deny his faith, urging, 'Have respect to your old age,' and the rest of it, according to the customary form, 'Swear by the genius of Caesar; change your mind; say, "Away with the Atheists!"' Then Polycarp looked with a stern countenance on the multitude of lawless heathen gathered in the stadium, and waved his hands at them, and looked up to heaven with a groan, and said, 'Away with the Atheists.' The Proconsul continued insisting and saying, 'Swear, and I release you; curse Christ.' And Polycarp said, 'Eighty-six years have I served Him, and He has done me no wrong; how then can I blaspheme my King who saved me?'[2]

Presumably this refers to an early infant baptism for him some eighty-six years before. Otherwise the evidence for infant baptism is that it was only done from about the mid-third century as a rule. Even in the fourth century great Christians such as Basil, Gregory of Nyssa and Augustine were only baptized in their thirties. Small wonder that in the sixteenth century a small group in Zurich led by Conrad Grebel felt that believer's baptism should be the norm; as a result they baptized each other. This group was the first group of 'Anabaptists', so called because they baptized all over again after their initial baptism as infants, which of course was meaningless because not authorized in scripture. Even among the early Protestants of Zurich Grebel and his followers were thought to be a threat to the city's security and some were drowned for their obstinacy.

Thus a colloquy or disputation was called by the council for 17th January [1525], to be held in the City Hall before councillors and Zurich citizens as well as scholars. At that time . . . Mantz, Grebel, and also Reublin were present to argue their case that children could not believe and did not understand the meaning of baptism. Baptism should be administered to believers to whom the Gospel had been preached, who understood it, and who therefore desired baptism, wanting to kill the old Adam and live a new life. Of this children knew nothing; therefore, baptism did not belong to them. They quoted passages from the Gospels and the Acts of the Apostles and showed that the Apostles did not baptize children, but only mature and understanding people. Thus should it be done today. Since there had been no proper baptism, infant baptism was not valid and everyone should be baptized again.[3]

Anabaptist or Baptist groups in England had enormous difficulties at the start of their existence and several met their deaths by execution. It is a point of interest that the early English Baptists did not baptize by their later method of total immersion but were content to sprinkle their converts. The Baptist principle of believer's baptism is one major instance where scripture has been regarded as fundamental to the way in which the church must move. The tradition of infant baptism must give way to the biblical relevation of believer's baptism. The Bible indicates believer's baptism was the norm and must be preferred to infant baptism.

Inspired by the Spirit

Orthodox, Anglican and Catholic often find problems with Protestant services. They are, they say, totally unpredictable and you never know what is coming next, whereas with the eucharistic liturgy you always know what happens next. This lack of form, this lack of books of service, in many Protestant churches can be a problem even for other Protestants.

The reason usually given is that the form of service, the hymns, the prayers, perhaps even the preaching, must be open to the influence of the Holy Spirit. Too many services otherwise might seem lacking in warmth, with little involvement of the people, with no attempt to reach those who have come for the first time and are not already initiated into the churches. The openness to the Spirit, the spontaneity of the services, the feeling of not being constrained by a set form of service, these are crucial ingredients for many Protestant churches. Sometimes the service is even more open to the Holy Spirit of God and speaking in tongues may take place or healings of members of the congregation may occur, or people might be slain in the Spirit (the 'Toronto Blessing' as it has come to be called). This way of holding services may not always fit in with people who prefer things to be quiet and respectable, but for young people and others who are not hidebound by conventions it may be the main way of their reaching God. It has the great advantage, too, that there are no class or colour barriers in this more open worship. In fact it is interesting that a great many of the black people of England prefer the open charismatic, non-liturgical style to the conventional liturgy of either the Church of England or the Roman Catholics.

Good fun and fellowship

People who have not been to church for a long time on their return want to hide in the back pews and probably do not want a handshake. They sometimes complain that Christians can be too friendly. I remember how for years I had gone to a high Church of England church, had always taken my own book from the back of the church and never had a handshake. I was then amazed when at the local Methodist church a hymnbook was put into my one hand while the other was grasped in a handshake and I was welcomed with, 'Good evening, young man'. What to me was very impressive could of course be off-putting to others.

The handshake and the welcome are really part of a theological package that many Protestant churches offer to people. These churches believe that Christianity, even while being fundamentally serious, should be fun and be enjoyable. Christians should actually like being together in worship and in groups for fellowship. They do not need to keep each other at arms length but can be honest to each other in conversation, knowing that other Christians will hear and understand. At their best such churches can be fine examples of how church can really be the people of God. If there is one small drawback, it is that fellowship with other believers, including groups for spiritual conversation as well as social and informal groups, can take the whole of people's existence. I know of one person who was so committed to the life of the local church that her father remarked to her, 'You might as well take your bed down there as well – you're never here.' Being a member of a local church can then take the whole of one's time when not gainfully employed. This sometimes means that when people leave a particular office in the church which has taken a large commitment of time, they take the opportunity to leave that church altogether. In the end they refuse to continue to take their beds to the church building with them.

Hymn-singing

Some Christians are horrified when they come to, say, a United Reformed, or a Baptist or a Methodist Church to find that they have to sing five or six hymns, sometimes with repetitions. This seems a disproportionate amount of time, say twenty minutes, to take out of what it might be hoped will be an hour's service. If the prayers are short, the readings short, and only the sermon and the hymns are long, it looks as if major parts of the Christian way of doing things are being neglected. After all, Christianity is about prayer and Bible reading as much as about hymns. And of course even the hymns they do sing have had the tunes changed from the ones we used to sing at school assembly.

An old maxim is that 'the law of praying is the law of believing'. Many Protestants would want to make this into 'the law of singing is the law of believing'; we sing what we believe and experience. When Methodists sing:

> Jesus – the name that charms our fears,
> That bids our sorrows cease;
> 'Tis music in the sinner's ears,
> 'Tis life, and health, and peace

they are singing of a Methodist experience in the past that has become theirs and that they hope will be the experience of others in the future. Other hymns of course are about Christian belief rather than direct experience but the hymns which affect people most are those that tie in with their own Christian experience. Others can sing with the utmost seriousness:

> Majesty, worship his majesty
> Unto Jesus be glory, honour and praise

because this is what they believe and this is what the scriptures affirm. It may be that for some Christians the singing of hymns and songs is a better realized form of praying and a more easily approached method of Bible reading. Which means of course that Christian hymn writers need to be very careful about what they write, and ask themselves, is it good doctrine? A thought that might help was once offered in a book of Christian definitions:

Hymn: a song with good theology and a poor tune.

Chorus: a song with a good tune and poor theology.

Perhaps every hymn book ought to be carefully examined to see whether it does in fact offer in verse form what we believe.

Many of the above emphases of Protestantism would have seemed strange to Roman Catholics before the period of the Second Vatican Council, 1962–65. Since the council, so many things that would have had a 'Protestant only' label have been taken into the Roman Catholic Church that to Roman Catholics of a previous generation the church might seem to have gone Protestant. The emphasis on Bible study in spiritual formation has become central, the Rite for the Christian Initiation of Adults has centred on baptism as the means of admission into the church, Roman Catholics are committed to the Charismatic Movement as much as are Protestants, Catholic parishes are much more likely to be welcoming than they were, and hymnody has become central to many parishes. But there are still some obvious differences between Roman Catholics and Protestants, as we shall see.

7

Strange Ideas: Catholic

Idolatry?

Around 1970 an Anglican bishop revisited a Catholic church where he had last preached at a time just after the Second Vatican Council had begun. He noticed the difference of 'after' from 'before' the Council. He turned to the parish priest in the crowded vestry and asked loudly, 'Peter, where are all your idols?'

To sound Protestants the average Catholic church is still a place where statues and religious pictures (sometimes called 'icons' if they are painted according to the conventions of the Orthodox Churches) are far too apparent. They feel that the only relevant illustration of Christianity should be an empty cross, as a symbol of Christ's work and a sign of his resurrection. Statues and pictures of the Virgin Mary and the saints seem to take the prior place of Christ in Catholic Christianity. Since it seems that these objects replace Christ as the central person of Christianity they are thought to be idolatrous.

The Catholic response might be expressed as follows. Christianity is a religion that is based on the coming of God into human form – incarnation is the technical word which means God taking on flesh. If this is true then the ordinary stuff of matter can be used to depict this. Human beings who have reached a particular level of holiness are examples to other Christians, so that pictures and statues of the saints may help to remind us of the life of perfection that is possible. It has to be remembered that Christianity is not just verbal and written but needs to have an embodiment in people. For most of the Christian centuries, through lack of literacy and the cost of literature, the written word was not available to most Christians. These had the faith depicted for them in their churches in stained glass, rood screens, statues and paintings.

A dispute about the use of paintings and statues arose in Eastern Christianity around the end of the seventh century. Because it was thought by one side that icons and images should be destroyed it was called the 'iconoclastic controversy'. It was eventually solved by an ecumenical council which met at Nicaea in 787, a council which was accepted by churches throughout the Christian world. The use of images to represent Jesus Christ, the Virgin Mary, the angels and the saints, is encouraged while an important distinction is made:

> The more frequently they are seen in representational art, the more are those who see them drawn to remember and long for those who serve as models, and to pay these images the tribute of salutation and respectful veneration. Certainly this is not the full adoration in accordance with our faith, which is properly paid only to the divine nature . . .

The council distinguished between 'adoration' or 'worship' which must be paid only to the Trinity, and 'veneration' which could be offered to the saints and the Virgin Mary by means of the images which represented them. Two points of interest arise. One is that Nicaea II is the last council to be acceptable to both the Eastern Orthodox and the Roman Catholics. As the last fully ecumenical council its conclusions deserve to be taken on board, not only by Orthodox and Catholic but by Protestants as well. Interestingly, some Protestants see the last council of the undivided church as Chalcedon in AD451. The second is that much has been made of Catholic 'adoration' of images. This stems from the unfortunate translation of the Latin *adoratio* which looks like 'adoration' when it ought to have been translated as 'veneration'.

Papal infallibility?

As Pius IX approached the end of his life in 1878 he had been for some eight years 'a prisoner in the Vatican' due to the reunification of Italy and the consequent collapse of Papal Rome in 1870 to the Italian forces. He had been pope for thirty-two years and such a long papal term of office had been thought impossible beyond twenty-five years, the time according to legend during which Peter was the leader of the church in Rome. Pius' successor Leo XIII was ninety-three when he died, having reigned for twenty-five years in his isolation in the Vatican.

'The old man in the Vatican' had of course been pronounced 'infallible' at the First Vatican Council just before the fall of Rome in 1870. To some it seemed as if it was no longer necessary for bishops and priests to teach the faithful the essence of the Catholic faith; it would come down in ready-made infallible parcels from the pope.

Maisie Ward describes her grandfather, William George Ward, a Roman Catholic convert from Anglicanism in 1845, as one with a complete adherence to the Roman obedience:

> The views he held on all these matters formed a complete pattern in his mind. He would have liked constant and daily guidance from Rome, 'a Papal Bull every morning with his *Times* at breakfast'. He interpreted all papal documents in the narrowest sense and to many of them he ascribed a degree of authority disavowed by the Roman theologians.[1]

Whatever her grandfather said about the state of the world or about how the church as a whole should think would have come from the pope, acting as it were as a spokesman from God. This was certainly the fear in England after 1870 and in 1874 W. E. Gladstone wrote an alarming pamphlet called *The Vatican Decrees and their Effect on Civil Allegiance*. For Gladstone, the Catholic acceptance of papal infallibility meant that Catholics would look to Rome for their allegiance rather than be good English citizens.

The Catholic response goes somewhat as follows:

1. The pope is infallible only under certain conditions laid down by Vatican I, e.g. when he speaks definitively on faith and morals (not just any old statement of faith and morals but one that has to be seen to be defined) and, when he speaks as chief pastor of the whole church (not just as the bishop of the diocese of Rome or even patriarch of the West).

2. Infallibility has only in fact been invoked once since 1870 when in 1950 Pius XII defined the Assumption of the Blessed Virgin Mary into heaven. The definition of the Immaculate Conception was of course made earlier, in 1854, by Pius IX.

3. Infallibility is a negative quality, i.e. the quality of not being

wrong, and it does not mean that the moral or doctrinal point at issue cannot at some future time be better expressed.

4. Infallibility has a sort of 'touch of Midas' feel to it and is hardly going to be used frequently. Once in 125 years is not too often and probably an average might be once every hundred years, e.g. the Immaculate Conception of the Blessed Virgin Mary was proclaimed by Pius IX in 1854 some ninety-six years before the proclamation of the Assumption.

5. The pope is morally obliged to sound out the faith of the Roman Catholic Church on matters which are defined, specifically from all the bishops of the church as to whether this definition is their faith and also the faith of the Catholic people as a whole.

The right of the pope to have jurisdiction in any part of the church is of course a wider question than that of infallibility. This was also stated in 1870 at the First Vatican Council. Sometimes it has been subject to some criticism, most of all when inappropriate episcopal appointments have been made.

To many people outside the Roman Catholic Church infallibility is much less of an issue than the papal power to intervene in the working of any diocese in the church. After all, the exercise of infallibility is very rare, whereas the exercise of papal jurisdiction is very common.

More than scripture

When the definitions about Mary were made in 1854 and 1950 they were said to be in accordance with scripture and to be part of the Christian tradition. Now tradition is a very slippery thing; it could mean a lot of different things. Sometimes it means the traditional teaching of the Fathers, those theologians and teachers of the first few centuries up to about the time of Gregory the Great (d. 604), particularly their understanding of the meaning of the Bible. Sometimes it means the teaching of the councils of the church from the first at Nicaea in 325 through the other six councils to the later purely Roman Catholic councils of Trent, Vatican I and Vatican II. Other times it has meant 'the way Catholics have always thought and how they have always done things'. In this latter sense tradition is applied to liturgy, to the popes, to the beliefs of the Catholic laity, to devotional practices. This 'more than just scripture' concept is indeed hard to pin down because it doesn't mean just one thing.

Catholics would argue that the faith has never been passed on by writing alone and that scripture alone is not enough for the life of the church. The Holy Spirit has matters concerning Christ that he continues to reveal to the church down the ages:

> But the Paraclete, the Holy Spirit, whom the Father will send in my name, will teach you everything and remind you of all I have said to you (John 14.26).

> However, when the Spirit of truth comes, he will lead you to the complete truth, since he will not be speaking of his own accord, but will only say what he has been told; and he will reveal to you the things to come (John 16.13).

There are things that have been done by most churches since the beginning of Christianity that have never had specific scriptural support, e.g. ways of doing the eucharist; the threefold ministry of deacon, priest and bishop; the custom of infant baptism; signing oneself with the sign of the cross; the use of a ring in marriage. Where the church has defined its faith it has not always found its terminology in scripture, the best example being the use in the creed we now call Nicene (in fact it dates from Constantinople in 381) of the term 'of one being with the Father' (in Greek *homoousios*) of the person of Christ. The papacy cannot be found in scripture (as was gleefully pointed out at the Reformation) although the primacy of Peter among the apostles is clear and the so-called 'Petrine texts' (Matt. 16.16ff., Luke 22.31ff., John 21.15ff., etc.) give a basis for what became more fully developed later. The idea of 'development' is in fact a very important one in Catholic theology. It implies that under the influence of the Holy Spirit the church will develop its doctrine from century to century and what was once implicit will eventually become explicit. The analogy often used is that of the acorn which over a long period develops into an oak tree. The acorn needs good fertile ground, heat and water in order to grow. A doctrine develops in the mind and hearts of the faithful people of God by devotional practice, by participation in the liturgy, by hearing the doctrine expounded by priests and bishops, until the Holy Spirit has brought the doctrine to such a state of maturity in the church that it can be defined as a dogma of faith. This process Catholics see as having taken place in the slow development of the two dogmas about Mary, the Immaculate Conception and the Assumption.

> Now what was handed on by the apostles includes everything which contributes to the holiness of life, and the increase in faith of the People of God; and so the Church, in her teaching life, and worship, perpetuates and hands on to all generations all that she herself is, all that she believes.

> This tradition which comes from the apostles develops in the Church with the help of the Holy Spirit. For there is a growth in the understanding of the realities and the words which have been handed down. This happens through the contemplation and study made by believers, who treasure these things in their hearts (cf Luke 21.19, 51), through the intimate understanding of spiritual things they experience, and through the preaching of those who have received through episcopal succession the sure gift of truth. For, as the centuries succeed one another, the Church constantly moves forward toward the fullness of divine truth until the words of God reach their complete fulfillment in her.

> . . . Consequently, it is not from sacred Scripture alone that the Church draws her certainty about everything which has been revealed. Therefore both sacred tradition and sacred scripture are to be accepted and venerated with the same sense of devotion and reverence.[2]

That such dogmas are not shared by most Protestants is because Protestants have not been part of the particular community of faith in which the definitions came to be. Had they shared, since say 1550, in the Catholic veneration of Mary, they too might have felt the Holy Spirit present in the church to make explicit the dogmatic affirmations about Mary of 1854 and 1950.

That Catholics have always regarded the Bible as the most important source is shown by many interesting facts. During the period just before the English Reformation, because of the danger of heresy in the fifteenth century due to followers of Wycliffe (often called 'Lollards'), the vernacular Bible was not permitted in England from 1408. However, in Germany, where the Reformation began, some twenty German versions were published between 1466 and 1522. During the penal period in England the Catholics had the Douai Bible (1609) and later Bishop Challoner produced a new English translation in 1750. It is of interest that Challoner cautioned his own Catholic people about the Methodists in 1760 in a small work that abounded in scriptural quotations to support Catholic doctrine. Recent Catholic documents have put scripture in the forefront in an amazing way. For example, see the Vatican II Dogmatic Constitution on the Church (*Lumen Gentium*) and also the recent papal encyclicals on morals (*Veritatis Splendor*) and ecumenism (*Ut Unum Sint*).

> Thus, the Church is the sheepfold whose one and necessary door is Christ (John 10.1–10). She is the flock of which God Himself foretold that He would be the Shepherd (cf Is. 40.11; Ez. 34.11ff.). Although guided by human shepherds, her sheep are nevertheless ceaselessly led and nourished by Christ Himself, the Good Shepherd and the Prince of Shepherds (cf John 10.11; 1 Pet. 5.4), who gave His life for the sheep (cf John 10.11–15).

> The Church is a tract of land to be cultivated, the field of God (I Cor. 3.9). On that land grows the ancient olive tree whose holy roots were the patriarchs and in which the reconciliation of Jew and Gentile has been brought about and will be brought about (Rom. 11.13–26). The Church has been cultivated by the heavenly Vinedresser as His choice vineyard (Mt. 21.33–43 par; cf Is. 5.1ff.). The true Vine is Christ who gives life and fruitfulness to the branches, that is, to us. Through the Church, we abide in Christ, without whom we can do nothing (John 15.1–5).[3]

The place of Mary

'Mary has taken Christ's place as the centre of Christian life in the Catholic Church.' 'There are more lights in front of the statue of Mary than there are in front of the reserved sacrament.' 'You hear the Hail Mary more than you hear the Lord's Prayer in the Catholic Church.' Protestants have for many centuries used these complaints against what they see to be excessive veneration for Mary. They have objected to England being called 'the dowry of Mary' as if extra prayers to Mary might one day make England a fully Catholic country. The Marian shrines at Walsingham, Egmanton and Willesden were some of the first places to be destroyed at the English Reformation. They say that prayers should be addressed not to Mary but to God through Jesus Christ by the help of the Holy Spirit. She has almost become a fourth person in the godhead in Catholic spirituality, as in one of the writings of Leonardo Boff:

> The mysterious reality of Mary's divinization has not gone unnoticed in the collective unconscious of the Church – the *sensus fidelium*. In his analysis of the elements of the unconscious and our interior archetypal archeology, Carl Jung has demonstrated an unconscious demand for the divinization of the feminine. Simple folk, in the innocence of an unarticulated faith and far removed from the discourse of official othodoxy, have always rendered Mary the homage of adoration.
>
> If Mary has been spiritualized by the Third Person of the Trinity, then everything that can be predicted of the Holy Spirit can be predicted of Mary and vice versa, by virtue of the general theological principle of the *perichoresis*.[4]

They argue that the definitions of the Immaculate Conception and the Assumption are totally unscriptural and only have a basis in an extravagant devotion that made Mary a mediatrix between Jesus and humanity because it was falsely thought that she would be kinder as a woman than her Son would be. Some of the devotions offered to Mary such as the *Salve Regina* and *Mater Coeli* are frankly idolatrous.

Catholics do have a strong devotion to the Virgin Mary. They do not pray to her as some seem to think. They ask for her prayers to God on their behalf. She is able to be a strong intercessor because she is in heaven and because as Mother of God she is closest to her Son. Why Protestants do not hear more about Mary they fail to understand. There is far more about her (129 verses) in the New Testament than there is about the eucharist (29 verses). She takes a leading part in the Christmas story when she gives birth to the incarnate God. She was there at Jesus' death and was in Jerusalem at Pentecost when the Holy Spirit was poured out. Yet Protestants seem embarrassed to mention her. Far from taking the place of

Christ, she was the first to benefit from the salvation that he came to offer. Because of the merits of Christ, before she gave birth she was already preserved from the stain of original sin (her Immaculate Conception). After her life on earth she was assumed body and soul into heaven (the Assumption), again because of the merits of Christ. Mary was in fact the first believer and could be thought of as the first to experience what has always been known as justification by faith. Can veneration towards the one who was the Mother of God ever be excessive? She knew Christ better than any other person, and was responsible for his early upbringing. When Catholics say the *Ave Maria* they are quoting scripture for the most part.

> Hail Mary, full of grace,
>> the Lord is with thee; (Luke 1.28)
>> blessed art thou among women,
>> and blessed is the fruit of thy womb, Jesus. (Luke 1.42)
> Holy Mary, Mother of God,
>> pray for us sinners
>> now and at the hour of our death.
>>> Amen.

When they cease to quote scripture in the prayer they ask Mary as Mother of God to pray for us now and at the hour of our death. It was the Council of Ephesus in 431 that defined Our Lady as Mother of God (*theotokos*), a council which is accepted by most churches as ecumenical. Perhaps Protestants need to look at Mary again.

The saints

It's interesting that not many Protestant people bear the names of the great saints of the church, e.g. Francis, Dominic, Ignatius, Gregory, Benedict, Teresa, Hilda, Rita. They tend to prefer biblical names such as John, Paul, David, Ruth, Rachel, Sarah, etc. The Catholics have made saints of so many people down the centuries that there is more than one for each day of the week. On 16 May for example they have Saints Brendan, Carontoc, Honoratus of Amiens, John Nepomucen, Peregrine of Auxerre, Possidius and Ubald of Gubbio. Any other day chosen arbitrarily would yield similar numbers. Some saints of course were canonized by the papacy because they had been anti-Protestant, for example the Forty English Martyrs (though it is only fair to say that at the canonization ceremony there were representatives of the Church of England and that Protestant martyrs also got a mention). But don't all these people, good as they may have been, stand in the way of Christ? If we have so many good examples of Christianity (of a sort) aren't we tempted to lose sight of Jesus and all he has done for us? In any case, the word 'saints' is used in the New Testament for all Christian people and not just for a selected few. Who knows who is in heaven? When we say 'we believe in the communion of saints' we mean that there is a communion which we see here on earth which we believe will be continued in heaven. But who will be there we don't know. We can only hope we might arrive there after death. Such is the Protestant argument concerning the saints.

The Roman Catholic response goes something like this. Saints are the great examples of the life of faith. They are 'the great cloud of witnesses' who have made it to heaven (Heb. 12.1). Because they have been canonized we are sure that they are in heaven with God and can ask for their prayers. Calling ourselves by their names means that they in particular can help us in our pilgrimage on earth as we go towards heaven. The English saints are interesting because there were so many of whom we know so little (e.g. the saints of Cornwall) and yet there were some remarkable ones (Chad, Cuthbert, Hilda, Julian of Norwich, Hugh of Lincoln, etc.) that belong to pre-Reformation times. There might be interest in veneration of post-Reformation people, e.g. the Wesleys, Wilberforce, Temple, etc. We all need our saints, whether they be Catholic or Protestant ones.

8

Is there Convergence
about the Bible?

We begin with a parody of positions about this:

1. The Bible is the Word of God to us. Not only is it the greatest authority in Christianity but it has come down to us with no mistakes nor confusion about its meaning. Although human writers were responsible for it the Holy Spirit was its inspiration to safeguard it from error.

2. The Bible was written in different places and by diverse people. There is no one overall principle to it as it is a human product. There will be differing views of God in it as seen in both the Testaments. There will be different pictures of Jesus Christ in it; Matthew and John for example give very different accounts of him. Because it is a very human book and an ancient one too, it is difficult to see clearly how it applies to the twentieth century.

3. The Bible belongs to the church and can only be understood within the church. Thus the interpretation of the scriptures belongs to the church authorities and it is not a matter of private judgment. Members of the church should therefore not be encouraged to read the scriptures except with the guidance of authorized teachers of the faith. Unauthorized interpretation of the scriptures has often led Christians into heresy.

As indicated, these are parodies of positions held by Christians and it is doubtful if anybody could be found who holds any of the three as stated above. The first one might be described as the 'fundamentalist' position which sees scripture as in some definite way safeguarded from error in that what we read can be believed as from the mouth or mind of God. It is only fair to say that it only arose in its present form as a reaction against nineteenth-century biblical scholarship and is quite a recent thing, having its major exponents in the so-called 'Bible belt' of the USA. The second position is the 'liberal' one and might only be held by those few scripture scholars who are on the borders of church life. The ideas of human production and differing theological positions about God and Jesus Christ are however held by nearly all scripture scholars. How an ancient book can be applied to the twentieth century is the problem usually called 'hermeneutics', itself now an important branch of theology and vital of course for preachers. The third position might be called 'pre Vatican II Roman Catholic', though even this description is unfair to Roman Catholic thought before 1962. It regards the Bible as leading people into heresy if read outside the direction of the *magisterium* (teaching authority) of the priests and bishops of the church. 'Private judgment' was the accusation thrown at Protestants at the time of the Reformation. This is implied by the Introduction to the New Testament in the Douay version of 1582:

> We must not imagine that in the primitive church . . . the translated Bibles into the vulgar tonges were in the hands of every husband-man, artificer, prentice, boies, girles, mistresse, maide, man: that they were sung, plaied, alleaged of every tinker, taverner, rimer, minstrel: that they were for table talk, for alebenches, for boates, and barges, and for every prophane person and companie.

The Douay translation offered Roman Catholics a faithful rendering in place of the impure versions of the Protestants which would harm their souls. If the Bible is read within the church's life and worship, it is read aright, says this position.

Samuel Taylor Coleridge, the poet and philosopher, once wrote that people are usually right in what they affirm but wrong in what they deny. This might be a useful guideline for ecumenical dialogue that we could apply to biblical interpretation. Let us see where it takes us.

1. The 'fundamentalist' position is right in its affirmation that the Bible is the Word of God to us. The denial that the Bible can be regarded as a human book is the problem with the position. The affirmation that the Holy Spirit is present is best seen as his presence when the Word is read and heard rather than his presence to ensure that no errors creep into its writing.

2. The 'liberal' position affirms the diversity of the Bible, different authors, different contexts, different dates of composition, etc. The implicit denial of any 'divine' element in it is one that we do not need to go along with. Different pictures of Jesus and different theologians should be a helpful affirmation. The denial of its authority for the twentieth century goes too far, especially when it is expressed in such terms as these, which are not uncommonly heard: 'How can a book composed mainly in the first hundred years after Christ have authority for me in the late twentieth century? It addresses different contexts from my context, its thought world is totally alien, its morals are not as nuanced as mine in the twentieth century. It has no more authority than a twentieth-century book on theology and ethics, perhaps, since the latter can at least speak to my context, it has even less.'

3. The 'pre-Vatican II' view of the Bible affirms that the Bible belongs within the church community if it is to be understood rightly. The denial of the right of private judgment forgets that most people who read the Bible actually belong to churches where individual interpretations can be corrected against the normal teaching and preaching heard there. The laity are not seeking to go off and look for new heresies but are actively concerned to understand the faith better. The Constitution on Divine Revelation from the Second Vatican Council encouraged Roman Catholics to more regular and sustained Bible reading and gave encouragement to translations done ecumenically.

Easy access to sacred Scripture should be provided for all the Christian faithful . . . But since the word of God should be available at all times, the Church with maternal concern sees to it that suitable and correct translations are made into different languages, especially from original texts of the sacred books. And if, given the opportunity and the approval of Church authority, these translations are produced in cooperation with the separated brethren as well, all Christians will be able to use them.[1]

But what about biblical scholarship? In the nineteenth century arguments ranged far and wide about matters of biblical interpretation. Was there a first man called 'Adam' and was there really a 'Fall' when it was clear that human beings had evolved from ape-like creatures?

Did the universal flood really happen; was there a Noah and an Ark when signs of a world-wide deluge are in fact very sparse? If the Gospel writers were interpreters and not historians of the life of Jesus, how could we be sure that Jesus said this or that? More importantly, could the story of the events of redemption, the passion, the crucifixion, the resurrection, be trusted as historical if the biblical writers were separated by over thirty or more years from them and had in any case used the Old Testament to illustrate the events? If there really was doubt about the authorship of Ephesians, Colossians, II Thessalonians, Hebrews, James, I, II, III John, I, II Peter and Revelation, where did that leave the inspiration of the Bible?

It is interesting that the early church had quite similar problems with scriptural interpretation and its authority. The Alexandrian Christian Origen had pointed out as early as the third century that to attach the names of Paul and John to Hebrews and Revelation respectively was nonsense since the Greek style differed so greatly from the other pieces attributed to them. Eventually some four levels of interpretation were thought in the early church to lie in scripture:

1. The literal explanation of the passage.

2. The allegorical explanation, e.g. Augustine took the parable of the Good Samaritan in the following way: the injured man was the Christian on his/her pilgrimage, the Samaritan was Christ, the inn was the church, the oil and wine were the sacraments which healed the soul.

3. The moral explanation: the scriptures are showing us how we should live as Christians in the world.

4. The spiritual explanation: the scriptures show us the way to heaven and therefore there is a level of explanation which relates to our pilgrimage to the heavenly destiny God has prepared for us.

All these levels had become standard exegesis in the church by the start of the seventh century. Luther in the sixteenth century felt obliged to reject this fourfold exegesis of scripture and preferred if possible the literal sense to be applied.

When I was young I was learned, especially before I came to the study of theology. At that time I dealt with allegories, tropologies, and analogies and did nothing but clever tricks with them . . . I know they're nothing but rubbish . . . The literal sense does it – in it there's life, comfort, power, instruction, and skill. The other is tomfoolery, however brilliant the impression it makes.[2]

But even he could not completely reject the past great interpreters of scripture such as Augustine and the literal sense did not always dominate Luther's exegesis of scripture.

The period called the Enlightenment probably caused the most problems for the Christian interpretation of the Bible. There was a polarization of that which could be taken as 'true' and that which was 'false'. The whole Bible had to be either 'true' or 'false'. When Jesus walked on the water, for example, was this 'true'? Since people do not usually walk on water the usual answer was 'false'. Some rational interpreters, however, were not content to leave it there, and Carl Friedrich Bahrdt, *c.*1782, suggested that some planks were available on the water and Jesus made use of them, unknown to his disciples who interpreted it as miraculous. In similar rational ways the feeding of the five thousand was explained as the boy with five loaves and two fishes so shaming the gathering with his display of generosity that they all shared what they had with each other. This 'sharing their sandwiches' view of the feeding is still sometimes heard from pulpits. What the Gospel writers would have said in response to it can only be guessed. The Enlightenment seems to have led to an 'either it is the Word of God or it isn't' view of the Bible. In England before the rise of the geological sciences and the evolutionary theory of Darwin, 'it is the Word of God' seems to have held sway. What geology and evolution did to this view is now well known. The age of the earth was not dateable from 4004 BC, as Archbishop Ussher had painstakingly calculated in the seventeenth century, but was many millions of years before and the large movements of the earth had taken millions of years to occur.

In the absence of any other data, efforts were made to derive a possible age for the earth from chronologies of the patriarchs in the book of Genesis (plus a good deal of imaginative guesswork). On this slender basis James Ussher, Archbishop of Armagh, and John Lightfoot, Chancellor of Cambridge University, jointly concluded that the date of Creation was 400 BC – a piece of misinformation printed in successive editions of the Authorized

Version of the Bible from 1701 onwards (and thereby given a quite spurious degree of authority).[3]

Darwin seemed to show, as a few others had indicated before him, that evolution and 'the survival of the fittest' was the way in which life had come about on earth. It seemed that there was now no place for the heavenly Designer as there had been in the previous centuries. In the meantime the Bible was under threat from within the church. *Essays and Reviews*, published in 1860, the year after Darwin's *Origin of Species*, suggested that the human authorship of the Bible must be taken seriously. In South Africa, in 1863, Bishop Colenso threw doubt on the early history of Genesis. In England F. D. Maurice was brought before the Privy Council for denying the usual teaching about hell but was allowed to continue his professorship at King's College, London.

Sensible attitudes did prevail, however, and much credit for this goes to the 'Cambridge Triumvirate' of B. F. Westcott, J. B. Lightfoot and F. J. A. Hort. These Anglican biblical scholars in their lectures and biblical commentaries showed that textual work on the Bible did not militate against the faith of the Christian church but rather reinforced it. Their work can still be read with profit. Biblical scholarship was strong also in the Free Churches in the late nineteenth century and mention must also be made of the Methodist A. S. Peake, and the Baptists Wheeler Robinson and John Clifford. A lot of Wesleyan Methodists and such Baptists as C. H. Spurgeon, however, would not espouse this new view of the Bible.

Modern scholars have pointed out the pretty obvious fact that the Bible is not a scientific textbook. As Galileo said in the seventeenth century, 'the Bible points to where the heavens are, not the way the heavens move'. Perhaps we should not look for the origins of the earth in its pages except the affirmation 'in the beginning God . . .' The Big Bang and the Big Crunch, the wave corpuscular theory of light, the periodic table of the elements, and the primaeval soup are not there in Genesis and it would be unrealistic to expect the Old Testament which reached almost its present state in about the fifth century before Christ to contain the findings of twentieth-century science. Scholars have been exercised to remind readers of the Bible to find different levels of writing there. As children we were all told that the Bible contained stories (not the same as histories), poems, proverbs and wise sayings, letters, apocalyptic, prophecy, as well as history and myth. To see only one level of writing in the Bible, direct verbal contact between God and humanity, is clearly to go against what we learned as children. Any immature attitude to the Bible will leave us with an inadequate understanding of what it has to say to us.

Until fairly recently it was thought that there could be no concensus about biblical authority or the place of biblical scholarship in the life of the church. For example, it was thought that Roman Catholics rejected the usual methods used by mainline Protestants to interpret the Bible, namely what has been called the 'historical–critical' method. It was also thought that there would be no agreement between the 'historical-critical method and the work of scholars from the more openly evangelical parts of the churches. It has been made clear from recent work that Roman Catholic biblical scholars, e.g. Raymond Brown in his works on the birth and death of Jesus and in his commentaries on the Johannine works, have taken the historical–critical method totally seriously. A look at some of the commentaries on the Bible from the evangelical camp shows that this is also true of that constituency.

In 1993 a document came from Rome that received little publicity and yet is of first importance. It was called *The Interpretation of the Bible in the Church*[4] and came from the Pontifical Biblical Commission, the work of authorized Catholic biblical scholars worldwide. The Commission document begins by reminding readers that the Bible has a human side and a divine side. While human authors were clearly responsible for the writings, the understanding the church has is that God communicates through the text by the operation of the Holy Spirit. The text of the document accepts the critical –historical method. This is applied in several ways. The first is that by means of 'textual criticism' a text is put forward which comes as near as scholars can come in the present state of the subject to the original texts of the biblical books. Next by 'literary criticism' scholars come to see the original sources of the texts. The best two examples of this are: the documentary hypothesis which finds four different sources in the first five books of the Old Testament, usually described as J, E, D and P; the 'two sources' theory of the First Three Gospels whereby the Gospels are derived from Mark as the first with additional material from a source called 'Q' (from German *Quelle*) which is used in different ways in Matthew and Luke. Next the method of 'form criticism' indicated the situation of the Gospels in life (German *Sitz in Leben*). Form criticism was then supplemented by 'redaction criticism' which helped by showing how the Gospel writers formed their material according to their own particular theological tendencies which shaped their work. This enabled scholars to show why the Jesus of Mark was different from the one of Luke who was different from the one of Matthew. The document of the Pontifical Commission is anxious that deeper meanings of scripture are to be allowed so that the critical–historical method does not have total dominion. For example, while the biblical sense of the texts are paramount, the 'spiritual' sense is also essential for Catholic exegesis. The Old Testament can thus be spiritualized in those parts which seem to have reference to Christ while written before the time of Christ. The grounds for this are that scripture is read under the influence of the Holy Spirit and in the context of the death and resurrection of Christ from which new life flows. The commission also wants to urge a 'fuller sense' as a deeper meaning intended by God but not expressed by the original author. Thus it states that the definition of original sin by the Council of Trent gives the fuller sense to Paul's teaching in Rom. 5.12–21 about the consequences of the sin of Adam for humanity. While individual Protestant scholars would have some problems with the spiritual sense, it is almost certain that most would not have time for the fuller sense as described above. This seems to lift important texts out of time altogether and introduce God the Holy Spirit to confirm what the Roman Catholic church has decided by a human process of consultation.

> In a word, one might think of the 'fuller sense' as another way of indicating the spiritual sense of a biblical text in the case where the spiritual sense is distinct from the literal sense. It has its foundation in the fact that the Holy Spirit, principal author of the Bible, can guide human authors in the choice of expressions in such a way that the latter will express a truth the fullest depths of which the authors themselves do not perceive.[5]

Finally, the document accepts that the theology of liberation and the feminist approach to the Bible have important parts to play in the full exegesis of God's work. But there is no tolerance for a fundamentalist interpretation which is defined as starting from the principle that 'the Bible, being the word of God, inspired and free from error, should be read and interpreted literally in all its details'.

The fundamentalist approach is dangerous, for it is attractive to people who look to the Bible for ready answers to the problems of life. It can deceive these people, offering interpretations that are pious but illusory, instead of telling them that the Bible does not necessarily contain an immediate answer to each and every problem. Without saying as much in so many words, fundamentalism actually invites people to a kind of intellectual suicide. It injects into life a false certitude, for it unwittingly confuses the divine substance of the biblical message with what are in fact its human limitations.[6]

Fundamentalism is opposed to the historical–critical method and all other scientific methods of biblical study. The basic problem is that because it refuses to take account of the historical nature of biblical revelation, it is incapable of believing in the incarnation where the divine and the human came together. By its emphasis on one fixed translation it dismisses the value of textual criticism; by equating the final shape of the Gospels with the historical figure of Jesus it forgets the historical process; by accepting the cosmology of the early chapters of the Bible it loses contact with modern science and culture.

Since the Bible is the common basis of the rule of faith, the ecumenical imperative urgently summons all Christians to a rereading of the inspired text, in docility of the Holy Spirit, in charity, sincerity and humility; it calls upon all to meditate on these texts and to live them in such a way as to achieve the conversion of heart and sanctity of life. These two qualities, when united with prayer for the unity of Christians, constitute the soul of the entire ecumenical movement (cf. *Unitatis Redintegratio* no. 8). To achieve this goal, it is necessary to make the acquiring of a Bible something within the reach of as many Christians as possible, to encourage ecumenical translations – since having a common text greatly assists reading and understanding together – and also ecumenical prayer groups, in order to contribute, by an authentic and living witness, to the achievement of unity within the diversity (cf. Romans 12.4–5).[7]

The positions indicated at the beginning of this chapter are still held however. We have tried to show that they do not make sense in the light of modern science and in the light of biblical scholarship. The work of the Pontifical Biblical Commission has put the ecumenical movement into its debt.

9

The English Scene: Why are
Protestants so Suspicious
of Catholics?

'Henry VIII saw the Church of England in the eyes of Anne Boleyn and as a result in 1533 England became a Protestant country.' That is the myth that still walks about in England and prevents a proper examination of the true issues. Henry was of course concerned for a male heir because of the future of the kingdom, and Katherine of Aragon had only produced Princess Mary. When the new Archbishop of Canterbury, Thomas Cranmer, allowed the King's divorce in 1533, against the will of the pope, it did of course mean a schism with Rome. But from 1533 to the death of Henry it is better to describe English Christianity as 'Catholicism without the pope' than as Protestantism. Despite the work of Cranmer in the reign of Edward VI and the return of the Protestant way of life after the death of Mary in 1558, it has often been remarked that England did not become truly Protestant till about 1580. Catholicism in England died hard as recent authors such as Scarisbrick and Duffy have shown. That is not to say that England was always happy about Rome and the claims about the papacy.

The early period of Christianity in Britain shows that Rome had no important part in the beginnings of Christianity in the island. When Augustine arrived in 597 from Rome Christianity had already been around for over three hundred years. The early Celtic church seems to have been independent of Rome on the whole and the Celtic bishops did not feel that their authority derived from Rome. Bede gives an account of Augustine's reception:

Augustine summoned the bishops and teachers of the nearest British province to a conference at a place still known to the English as Augustine's Oak ... He began by urging them to establish brotherly relations with him in Catholic unity, and to join with him in God's work of preaching the Gospel to the heathen.

The British bishops then consulted a hermit:

'Arrange that he and his followers arrive first at the place appointed for the conference,' answered the hermit. 'If he rises courteously as you approach, rest assured that he is the servant of Christ and do as he asks. But if he ignores you and does not rise, then, since you are in the majority, do not comply with his demands.'

The British bishops carried out his suggestion, and it happened that Augustine remained seated in his chair. Seeing this, they became angry, accusing him of pride and taking pains to contradict all he said.

... But the bishops refused these things [agreement on the date of Easter, to complete baptism by the Roman rites, to join in preaching to the pagan English], nor would they recognize Augustine as their archbishop, saying among themselves that if he would not rise to greet them in this first instance, he would have even less regard for them once they submitted to his authority.[1]

A letter dating from 613 indicates that Columbanus the Irish missionary believed that the church must correct the Bishop of Rome if he were in the wrong, indicating the Celtic belief that the papal power depended on papal orthodoxy. By 664 and the Synod of Whitby the church in England was, at least in theory, committed to the ways of Rome, as shown in the debates over the date of Easter and over the authority of the successor to Peter. During this period we have a large number of records of visits of the English to Rome but it was not usually to pay a papal visit that the English went but to do the pilgrimage of the early Christian areas of Rome and their saints. Relics and their attendant benefits were at stake, not conversations with the popes. In the period before the time of Pope Gregory VII (1073–1087) England had proved very reluctant to take on celibacy for the priesthood; after Gregory VII it was more rigorously enforced, but even then followed with great reluctance. During the rise of papal supremacy over the whole church, roughly the period from Gregory VII to Innocent III, 1073–1216, the closest contacts were made with Rome. Yet even in this period during which an English cardinal Nicholas Brakespeare became Adrian IV (1154–1159), the English church relaxed the papal decrees against clerical marriage, declared Gregory VII's view of papal primacy impossible, while William I insisted on appointing his own bishops and important abbots, and refused to be subject to Gregory VII. During his reign Archbishop Anselm (1093–1109) insisted against William II and Henry I on the papal authority over episcopal appointments. Henry in response refused to allow papal letters from papal legates in England without his permission. The conflict between Henry II (1154–1189) and his archbishop Thomas Becket (d. 1170) has been well documented. Becket fought for the rights of Roman obedience against the king and was eventually assassinated at Canterbury, achieving by this the status of a martyr. In the reign of John (1199–1215) Stephen Langton was chosen by Innocent III as the Archbishop of Canterbury. John refused to accept Langton and seized many of the assets of the English church. Innocent put England under an interdict in 1208 whereby all public worship and sacramental life had to cease. John eventually gave in after an enormous struggle and in 1213 Langton came to England to be enthroned and to absolve John, who was obliged to take an Oath of Fealty.

I, John, by the grace of God king of England and lord of Ireland, from this hour forward will be faithful to God and the blessed Peter and the Roman Church, and my lord the Pope Innocent and his successors who succeed in catholic manner: I will not be party in deed, word, consent, or counsel, to their losing life or limb or being unjustly imprisoned. If I am aware of anything to their hurt I will prevent it and will have it removed if I can; or else, as soon as I can, I will signify it, or will tell such persons as I shall believe will surely tell them. Any counsel they entrust to me, whether personally or by their messengers or their letter, I will keep secret, and will consciously disclose to no one to their hurt. The patrimony of blessed Peter, and specially the realm of England

and the realm of Ireland, I will aid to hold and defend against all men to my ability. So help me God and these holy gospels.[2]

By the mid-thirteenth century the decline of the mediaeval papacy had begun which ended with the 'Babylonian Captivity' of the popes at Avignon. In 1250 the Bishop of Lincoln, Robert Grosseteste, protested to Innocent IV at the exactions of Rome from England and the suggestion that the Pope's nephew should be a canon at Lincoln; the revenue of the crown was not a third of the money claimed yearly to Rome, the demand for a canonry was not in line with the doctrine of the apostles. In 1256 the new pope, Alexander IV, demanded from the church a charge of annates or first fruits, the first year's income from new abbots and bishops, allowing huge sums to leave England for Rome each year. During the papal sojourn in Avignon, 1305–1376, the papacy declined in authority in England, so much so that two important statutes were passed that limited papal influence. By the Statute of Provisors in 1351 (repeated in 1353, 1365 and 1389) it was forbidden to allow bishoprics and other important posts in the English church to be filled or 'provided' by the papal court. The Statute of Praemunire in 1353 (repeated in 1365 and 1393) curbed appeals from England to the papal legal courts.

By 1378 there were two rival popes claiming to be Peter's successor and by 1409 there were three. This situation was only resolved by the election of Martin V at the Council of Constance in 1417. The Great Schism after the Babylonian Captivity did not enhance the papacy in the eyes of the English, nor did the reputation of some of the popes on the eve of the Reformation, Alexander VI (1492–1503) and Julius II (1503–1513) being particularly notorious. In the fifteenth century popes asked at least fifteen times for the taxes which had been imposed on the English church; on the whole their pleas were not heard.

On the eve of the English Reformation it is thus clear that England did not love the papacy or what were held to be the exactions of Rome; annates payable on major incomes of abbots and bishops; the way in which some dioceses were still held by foreigners despite the statutes of Provisors; the payment of 'Peter's Pence' for the running of the papal curia. It is reckoned that an average sum of £4,800 per annum was leaving England for Rome in the period 1485–1533.

This was a very significant sum, and yet it is only the gross value of the two major monasteries of Christchurch at Canterbury and St Mary at York. It is also only 10% of the annual sum taken by Henry VIII from the English church from 1535 to 1547. To say that the English were milked by greedy Roman hands in this period is then a vast exaggeration. When Henry VIII began to put pressure on Rome over his divorce, he was acting as many of his English predecessors had done. First he brought the charge of Praemunire against the clergy of Canterbury and York in 1531. They had accepted the legatine authority of Wolsey and had therefore allowed appeals to be made to Rome which should have gone to the king. The clergy purchased forgiveness for £118,840. Two years later the clergy in convocation stated that the marriage of Henry and Katherine was not legitimate as Katherine's previous marriage to Arthur, Henry's brother, had been consummated. The new archbishop, Thomas Cranmer, married Henry to Anne Boleyn in May 1533 and Elizabeth was born some four months later. The Succession Act ensured that the succession could pass to the heirs of Henry and Anne Boleyn while the Supremacy Act of 1534 acknowledged Henry as 'the only supreme head in earth of the Church of England'. For their refusal to acknowledge the Act of Supremacy and their advocacy of papal authority, Thomas More and John Fisher were beheaded and so were some Carthusians and Franciscans.

> The sixth day of July was Sir Thomas More beheaded for the like treason before rehearsed, which, as you have heard, was for the denial of the King's supremacy. This man was learned, and was Lord Chancellor of England, and in that time a great persecutor of those who detested the supremacy of the Bishop of Rome, which he himself so highly favoured. He stood to it until he was brought to the scaffold on the Tower Hill, where on a block his head was stricken from his shoulders.[3]

But few English Christians went to the stake or the block at this time for obedience to Rome. The dissolution of the monasteries in 1536 and 1539 was not an anti-Catholic piece of legislation but an attempt to raise money for the king's foreign wars. It has been looked on as an anti-Catholic act but it has been seen that way only with a great deal

of hindsight. Before Henry's death in 1547 the theological formulations which defined the faith of the English church varied somewhat,
but 'Reformed Catholicism' is as good as any other description of the
new structure.

With the advent of Edward VI (1547–1553), the boy king,
Cranmer took his opportunity to bring in an English Reformation.
Chantries, where mass had been offered for departed souls, were
abolished, a sign of where the new thinking was going. In 1549 came
the first Book of Common Prayer in English with the new services of
matins and evensong and a revised mass. The more traditional
Catholics regarded it as 'a Christmas game', while the newer
Protestants felt that it did not go far enough. As a result Cranmer
produced the 1552 Book of Common Prayer in which the sacrament
of the Lord's Supper no longer had the alternative title of 'mass' and
certainly had a distinctly un-Catholic looking eucharist which
seemed to owe more to Zwingli the reformer of Zurich than to
Luther and the Catholics.

Mary Tudor (1553–1558) brought Catholicism back to England
but it was of a strange kind. It is possible that her reign would have
been much happier had she accepted her father's title of 'Supreme
Head' of this church. But as the daughter of Katherine of Aragon
she reintroduced a papal Catholicism that England had not
experienced for twenty years. In Protestant understanding she has
gone down into history as 'bloody Mary' since 282 were martyred for
their Protestantism in her five years. The martyrs included Archbishop Cranmer and Bishops Ridley and Latimer, all of whom were
burned at the stake in Oxford. Although a similar number of
Catholic martyrs were executed under Elizabeth, Mary's short reign
made her and her bishops the chief enemies of English Protestantism. It could be that negative associations which attach to the
name of Mary are not principally aimed at the devotion to the
Mother of God but cling to the name of the Queen who restored
persecuting Catholicism to England. Foxe's *Book of Martyrs* (1563)
gave the Protestants an exalted status for the future and put the
Catholic persecutors in a bad light.

Elizabeth (1558–1603), given that her mother was the Protestant
Anne Boleyn, was bound to opt for a Protestant England. She
restored the Book of Common Prayer and accepted the title of

Supreme Governor of the Church of England. It was during Elizabeth's reign that anti-Catholicism in England put down its deep roots. There were fears which centred first in the possibility of Elizabeth marrying the Catholic Philip II of Spain and then in the person of Mary Stuart, Queen of Scots, who was a rival Catholic candidate to the throne of England. While some English Catholics kept chalices and vestments hidden in the hope of a restoration of Catholicism, from abroad William Allen fought a one-man crusade against Catholic attendances at the worship services according to the Book of Common Prayer. While Catholic books and pamphlets were printed on the continent and smuggled into England, the real problem for Catholicism was that it was a Christianity that had no priests. Not until 1574 were priests from the new seminaries able to find their way in secret to England. The years 1568–1570 were crucial for Catholics in England. In 1568 Mary Queen of Scots fled to England and, as next in line to the throne, she became the reason why Roman Catholics were identified with attempts to overthrow Elizabeth. In the same year Douai College was established by William Allen to train priests and scholars for the English mission and to educate Catholic boys. The rising of the Northern Earls in 1569 in an attempt to release Mary Stuart and recognize her as heir to the throne was crushed only after Catholic altars and the mass had been restored in Durham. Pope Pius V encouraged the rising in the mistaken hope that the English Catholics wanted to overthrow Elizabeth but were troubled about taking arms against the rightful Queen. In 1570 he signed the famous bull *Regnans in Excelsis*, claiming that Elizabeth could be lawfully deposed as a heretic, under the illusion that the English were waiting to rise up against Elizabeth.

3. We, seeing impieties and crimes multiplied one upon another – the persecution of the faithful and afflictions of religion daily growing more severe under the guidance and by the activity of the said Elizabeth – and recognizing that her mind is so fixed and set that she has not only despised the pious prayers and admonitions with which Catholic princes have tried to cure and convert her but has not even permitted the nuncios sent to her in this matter by this See to cross into England, are compelled by necessity to take up against her the weapons of justice, though we cannot forbear to

regret that we should be forced to turn upon one whose ancestors have so well deserved of the Christian community. Therefore, resting upon the authority of Him whose pleasure it was to place us (though unequal to such a burden) upon this supreme justice-seat, we do out of the fullness of our apostolic power declare the foresaid Elizabeth to be a heretic and favourer of heretics, and her adherents in the matters aforesaid to have incurred the sentence of excommunication and to be cut off from the unity of the body of Christ.

4. And moreover [we declare] her to be deprived of her pretended title to the aforesaid crown and of all lordship, dignity and privilege whatsoever.

5. And also [declare] the nobles, subjects and people of the said realm, and all others who have in any way sworn oaths to her, to be forever absolved from such an oath and from any duty arising from lordship, fealty and obedience; and we do, by authority of these presents, so absolve them and so deprive the same Elizabeth of her pretended title to the crown and all other the abovesaid matters.[4]

The bull proved a disaster and sadly was never withdrawn by the papacy; the bull showed the English that to be pro-papal was to be a traitor to the nation of England. Acts against English Catholics followed; it was treasonable to say that Elizabeth was not the lawful Queen; the bringing of papal bulls and Roman devotional aids into England was prohibited; stringent fines and terms of imprisonment were the fate of many. The first of the new seminary priests arrived in 1574 and there began the succession of English martyrs, the first being Cuthbert Mayne who in 1577 was hanged and quartered in Cornwall for having a papal bull, saying mass and wearing an *agnus dei* (a medal of the lamb of God). Jesuits such as Robert Parsons and Edmund Campion followed in 1580. Although Campion insisted that he had only come to save souls and acknowledged Elizabeth as Queen (the deposing power of popes was a matter of debate between scholars), he was hanged, drawn and quartered in 1581. In 1581 by acts of Parliament the saying of mass became punishable by death, Catholic recusants were severely fined for refusal to be at the services of the Church of England, and it became an act of treason to reconcile or be reconciled to the pope. Fear of invasion by Catholic powers was the reason offered for much persecution; Catholics would be disloyal if French or Spanish forces invaded England. It is reckoned during Elizabeth's reign that some 125 clergy and 63 lay people lost their lives for their Catholic profession; to the English government, to be a Catholic was to be a traitor. Some 146 Catholics were executed after the passing of an act of 1585 against Jesuits, seminary priests and other disobedient people and fines against recusants quadrupled after 1585.

The Armada of 1588 was a terrifying prospect when it gathered against the naval forces of Britain and it had the support of Pope Sixtus V who released Catholics from their allegiance to Elizabeth. Had the Armada landed and not been blown off course by providential winds, it is extremely doubtful whether the English Roman Catholics would have supported the invasion. The romance of Catholic resistance against Protestants begins about this time. On the one hand there are accounts of the sufferings of the Catholics as the government approved of torture to extract information; the Pit, some twenty feet deep with no light; the Little Ease, a cell in which prisoners could not stand erect; the Scavenger's Daughter, a ring which brought hands, feet and head together; the Rack; keeping prisoners in the same clothes for weeks on end and not allowing access to the lavatory. But if these horrors were to be avoided priests and others had to be hidden; the priests' holes of the large country houses, such as Harvington Hall with the remarkable work of Nicholas Owen, help create a romantic story. By the end of Elizabeth's reign the English Protestants were guilty of anti-Catholic paranoia.

Catholics had high initial hopes of James I (1603–1625) who was the son of Mary Stuart, but these were quickly dashed. By mid 1604 all the Elizabethan anti-Catholic acts were restated, a fine of £100 was payable by those who sent their children to Roman Catholic schools abroad, and fines of £20 per month were levied against those who refused to attend the services of the Church of England. The Gunpowder Plot of 1605 planted the 'conspiracy' theory of papists deep in the English consciousness. While it was unquestionably a Catholic conspiracy against James I hatched by Catesby, Winter, Percy and Fawkes, it is a fact that Henry Garnet the Jesuit leader had tried to stop it. It has been suggested that the Plot was used as a device by Henry Cecil, the king's chancellor, to discredit the Roman Catholics in England. That effigies of Guy Fawkes and the pope have been burned on 5 November every year since 1605 is a sign that the discredit has lasted a long time in the English memory. Catholics after 1606 had to take an oath against the deposing power of the pope, were made to receive communion at Anglican altars at least yearly or suffer large fines, and were obliged to give two-thirds of their estates to the king if convicted of recusancy. Interestingly only twenty-five Catholics died on the scaffold in James' reign and when James died in 1625 England had a Catholic queen in Henrietta Maria, the wife of Charles I.

Under Charles I (1625–1649) it seemed as if the Church of England had reverted to a more Catholic stance, and this was exemplified by William Laud who was Archbishop of Canterbury from 1633. Laud's concern was for the beauty of holiness in the church but this seemed to many to be a pathway back to Rome. Laud believed also in the divine right of kings as the answer to papal claims. The power of the Puritans in the Commons ensured that Laud would be impeached. He was imprisoned for four years before being executed in 1645. His monarch followed in 1649 and England became for a while limitedly Presbyterian with a large number of Independents, of whom Oliver Cromwell and John Milton were the most famous. During the Protectorate of Cromwell some freedom was offered to religious groups, but it was never extended to members of the Church of England nor to Roman Catholics.

Charles II (1660–1685) was certainly sympathetic to the Catholics of England. He was however forced to agree to legislation against them, most notably the act which disallowed Catholics from taking civil or military office on the grounds that they could not take the Oath of Supremacy. By this Act they could receive the Lord's Supper in the Church of England only after taking the declaration that no transubstantiation was believed. It is alleged that Charles was received into the Roman Catholic church on his deathbed. His successor and brother James II (1685–1688) was certainly a Catholic. During his reign the penal laws against Catholics were disregarded while James did his utmost to promote Catholics to high office. From 1685 he restored Catholic bishops to England with the creation of the offices of Vicars Apostolic of first the London region, then the Western region, the Midland region and the Northern region.

> The vast task of organizing the shattered Church in England, of nursing the flickering flame of Catholicism, of sowing the seed that would bring a worthy harvest of converts: this task was far too much for one man, and the King and his solitary bishop, Dr Leyburn, therefore petitioned the Holy See for the appointment of more bishops. The upshot was that in 1688 England and Wales were divided up into four 'Districts', each of which was given its own Vicar Apostolic, and they were known respectively as the London District, the Midland District, the Northern District, and the Western District . . . Dr Leyburn was henceforth to be in charge of the London District, and three new bishops were appointed for the remaining three Districts. Of these, the Northern District was given to James Smith, the Midland to Bonaventure Giffard, and the Western to Dom Michael Ellis, OSB.[5]

The invitation by Parliament to William of Orange and Mary, who began their reign in 1689, is well known. Into Protestant history in Ireland and some parts of England has gone the Battle of the Boyne, 1690, when the forces of 'King Billy' defeated the Catholics under James.

The reign of William and Mary (1689–1703) saw the last of the legislation against English Catholics, in particular an Act of 1700 which meant that anyone caught saying mass, bishop, priest or Jesuit, should suffer life imprisonment while the informers against them should receive £100. As far as the records suggest only one person ever brought a case against a priest who said mass and even then the case was not proved in law. Perhaps the failure of the 1700 legislation showed that England was becoming more tolerant towards Catholics. About three quarters of the way through the century it became clear that Catholic soldiers would be of use both to Scotland and to England. The first Catholic Relief Act of 1778 was designed to relieve Catholics of the disabilities resulting from the Act of 1700. By this Act the arrest of Catholic priests was no longer possible; Catholics could now freely keep schools in Britain; inheritance could pass to Catholic and not only to Protestant next of kin. Catholics were now to take an Oath of Allegiance which meant that they would be loyal to the Hanoverian succession; they would deny the principle 'no faith to be kept with heretics'; they would deny the deposing power of the pope and deny his jurisdiction in England. The Relief Act meant an end to official persecution and an increase in the building of Catholic chapels. The Act met little opposition in England but in Scotland a leader emerged who opposed the Act and became leader of the Protestant Association. Lord George Gordon with 60,000 marched on Parliament in 1780 to present a monster petition against the Relief Act. The mob began a riot that went on in London for some ten days and made London the scene for attacks on Catholics and on their chapels.

Two of the embassy chapels were attacked; the Sardinian embassy in Lincoln's Inn Fields had its chapel burned down; the Bavarian embassy chapel was ransacked and its furniture made into a bonfire in the street. Two days later, the Catholic chapel in Moorfields, the nearest Catholic place of worship to Wesley's new chapel in City Road, was attacked and its contents set on fire in the street outside. During the following days further Catholic property was attacked and burned, the most spectacular instance being Thomas Langdale's gin distillery in Holborn. Langdale, a noted Catholic, had at first tried to conciliate the mob with free gin, but in the end the mob set light to his house and the large gin vats. Men and women drank the flaming gin as it ran down the streets. Dickens, in *Barnaby Rudge*, offers the best description: 'The gutters of the street, and every crack and fissure in the stones, ran with scorching spirit, which being damned up by busy hands, overflowed the road and pavement, and forced a great pool, into which the people dropped down dead by dozens.' In all some 210 people were killed in the riots and some 450 arrested for their part in the disturbances. 'No popery' was the ostensible reason for the riots though since the richer supporters of the 1778 Act were the main victims along with the Catholics the antagonism of the mob was as much against the rich as against the Catholics of London. The Relief Act of 1791 caused very little disquiet in England and the Gordon Riots were never repeated. By the 1791 Act it was no longer an offence to be a Catholic or a priest or to perform Catholic rites, and the learned professions were opened up.

The request for Catholic Emancipation showed the depth of

anti-Catholic feeling in England. The spectre of the 1570 bull which deposed Elizabeth was still causing major fears. Orange Lodges and Brunswick Clubs sprang up all over the United Kingdom from about 1828 when emancipation was in the air. Although the reigning king, George IV, is supposed to have signed the Act of Catholic Emancipation in 1829 with tears in his eyes for the death of the British Constitution, the Act in fact safeguarded Protestantism. No Roman Catholic could become king or queen or take the major offices of state, Catholics entering Parliament were obliged to take an oath to the House of Hanover and against the deposing power of the pope. This oath was only removed in 1871. While the need for MPs to take the declaration against transubstantiation and the sacrifice of the mass was removed, it was nevertheless made illegal for any Catholic bishopric or deanery to have the same title as that in the Church of England. The existence of the titles of Liverpool, Birmingham, Portsmouth and Southwark in both the Roman Catholic Church and the Church of England indicates that the Catholic sees were founded before the Anglican ones. In 1838 and 1839 there appeared very similar articles in *Blackwood's Magazine* and *Fraser's Magazine* on the 'Progress of Popery'. The *Fraser's Magazine* consisted of two articles and was accompanied by a map with black crosses to indicate Catholic chapels and their increase. The *Blackwood's* article was reprinted in pamphlet form priced at 3d and sold several thousands, an indication of the fear of the rapid increase in Catholic numbers to certain Protestants. Some believed that at Emancipation Catholics formed about 10% of the English population; the actual figure was about 3%. *Blackwood's* suggested that by 1839 there were little short of two million Catholics, or about 15% of the population of England. The 1851 census showed that the figure was nearer one million practising Catholics in England and Wales.

Two major rows occurred later in the nineteenth century which showed the antagonism of Protestants towards Catholics in England. The Catholic bishops in England till 1850 were called vicars apostolic and were under the control of the missionary arm of the Roman Catholic Church called Propaganda. The new head of the Roman Catholics in England, Nicholas Wiseman, asked for the hierarchy to be restored to England. In 1850 the negotiations with

Rome were completed and in October Wiseman unwisely issued a pastoral letter called *From Out the Flaminian Gate*. The letter was extremely triumphalist and was seen as provocative in England. Wiseman was to be elevated to the rank of Cardinal and be Archbishop of Westminster. The choice of Westminster with its parliamentary associations was unfortunate, and so was Wiseman's claim to have authority over Middlesex, Hertfordshire, Essex, Surrey, Sussex, Kent, Berkshire and Hampshire. The Prime Minister, Lord John Russell, angrily answered Wiseman, claiming that the assumption of authority over England was incompatible with the authority of the queen and that of the bishops of the Church of England. Fears in England were increased because the Oxford Movement and the Ceremonialist Movement were causing defections from the Anglicans to the Catholics. John Henry Newman, W. G. Ward and F. W. Faber were some of the principal converts who were soon to be followed by Henry Manning and two of the Wilberforce brothers, sons of the great reformer. Riots over ceremonialist excesses in the Romeward direction had taken place at St Barnabas', Pimlico and St Paul's, Knightsbridge. But Wiseman had at least one logistical argument in favour of the restoration of the hierarchy, the need to give pastoral support to the larger number of Roman Catholics now in England due to Irish immigration; it was reckoned by 1861 for example that 600,000 Irish were living who had been born in England and Wales.

A new Archbishop of Westminster, Henry Manning, began his work in 1865. Shortly afterwards an ecumenical council was announced in Rome. Pius IX had already indicated in his pontificate the way that things might go at a council. Coming to Rome with a reputation as a liberal, it became clear that a liberal attitude could not deal with the problems of the Italian peninsula nor the increasingly freethinking Europe in which the papacy was set. The Syllabus of Errors of 1864 seemed to show that the papacy did not want to come to terms with modern civilization. In 1854 the pope had personally defined the Immaculate Conception of the Blessed Virgin Mary. The Vatican Council met only from 1869 till it was forced to end its deliberations in 1870 as Rome was threatened with invasion by the forces of Italy. In the end the matter of papal authority became the major issue and culminated in a definition of the pope's infallibility and an indication of the extent of his jurisdiction. Papal infallibility was carefully defined and safeguarded from misinterpretation. But some bishops took a maximalist view of the extent of infallibility, including Archbishop Manning who was one of the chief instigators of the definition. When news of the 1870 definition was heard in England all the fears of papal domination were raised once again. Gladstone wrote a vehement pamphlet against 'the oracle of the Vatican' asking how the Vatican decrees affected civil allegiance for English Catholics. Newman in his *Letter to the Duke of Norfolk* (1874) explained how much Catholic understandings of authority had been misunderstood in England. One of his sentences was very telling:

> I add one remark. Certainly, if I am obliged to bring religion into after-dinner toasts, (which indeed does not seem quite the thing) I shall drink, – to the Pope, if you please, – still, to Conscience first, and to the Pope afterwards.[6]

While some Catholics would have been happy to see an extension of papal authority (as we have seen, W. G. Ward stated that he would have liked a papal bull with his *Times* at breakfast each morning), the fears of many English people were not realized. Papal infallibility has only been invoked once since 1870, when Pius XII proclaimed the dogma of the Assumption of Mary in 1950.

Historically, fear of Rome in England seems to have been mainly about the following matters:

1. The allegiance of Roman Catholics to the reigning monarch. Would English Catholics have murdered Elizabeth to get Mary Stuart on the throne? Did the Gunpowder Plot really implicate Catholics or was there some value to the government in proving Catholics disloyal? Did the Catholics consistently advocate the Catholic Stuart succession after the removal of James II or were they loyal to the Protestant succession? As late as 1929, a century after Emancipation, it was still suggested that the effect of the memory of the penal laws still prevented Catholics taking their full part in the public life of the country.

2. Did the removal of the penal laws against Catholics in 1778, 1791 and 1829 create problems for the Protestants of England? The Gordon Riots of 1780 and the furore concerning Catholic Eman-

cipation suggest that there was an underlying fear of Rome that could raise its head when the Protestants of England were provoked.

3. The fear of persecution by Catholics which was summed up in the Protestant mind by the phrase 'no faith is to be kept with heretics' had to be looked at in almost every period after the Reformation. John Wesley wrote about it on several occasions and the Catholic Emancipation Act deliberately asks Catholics to disown belief in the maxim. Of course persecution of Catholics had caused many to believe that 'no faith is to be kept with Catholics' was the maxim of the English Parliament and church.

4. The fear of a foreign import. It is fair to say that in the twentieth century most people have seen the English Roman Catholic Church as a religious way of life which is not truly English. From the last century into the present one Catholics have venerated statues in their churches (which by and large English Protestants have not) in the same way that holiday makers have noticed Catholics doing in Spain, Portugal and Italy. Catholics seem to have Irish or southern European names rather than English ones. If you call your local priest Father O'Reilly or Father Gentili rather than Father Robinson or Father Parsons, it feels as if you have imported your type of Christianity from overseas.

> That the Catholic Church stood on the doorstep was not always consciously held to be a threat by many Anglo-Catholics, despite the fact that it represented a goal which they themselves could never achieve. They might, sometimes seriously, at other times in jest, talk about the 'Italian [or Roman] mission' to England, implying that Catholicism was already in the country, a genuinely English Catholicism. The Church of England, through the efforts of Anglo-Catholics, had the responsibility for the nurture of Catholicism in England. The quip about the 'Italian mission' made those who used the phrase a laughing-stock rather than those whom they ridiculed.[7]

5. The fear of the power of priestly ministry, especially the confessional. This probably stems from 1605 when Henry Garnet almost certainly knew of the plot against James I but was unable to reveal it because of the seal of the confessional. This has helped to implant in the English consciousness a feeling that at bottom

Catholics and their priests might have a subtle way of avoiding the law of the land because they are in some way directly responsible to God for their actions. Thus the feeling of Catholic disloyalty to England has been reinforced by what is a sacrament of the Catholic Church.

6. The fear of a take over. This has dogged the ecumenical movement in England for at least a century and perhaps even longer. Leo XIII thought that the Church of England might be close to conceding the Roman claims in 1895, though he was misled by the success of some Catholic/Anglican conversations. But numbers have recently indicated another situation. In *Reflections*, 1987, published by the British Council of Churches and the Catholic Truth Society, Roman Catholic numbers for England and Wales were given as about 1,500,000 while Church of England numbers were 1,725,000, a difference of only 225,000. Anglican numbers as is well known are based on Easter communicants, a figure which does not really tell the week-to-week story. Even if Catholic numbers are based on Easter mass attendances it is likely that the regular attenders at mass are at least one and a half times the Anglican numbers. This makes it fairly likely that at the moment the Roman Catholic Church in England has the largest effective membership of the churches of England. While this does not mean that England is a Catholic country it does mean that the Roman Catholics in England do have the same right to be heard as do members of the Church of England. It was not so in the past and this new situation could cause some anxiety in some parts of the Protestant life of England. Is some sort of take-over in the pipeline? The fear of Roman Catholicism still remains for many in England.

7. The fear of the papacy. This probably dates from *Regnans in Excelsis* of 1570 when Pius V excommunicated Elizabeth I and implied that causing her death would not be a mortal sin for a Roman Catholic. Interference in the affairs of England by the papacy has of course been minimal since 1570 and perhaps only in 1850 with the restoration of the hierarchy by Pius IX was there another whiff of danger to the English constitution. While a John XXIII was in the seat of Peter there seemed a genuine pastor in the Vatican who was recognized by all. With Paul VI and John Paul II a different and perhaps even hard-line papacy has seemed to take over. That this is

not so was shown by the pastoral nature of the papal visit to Britain in 1982. That the pope is concerned that he may be seen as a major stumbling block to unity is clear from his remarks in *Ut Unum Sint*, and it has to be noted that some English non-Catholics are responding to the encyclical.

> . . . as I acknowledged on the important occasion of a visit to the World Council of Churches in Geneva on 12 June 1984, the Catholic Church's conviction that in the ministry of the Bishop of Rome she has preserved, in fidelity to the Apostolic Tradition and the faith of the Fathers, the visible sign and guarantor of unity, constitutes a difficulty for most other Christians, whose memory is marked by certain painful recollections. To the extent that we are responsible for these, I join my Predecessor Paul VI in asking for forgiveness.[8]

But it has to be noted that the fear of the possible tough line that might be taken by the papacy on many issues is a constant one for many English Christians.

10

Why Can't Anglicans
and Methodists Make It?

In 1946 Archbishop Geoffrey Fisher preached a sermon at Great St Mary's in Cambridge on Christian unity. In his sermon he invited the nonconformists in England to take episcopacy into their systems.

> The Church of England has not yet found the finally satisfying use of episcopacy in practice, nor certainly has the Church of Rome. If non-episcopal churches agree that it must come into the picture, could they not take it and try it out on their own ground first? . . . If then non-episcopal churches could thus take episcopacy into their systems . . . What I desire is that I should be able freely to enter their churches and they mine in the sacraments of the Lord and in the full fellowship of worship, that His life may freely circulate between us.[1]

He was going along with the worldwide Anglican ideas in this because according to the famous Lambeth Quadrilateral formulated in 1888 the acceptance of bishops was one of the four main planks for Anglicans in any unity negotiations. Fisher's idea of Christian unity was a somewhat limited one; he only saw intercommunion as the end of the process and not a complete integration of the English churches.

In the end only one of the free churches in England felt in a position to proceed with further talks towards the goal of unity. This was the Methodist Church. Small wonder, some said, for hadn't the Methodist Church sprung from the soil of Anglicanism and weren't some particles of that soil still visible, in the use of Anglican matins in some Methodist churches, in the communion service in the 1936 Methodist Service Book which differed little from the one in the

Book of Common Prayer. Others saw vast differences in some areas where Methodist churches were fiercely independent communities where 'chapel' people were very different from 'church' people and certainly would have had no dealings with official prayer books, whether Methodist or Anglican.

> I believe there is no liturgy in the world, either in ancient or modern language, which breathes more of solid, Scriptural, rational piety than the Common Prayer of the Church of England; and though the main of it was compiled more than two hundred years ago, yet is the language of it not only pure, but strong and elegant in the highest degree.[2]

A brief historical survey may help to clarify the situation.

John Wesley, like his younger brother Charles, was an Anglican clergyman, the son of the Anglican rector of St Andrews Church in Epworth, Lincolnshire. Both John's father, Samuel, and mother, Susanna, had been brought up in the dissenting or nonconformist traditions but had changed to the Church of England in their teens. After Epworth the two Wesley brothers had gone to Oxford. John was ordained to the diaconate in 1725 and became his father's curate for a time. When he returned to Oxford as a fellow of Lincoln College he found that his brother had become the leader of a small group of religiously disposed young men who were taking Christianity seriously, being assiduous readers of the Bible, meeting regularly for spiritual conferences, constantly attending the sacraments, visiting the prisoners in Oxford jail, and helping the poor. The group became known as 'Bible Moths', 'Sacramentarians', 'Supererogation Men', 'the Holy Club', and the name that became their title, 'Methodists'. In 1735 John and Charles were induced to join the Society for the Propagation of the Gospel work in Georgia, America, and on the way there they came into close contact with the Moravians, a group of Christian refugees from central Europe, who were of the 'pietist' type. This group were concerned with the priority of personal conversion to Christ, with Bible study and with group experience to encourage Christian growth. When John and Charles returned to England in 1738 they were ready to take on board the emphases of the Moravians. They were converted to this new way of thinking on 21 May (Charles) and on 24 May (John) of that same year.

What occurred on *Wednesday the 24th.* I think best to relate at large . . . I think it was about five in the morning, that I opened my Testament on those words, 'There are given unto us exceeding great and precious promises, even that ye should be partakers of the divine nature' (2 Pet. 1.4). Just as I went out, I opened again on those words, 'Thou art not far from the kingdom of God.' In the afternoon I was asked to go to St Paul's. The anthem was, 'Out of the deep have I called unto Thee, O Lord; Lord, hear my voice. O let Thine ears consider well the voice of my complaint. If Thou, Lord, wilt be extreme to mark what is done amiss, O Lord, who may abide it? For there is mercy with Thee; therefore shalt Thou be feared. O Israel, trust in the Lord: for with the Lord there is mercy, and with Him is plenteous redemption. And He shall redeem Israel from all his sins.'

In the evening I went very unwillingly to a society in Aldersgate Street, where one was reading Luther's preface to the Epistle to the Romans. About a quarter before nine, while he was describing the change which God works in the heart through faith in Christ, I felt my heart strangely warmed. I felt I did trust in Christ, Christ alone for salvation; and an assurance was given me that He had taken away *my* sins, even *mine*, and saved *me* from the law of sin and death.

I began to pray with all my might for those who had in a more especial manner despitefully used me and persecuted me. I then testified openly to all there what I now first felt in my heart. But it was not long before the enemy suggested, 'This cannot be faith; for where is thy joy?' Then was I taught that peace and victory over sin are essential to faith in the Captain of our salvation; but that, as to the transports of joy that usually attend the beginning of it, especially in those who have mourned deeply, God sometimes giveth, sometimes withholdeth them, according to the counsels of His own will.[3]

The experiences took John and Charles into a new proclamation and into new avenues to make that proclamation. They became open air preachers and travelled the length and breadth of the British Isles, John himself travelling some 225,000 miles, mainly on horseback. Charles became the hymn writer of the movement and later did far less travelling. This hymn for many years appeared first in every Methodist hymn book.

> O for a thousand tongues to sing
>   My great Redeemer's praise,
> The glories of my God and King,
>   The triumphs of his grace!
>
> Jesus – the name that charms our fears,
>   That bids our sorrows cease;
> 'Tis music in the sinner's ears,
>   'Tis life, and health, and peace.
>
> See all your sins on Jesus laid;
>   The Lamb of God was slain;
> His soul was once an offering made
>   For every soul of man.

And this, when sung to the tune *Sagina*, has become an anthem for Methodists.

> And can it be that I should gain
>   An interest in the Saviour's blood?
> Died he for me, who caused his pain?
>   For me, who him to death pursued?
> Amazing love! How can it be
> That thou, my God, shouldst die for me?
>
> Long my imprisoned spirit lay
>   Fast bound in sin and nature's night;
> Thine eye diffused a quickening ray –
>   I woke, the dungeon flamed with light,
> My chains fell off, my heart was free,
> I rose, went forth, and followed thee.
>
> No condemnation now I dread;
>   Jesus, and all in him, is mine!
> Alive in him, my living Head,
>   And clothed in righteousness divine,
> Bold I approach the eternal throne,
> And claim the crown, through Christ, my own.

By the time of the death of John Wesley in 1791 some 72,000 people were members of local Methodist societies (about 1% of the population) who met regularly in classes for spiritual enrichment. John died a clergyman of the Church of England but at least four matters had put him at odds with the Anglican establishment which were unresolved at his death:

1. The problem of field preaching which Wesley had begun in April 1739 at the request of George Whitefield. Did the Methodists have the right to preach in other men's parishes? A lot of clergymen were annoyed at the trespassing on their pastoral domains.

2. The problem of lay preaching. This began at the Foundery in Moorfields, London, *c.*1740, and Wesley saw that through lay preachers people were converted. At Wesley's death there were 282 of these, arranged in 'circuits' where they itinerated from place to place. John Wesley once said, 'soul damning clergymen lay me under more difficulties than soul saving laymen'. But they were not approved by episcopal authority.

3. The use of Methodist buildings. Were these, such as the Horsefair in Bristol, the Foundery in London and the later Wesley's Chapel in London, really Anglican buildings or were they sectarian? That they were founded with their own model trust deeds seemed to indicate that they were sectarian.

4. Methodist ordinations. Wesley approached the Bishop of London to request him to ordain some of his lay preachers for America where the recent War of Independence had left the Anglicans without pastors. The Bishop refused whereupon Wesley ordained two of his own men for America and set apart another clergyman as a superintendent. He claimed that his authority for doing this was to be found in the history of the early church where 'bishop' and 'presbyter' were the same order of ministry.

> On the road I read over Lord King's *Account of the Primitive Church*. In spite of the vehement prejudice of my education, I was ready to believe that this was a fair and impartial draught; but if so, it would follow that bishops and presbyters are (essentially) of one order, and that originally every Christian congregation was a church independent on all others.[4]

But his action in 1784 precipitated a crisis not only with the Church of England but with his own brother. Pastoral need seemed to have been more important to Wesley than church order.

It was once said that Mr Wesley was like a skilled rower who faced the Church of England while every stroke of his oars pulled his boat in the opposite direction. After his death, from 1795 local societies of Methodists were allowed to have communion from the itinerant preachers if the local people demanded it. Perceived lack of lay involvement led to the first schism from the Methodists in 1797 when Alexander Kilham founded the Methodist New Connexion. By 1810 the Primitive Methodists (in the sense that John Wesley meant, as those who stood for the earliest ideals of the movement) began under Hugh Bourne and William Clowes. The Bible Christians founded by William O'Bryan in 1815 began as an attempt to evangelize areas that other Methodists could not reach but ended in schism. Other schisms arose when Methodist members found the Conference too clerical and authoritarian; one was over the placing of an organ in a Leeds church, another concerned the opening of a

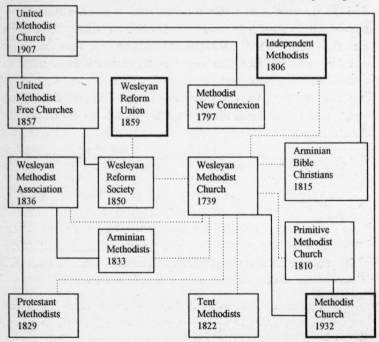

Dotted lines indicate divisions. Unbroken lines show unions. Heavy lines around groups indicate an existing Methodist denomination, while lighter lines indicate a group that united with other Methodist denominations.

theological college, while a further schism came about after anonymous fly sheets accused the Conference of having an almost Roman Catholic concept of power. By about 1850 only half the Methodists in England were labelled 'Wesleyan'. The early nineteenth century had ensured that Methodists would move away from Wesley's Anglicanism. The history of Methodism after 1850 is the story of attempts to reunite the parties within Methodism but Methodist Union was only realized in 1932.

After Geoffrey Fisher's initiative, preliminary talks took place between the Church of England and the Free Churches. The Methodist Church agreed to have deeper conversations that resulted in several important publications in the 1960s. Eventually *The Scheme* of unity was produced and an *Ordinal* was agreed for future ordinations. The Scheme was not agreeable to all Methodists on the unity commission and four dissidents indicated their shared misgivings about it:

1. The place of Tradition in the document seemed to militate against the primacy of scripture in the Methodist Church.
2. The high regard for the place of bishops in the church was not seen to be in accordance with scripture and the history of episcopacy was not reassuring for Methodists. As Gordon Rupp, President of the Methodist Conference for the year 1968–69 remarked: 'The Anglicans have asked us to take episcopacy into our system. It would help us if they would get some system into their episcopacy.'

   Historic episcopacy is so essential to the proposals contained in this report that it is necessary, in all charity, to make a few comments on it:
   a) Historically it is incapable of proof – 'a fable which no man ever did or could prove' as John Wesley said of the apostolic succession.
   b) It has notoriously failed to act as the safeguard it is claimed to be. This is sufficiently illustrated by the history of the mediaeval and renaissance papacy.
   c) Methodists have consistently, and rightly, claimed that their church is one with the church of the apostles, saints, and martyrs, without the aid of any material succession.

The Christian heritage is in faith and life, not in institutions.

d) For what outward continuity may be worth, most Methodists would prefer to be visibly one with the churches of the Reformation than with mediaeval and un-reformed Christendom.

e) If the hope of further union, on the basis of the historic episcopate, is canvassed, it must be recalled that the largest episcopal church in the world believes that the Church of England does not have, and therefore cannot impart, the historic ministry.

f) Far more important than any of these points is the fact that historic episcopacy is completely without support in the New Testament. This negative observation is itself sufficient to show that no ecclesiastical body has the right to demand participation in historic episcopacy as a qualification for communion or union with itself. Further, we are bound to conclude that the belief that the full and true being of the church is dependent upon its possession of historic episcopacy is inconsistent with the New Testament doctrine that the existence of the People of God depends wholly upon God's gracious election, grasped by faith only.

g) There is little help in the (limited) 'liberty of interpretation' offered. Actions speak louder than words, and an interpretation of episcopacy as (i) the historic episcopacy, and (ii) absolutely indispensable to the church of the future, is presupposed by the proposals contained in the report.[5]

3. The Methodists would lose the important lay involvement in the organization and sacramental life of their church.

4. The method whereby the Anglican priesthood and Methodist ministry would be reconciled was being interpreted as reordination of the Methodists by some Anglicans. This ambiguity in the Service of Reconciliation was a major fault in the Scheme.

Then shall the President and other Ministers lay hands on them in silence, after which he shall say:

We welcome you into the fellowship of the Ministry in the Methodist Church, to preach the Word of God and minister the holy sacraments among us as need shall arise and you shall be requested so to do. We repeat our pledge that we will serve with you as fellow-workers in Christ and that we will never rest until we have found that fuller unity in him which we believe to be God's will.

Then the Archbishop and the four priests shall lay hands on them in silence, after which he shall say,

We welcome you into the fellowship of the Ministry in the Church of England, to preach the Word of God and minister the holy Sacraments among us as need shall arise and you shall be requested so to do. We repeat our pledge that we will serve with you as fellow- workers in Christ and that we will never rest until we have found that fuller unity in him which we believe to be God's will.[6]

It is interesting that these criticisms were put forward by Anglicans as well as Methodists. Voting on the scheme of union was to be by 75% majorities of the Methodist Conference and the Houses of Convocation. The 1969 Conference achieved the 75% but the Church of England vote only reached 69%, the majority of dissentient votes coming from the House of Clergy.

Discussion of plans for union is an interesting and at times enjoyable form of intellectual dissipation. To face the actual plunge into the cold water of unity is a very different thing.[7]

Three years later in 1972 the vote was put again to the newly-formed General Synod which achieved only 66%. Two matters are of interest here. One is that a coalition of high-church and low-church parties torpedoed the Scheme in the Church of England and for opposite reasons; one thought that the Scheme did not make it clear that Methodist ministers were being reordained, the other thought that Methodist ministers did not need to be reordained. The other matter concerns the crucial decision taken in 1992 by the General Synod to ordain women to the priesthood. The vote was not by a bare majority, but two-thirds was needed for it to pass. Everyone knows now that it just passed and became legislation. If the same majority had been requested in 1969 Methodists and Anglicans in England would now be part of the same Church.

That there are other issues than those of theology and church order is clear and it is only fair to put these forward so that they can be avoided in future negotiations:

1. 'Church' and 'chapel' were terms often used in the past and described differences between Anglicans and Methodists. The differences were cultural; the chapel culture was a style of life that meant that all leisure time was spent at the various guilds, uniformed organizations, youth clubs, Bible groups etc. that were offered for every week night. Church people were 'Sundays only' people who seemed not so involved in Christianity.

2. The social group in the parish church was often regarded as somewhat higher in class than the people of the chapel. Some moved over as they prospered. 'The coach and pair does not pass the church door for more than a generation.' 'Them' and 'us' became part of Methodist vocabulary.

3. Rupert Davies talked about 'the effortless superiority' of some Anglican clergy when unity talks were proceeding. Rupert was a Methodist minister who became the principal of a theological college, was a graduate of both Oxford and Cambridge, spent time as chaplain to a public school, and yet still felt the superiority of some Anglican clergy. Small wonder that lesser mortals might feel it too.

4. The Church of England as the established church owns the ancient churches that are so much a part of the British scenery. They are the obvious places to which people turn on special occasions, whether they be Christian festivals such as Christmas and Easter, or Civic Services and Remembrance Day services. Some Methodists wonder whether Anglicans might not use their buildings and these occasions for more obvious Christian outreach than they do at the moment. For example, it is possible to enter major cathedrals and find no information sheets on what Christianity means. John Wesley would be appalled that such evangelical opportunities are not grasped with both hands!

These are often described as 'non-theological' factors' and to some extent they are. But they can be what makes local unity difficult.

And the inertia in the minds of many people of many denominations as regards steps to unity is due less to theological reasons than to dislike of a merging of domestic habits.[8]

The local Methodist minister may regard herself as a very ordinary woman who tries to minister to the best of her ability. If her local Anglican clergyman lives in a totally different 'gin and Jag' culture, makes it clear that he attended an important public school, and never invites her to preach at the Civic Service, relations may be cool between the two ministers. And it is likely that the coolness between the ministers will have led to frigidity between the Methodist and Anglican communities.

Talks have recently taken place on an international scale between Anglicans and Methodists. In 1993 a report called *Sharing in the Apostolic Communion* was published. The following important matters were thrown up by it:

1. The elements required for full communion in faith, mission and sacramental life would include a necessary and sufficient measure of doctrinal agreement, eucharistic sharing, mutual recognition and interchange of ministry, Christian fellowship and collaboration in evangelism and service.

2. Convergence has been brought about by the ecumenical movement, by scholarly work on the Bible and Christian origins, by the liturgical movement, by the perceived need for evangelism and the call of the Church to mission, and by the needs of the world.

3. Affirmation is needed of each other's contributions to the church in separation.

4. One significant area is in the relations between the Church of England and the British Methodist Church. Here the Methodists agreed to the doctrine contained in the Scheme of 1968 in both the Conferences of 1969 and 1972. In 1978 the General Synod agreed that no further doctrinal assurances were needed from British Methodists.

5. The significance of the historic episcopate is affirmed along with the threefold ministry. In 1981 British Methodism affirmed itself ready to receive the historic episcopate into its life and ministry.

6. Interim possible paths towards reconciliation could include mutual eucharistic hospitality, invitation to participate in ordinations

and consecrations, joint courses in theological colleges and the creation of local covenants or local ecumenical partnerships.

In autumn 1994 the Church of England and the Methodist Church began exploratory talks together and these are likely to be continued. The main obstacle to Anglican–Methodist union in England is not in the end likely to be a theological one but the sheer unwillingness of many local Anglican and Methodist congregations to go down a road again that in 1969 and 1972 led nowhere. I for one hope that this is being unduly pessimistic.

11

What of Catholics and Anglicans?

Almost everyone these days seems to have heard of ARCIC, the Anglican–Roman Catholic International Commission. But Anglicans and Catholics were in dialogue long before Paul VI and Archbishop Ramsey set up ARCIC after the Second Vatican Council. During the English Reformation, and after, there was of course little dialogue but more of a slanging match where one side made points against the other, for example the long dispute between William Laud and the Jesuit John Fisher in 1622. By the time of James II, the Catholic king, it was even more important for the two sides to be clear about what divided them. For example John Williams, later to be Bishop of Chichester, produced a point-by-point refutation of the Roman Catholic Catechism of the Council of Trent in 1686. Later on in 1717 a French Roman Catholic, Ellies du Pin, had a two-year correspondence with the Archbishop of Canterbury, William Wake, in which he worked on a draft scheme for union between the Church of France and the Church of England. Du Pin's ideas were possible because the French church was at this time concerned about the intransigence of the eighteenth-century papacy and it was felt that the Western churches could unite on the basis of antagonism towards the papacy.

... with respect to the jurisdiction of the pope in regard to our kingdom, it is confined within such narrow limits that it cannot do anything to our hurt; for he can do nothing in regard to temporal matters, and in regard to spiritual matters, he is confined within the rules of the ancient canons ... The other things which belong to him by human ordinance, are not necessary, and each Church ought to enjoy its own liberties, rights and customs, which ought to continue unshaken and which cannot be infringed by the Roman pontiffs.[1]

Although the attempt came to nothing due to opposition from both sides, there was significant agreement on as many as twenty-three of the Thirty-Nine Articles of the Church of England. Another French priest, Pierre le Courayer, shared an interest in Anglican orders in correspondence with Wake and in 1723 wrote a book in which he pronounced them valid. He was censured by twenty-two of his bishops but approved by the Archbishop of Paris for his work. By 1728 he had been excommunicated and retired to England, where he died. He ws buried in Westminster Abbey although he had never rejected his Catholic faith.

The Oxford Movement of 1833–1845, under the leadership of Pusey, Newman and Keble, interested many members of the Church of England in the Roman Catholic Church and its claims. It is well known that Newman wrote Tract XC in 1841 as an attempt to interpret the Thirty-Nine Articles in a Catholic sense. The response to Tract XC and further reflection led Newman to become a Roman Catholic in 1845, to be followed by several others who were important in the Movement. In 1857 a Catholic and an Anglican founded the short-lived Association for Promoting the Unity of Christendom. This was condemned by Rome in 1864 due to the opposition of Manning and others who believed that the true church had never lost its unity and that the only option for the other so-called churches was to return to the true church. At the time APUC had some 7,000 members, mainly Roman Catholic and Anglican. Some Anglicans at this time were so close to Rome in both theology and ceremonial practice that they accepted all the articles of the Roman Catholic creed except papal supremacy.

> Contrast the churches of the establishment of sixty or seventy years ago ... – with the present churches, which are often distinguishable only with extreme difficulty from those belonging to the Church of Rome ... the Thirty-Nine Articles have been banished and buried as a rule of faith. The Real Presence, the Sacrifice of the Mass offered for the living and the dead – sometimes even in Latin – not infrequent Reservation of the Sacrament, regular auricular Confession, Extreme Unction, Purgatory, prayers for the dead, devotions to Our Lady, to her Immaculate Conception, the use of her Rosary, and the Invoca-

tion of Saints are doctrines taught and accepted, with a growing desire and relish for them, in the Church of England.[2]

Catholic leaders in England such as Manning and Vaughan saw that reunion was not realistic unless the Church of England could accept the main doctrines of Rome including transubstantiation, the intercession of the Saints, purgatory, the Immaculate Conception, confession and papal infallibility. Some Anglicans no doubt could go almost this far, but the Church of England was a comprehensive church and the evangelical wing would certainly have resisted closer conversations with Roman Catholicism.

When the Abbé Fernand Portal first met Lord Halifax, the President of the Church Union and a convinced Anglo-Catholic, he was certain that Halifax was within a whisker of Roman Catholicism. Both Portal and Louis Duchesne in France believed in the validity of Anglican orders. By 1895 even Pope Leo XIII was convinced that reunion was a possibility and he said to Cardinal Vaughan, the Archbishop of Westminster, 'I hear they are on the point of coming over.' An international commission was formed in Rome to look at Anglican orders. The result was the infamous bull of 13 September 1896 called *Apostolicae Curae*. After a full discussion of the points at issue: was the Anglican priesthood a sacrificing priesthood?, did their priests intend to do what Catholic priests did?, etc, the Bull pronounced that Anglican orders were defective in form and intention and 'absolutely null and void'.

> Therefore adhering entirely to the decrees of the Pontiffs Our Predecessors on this subject and fully ratifying and renewing them by Our authority, on Our own initiative and with certain knowledge, We pronounce and declare that ordinations performed according to the Anglican rite have been and are completely null and void.

It was a major blow to the careful work of Portal and Halifax, but could a Church of England who had only three 'high' or ceremonialist bishops in its episcopal ranks really profess to have a ministry akin to that of the Roman Catholics?

The 1920 Lambeth Conference of the Anglican churches made *An Appeal to All Christian People* for talks about unity to proceed with other churches on the basis of the famous Lambeth Quadrilateral of 1888 (the four themes being: the scriptures; the creeds; the two sacraments; the episcopate).

> We believe that the visible unity of the Church will be found to involve the whole-hearted acceptance of:–
> The Holy Scriptures as the record of God's revelation of Himself to man, and as being the rule and ultimate standard of faith; and the Creed commonly called Nicene, as the sufficient statement of the Christian faith, and either it or the Apostles' Creed as the Baptismal confession of belief.
> The divinely instituted sacraments of Baptism and the Holy Communion, as expressing for all the corporate life of the whole fellowship, in and with Christ.
> A ministry acknowledged by every part of the Church as possessing not only the inward call of the Spirit but also the commission of Christ and the authority of the whole body.
> May we not reasonably claim that the Episcopate is the one means of providing such a ministry?

Although the hope was that the Free Churches might take up the offer, the appeal was clearly extendable to Rome. By 1921 Cardinal Mercier of Malines in Belgium agreed to host another set of conversations. Once again Abbé Fernand Portal and Lord Halifax took part and discussion ranged over the nature of the church and sacraments with the Anglicans agreeing that papal primacy was not necessarily a barrier to unity. The talks went on with other participants included for some five years until the deaths of Portal and Mercier in 1926. The majority of English Catholics were not in favour of the talks and preferred the stance that Anglicans should submit to Rome. When Pope Pius XI issued the encyclical *Mortalium Animos* in 1928, it was clear that Rome stood with the English Catholics; the Anglicans should return to Rome. The text should be read in the context of the understanding that the Roman Catholic Church was *the* Church of Christ as it was understood in 1928:

> It is clear, therefore, Venerable Brothers, why this apostolic See has never permitted its subjects to take part in the congresses of

non-Catholics. The union of Christians cannot be fostered otherwise than by promoting the return of the dissidents to the one true Church of Christ, which in the past they so unfortunately abandoned; return, we say, to the one true Church of Christ which is plainly visible to all and which by the will of her Founder forever remains what He Himself destined her to be for the common salvation of men. For the mystical Spouse of Christ has never been contaminated in the course of centuries, nor will she ever be contaminated . . . No one is in the Church of Christ, and no one remains in it, unless he acknowledges and accepts with obedience the authority and power of Peter and his legitimate successors.

Although there were times when Catholics and Anglicans moved closer, for example when Cardinal Hinsley was at Westminster, in general things moved very slowly until Vatican II began a new era in Anglican–Catholic relationships. Archbishop Geoffrey Fisher and Pope John XXIII met in 1960 just before the Vatican Council, but it was not until after the Council in March 1966 that Paul VI and Archbishop Michael Ramsey gave their approval for a serious dialogue in the Common Declaration issued at St Paul's Outside-the-Walls. The new dialogue was to be founded 'on the Gospels and on the ancient common traditions'. The Anglican–Roman Catholic International Commission, ARCIC, began its work in 1967 and produced in 1971 the Windsor Statement on Eucharistic Doctrine, the Canterbury Statement in 1973 on Ministry and Ordination, Authority in the Church I at Venice in 1976 and Authority in the Church II in 1981. When the Final Report of what came to be called ARCIC I came out in 1982, important Elucidations which had been published separately were added to the agreements on Eucharist, Ministry and Authority.[3]

Perhaps a few of the more important points of ARCIC I ought to be set down here, although it will be obvious that the reader needs to refer to the Final Report for the full story. On the question of the eucharist, the disagreements between Catholics and Anglicans appeared to centre around the questions: do Catholics attempt to add in some way to the 'once for all' sacrifice of Christ on the cross?, what is the true presence of Christ, is it in the mind of the receiver or is it a fact which does not depend on experience?

ARCIC gave some answers as follows:

5. ... There can be no repetition of or addition to what was then accomplished once for all by Christ ...

6. Communion with Christ in the eucharist presupposes his true presence, effectually signified by the bread and wine which, in this mystery, becomes his body and blood ...[4]

ARCIC I used the important word 'memorial' (Greek, *anamnesis*) which means 'making effective in the present an event of the past' to explain in a clearer way what happens in the eucharist. The Elucidation explains more fully the implications of *anamnesis* which affirm a strong conviction of sacramental realism and reject mere symbolism (para 5). In section 6 the Elucidation makes it clear what 'become' means in the quotation above concerning bread and wine:

Before the eucharistic prayer, to the question: 'What is that?', the believer answers: 'It is bread.' After the eucharistic prayer, to the same question he answers: 'It is truly the body of Christ, the Bread of Life.'[5]

The Statement and Elucidation on Ministry and Ordination called for a reappraisal of the verdict on Anglican Orders given in the Bull of 1896, *Apostolicae Curae*. After a historical introduction which acknowledged that 'bishop' and 'presbyter' could be applied to men doing the same work, the Statement concludes that after the apostolic age the threefold structure of bishop, presbyter and deacon became universal. The Christian community exists to give glory to God as a royal priesthood and it follows:

7. ... The goal of the ordained ministry is to serve this priesthood of all the faithful. Like any human community the Church requires a focus of leadership and unity, which the Holy Spirit provides in the ordained ministry ...[6]

The functions of the ministry are those of service, proclamation of the message of reconciliation, teaching, pastoral care, stewardship and to exemplify the Christian life (8). After the obvious points that ministers celebrate the sacraments and proclaim the word, they also are said to perform the work of restoring the fallen:

11. . . . Authority to pronounce God's forgiveness of sin, given to bishops and presbyters at their ordination, is exercised by them to bring Christians to a closer communion with God and with their fellow men through Christ and to assure them of God's continuing love and mercy . . .[7]

The question of the priesthood of the ministry is explained:

13. . . . Despite the fact that in the New Testament the ministers are never called 'priests' (*hiereis*) Christians came to see the priestly role of Christ reflected in these ministers and used priestly terms in describing them . . . Nevertheless their ministry is not an extension of the common Christian priesthood but belongs to another realm of the gifts of the Spirit . . .[8]

The Elucidation to 13 above explained that the ordained ministry was called priestly principally because it had a particular sacramental relationship with Christ as High Priest (2). Towards the end of the Elucidation the question of the ordination of women came up with this comment added:

5. . . . Objections, however substantial, to the ordination of women are of a different kind from objections raised in the past against the validity of Anglican Orders in general.[9]

The two Statements on Authority would obviously be more difficult to formulate and arrive at a consensus. The issues here were the problem of papal primacy, the authority of councils held after the break up of East and West, and the authority of scripture within the two traditions. There were important points made in Authority I:

7. . . . The authorities in the Church cannot adequately reflect Christ's authority because they are still subject to the limitations and sinfulness of human nature. Awareness of this inadequacy is a continual summons to reform.[10]

On the Bishop of Rome:

12. . . . Sometimes functions assumed by the see of Rome were not necessarily linked to the primacy: sometimes the conduct of the occupant of this see has been unworthy of his office: sometimes the image of this office has been obscured by

interpretations placed upon it: and sometimes external pres-
sures have made its proper exercise almost impossible. Yet
the primacy, rightly understood, implies that the bishop of
Rome exercises his oversight in order to guard and promote
the faithfulness of all the Churches of Christ and one
another . . .[11]

Since only one see has claimed and now exercises universal primacy:

23. . . . It seems appropriate that in any future union a universal
primacy such as has been described should be held by that
see.[12]

Infallibility, the Marian definitions and papal jurisdiction are the
main difficulties that remain to be resolved. In Authority II more
detailed work was done on the texts about Peter in the New
Testament, the place of papal jurisdiction in so far as it might be seen
to threaten the theological and liturgical traditions of the Anglican
Church, the place of infallibility in the papal office, and the
importance of the definitions of the Immaculate Conception and
Bodily Assumption of the Blessed Virgin Mary of 1854 and 1950.

It is well known that although ARCIC I on Eucharist and
Ministry was recognized by the 1988 Lambeth Conference as
'consonant in substance with the faith of Anglicans' and Authority I
and II welcomed as 'a firm basis for the direction and agenda of the
continuing dialogue on authority', nevertheless only in 1991 was
there an official response to ARCIC I from Rome. Further work
was suggested in the response before it could be said that the Final
Report corresponded to Catholic doctrine on the eucharist and
ordained ministry. Other problems mentioned in the official
response by the Congregation for the Doctrine of the Faith and the
Pontifical Council for Promoting Christian Unity included papal
infallibility, and the Petrine office, the Marian dogmas, the authority
of Ecumenical Councils, and the mode of the Real Presence in the
eucharist.

While this Final Report was awaited a new commission,
ARCIC II, was set up in 1982 by John Paul II and Archbishop
Runcie. So far this commission has produced three reports:
Salvation and the Church, 1987, *Church as Communion*, 1991, and *Life*

in Christ, 1993. The first report sets the Reformation question of salvation in a different context and produces an excellent consensus:

> 7. Although the sixteenth-century disagreements centred mainly on the relationship of faith, righteousness and good works to the salvation of the individual, *the role of the Church* in the process of salvation constituted a *fourth* difficulty. As well as believing that Catholics did not acknowledge the true authority of Scripture over the Church, Protestants also felt that Catholic teaching and practice had interpreted the mediatorial role of the Church in such a way as to derogate from the place of Christ as 'sole mediator between God and man' (I Tim. 2.5). Catholics believed that Protestants were abandoning or at least devaluing the Church's ministry and sacraments, which were divinely appointed means of grace; also that they were rejecting its divinely given authority as guardian and interpreter of the revealed Word of God.[13]

The second discusses the important question of *koinonia,* the Greek word for communion, and applies it to the churches as the essential word and method of advances in unity:

> 45. In the light of all that we have said about communion it is now possible to describe what constitutes ecclesial communion. It is rooted in the confession of the one apostolic faith, revealed in the Scriptures, and set forth in the Creeds. It is founded upon one baptism. The one celebration of the eucharist is its pre-eminent expression and focus. It necessarily finds expression in shared commitment to the mission entrusted by Christ to his Church. It is a life of shared concern for one another in mutual forbearance, submission, gentleness and love; in the placing of the interests of others above the interests of self; in making room for each other in the body of Christ; in solidarity with the poor and the powerless; and in the sharing of gifts both material and spiritual (cf. Acts 2.44). Also constitutive of life in communion is acceptance of the same basic moral values, the sharing of the same vision of humanity created in the image of God and recreated in Christ, and in common confession of the one hope in the final consummation of the Kingdom of God.[14]

The third is the first effort at a convergence on the moral life and suggests ways in which the two Christian churches might tackle moral problems from a similar starting point:

1. There is a popular and widespread belief that the Anglican and Roman Catholic Communions are divided most sharply by their moral teaching. Careful consideration has persuaded the Commission that, despite existing disagreement in certain areas of practical and pastoral judgment, Anglicans and Roman Catholics derive from the Scriptures and Tradition the same controlling vision of the nature and destiny of humanity and share the same fundamental moral values.

6. The true goal of the moral life is the flourishing and fulfilment of that *humanity* for which all men and women have been created. The fundamental moral question, therefore, is not 'What ought we to do?', but 'What kind of persons are we called to become?' For children of God, moral obedience is nourished by the hope of becoming like God (cf. I John 3.1–3).[15]

The work of ARCIC II was threatened by the decision of the Church of England in 1992 to follow some other Anglican provinces and ordain women to the priesthood.

The Pope and the Archbishop spoke of the question of the ordination of women to the priesthood. The Archbishop expressed his conviction that this development is a possible and proper development of the doctrine of the ordained ministry. The Holy Father reiterated what has already been said to Archbishop Carey's predecessors, that this development constitutes a decision which the Church does not see itself entitled to authorize, and which constitutes a grave obstacle to the whole process of Anglican–Roman Catholic reconciliation. It was agreed, however, that there must be further study of the ecclesial and ecumenical aspects of this question.[16]

But the important thing is that ARCIC continues.

One of the main blocks to Anglican–Catholic unity is the papal bull of 1896 *Apostolicae Curae* that proclaimed Anglican orders null and void. There have been several attempts to solve this problem in recent years. One has been to recognize the implications of the fact that the Old Catholics who left the Roman Catholic Church over papal infallibility in 1870 are in communion with the Church of England. Old Catholic priestly orders have never been regarded as invalid by Rome. As a result future Anglican ordinations which included an Old Catholic bishop, from say Holland, would make such ordinations valid in the sight of Rome. The Alternative Service Book ordination service of 1980 appears to contain all that Catholic theology would require to make a valid priest, whereas the Book of Common Prayer of 1662 and earlier editions did not seem to have the correct intention as far as Rome was concerned.

In 1990 George Tavard, a French Augustinian father of the Assumption, produced an important book which has been unjustly neglected. It was called *A Review of Anglican Orders: the Problem and the Solution.* Tavard had been a member of ARCIC I, a member of the Methodist–Roman Catholic international commission, and before that a theologian at Vatican II. Tavard claimed that the Catholic Archbishop of Canterbury of Mary's reign, Cardinal Pole, had not deposed deacons, priests and bishops ordained by Cranmer's ordination services of 1550 and 1552 but had merely asked bishops to supply what was wanting for their ministry: the ordinations were thus effective but not legal. Theologians from France just before 1896 such as Duchesne had claimed that Cranmer intended to do 'as the Church did' in ordination. Tavard thus came out with the solution that Anglican orders should be presumed valid by Rome, since Anglican bishops now intended to do 'as the Church does' in ordination, since Old Catholic bishops now take part in Anglican ordinations, and since ARCIC I theology of the priesthood is similar.

> The Catholic hierarchy could decide that there is, today if not in the past, a presumption of validity in favour of Anglican orders. From Paul IV to Leo XIII there was a presumption of invalidity. The circumstances having been drastically altered, this presumption of invalidity need not apply any longer. Arguments in support of a presumption of validity may be drawn from several areas: the general predominance, in contemporary Anglicanism, of 'high church' over 'low church' conceptions of the sacraments; the

present evidence that Anglican bishops intend to do what the Church does in ordination; the participation of Old Catholic bishops in Anglican ordinations; the growth of a theology of priesthood that is shared by Catholics and Anglicans alike, as illustrated by the Final Report; the increasing mistrust of the Aristotelian categories of form and matter in sacramental theology; the progressive abandonment of a 'pipe-line' conception of apostolic succession in Catholic theology; the recognition of Anglican orders by Orthodox Churches by virtue of the 'principle of economy'.

In a first step, this would allow Catholic bishops to ordain conditionally, rather than absolutely, those Anglican or former Anglican priests and deacons who ask for it. In a second step, it could allow the Catholic magisterium to declare that, given the contemporary evidence in favor of the presumption of validity, Anglican orders are now recognized, or regarded as valid.[17]

It is of interest that the former Bishop of London, Graham Leonard, on his recent reception into the Catholic Church, was ordained 'conditionally' to the Catholic priesthood. This meant that his orders might or might not have been valid but that the ordination took place in case they were not.

A paragraph belongs here to the work of English ARC, the national Anglican–Roman Catholic commission. It is the place where the work of ARCIC has been most discussed in England and where the national implications of the consensus and convergence statements have been fleshed out. ARC has been responsible for study guides on the work of ARCIC. It has also done work on twinning relationships between English towns and French towns where the dominant Christian churches are Anglican and Catholic respectively. Much discussion has also been held on the work and extension of the idea of joint schools between Catholics and Anglicans, several examples of which exist in England. Joint schools are an important way of focussing ecumenical issues locally.

Particularly in the last two decades, there have been energetic moves to set aside the animosities of the past and to witness together to the teaching of Christ in the community of faith. These efforts have resulted in the creation of a number of joint

Christian schools, notably those bringing together Anglican and
Roman Catholic (the two largest Christian bodies in England).
These schools have developed when in Britain there is increased
pressure on all schools to keep the curriculum abreast of modern
developments (e.g. in information technology), to ensure equal
opportunities, to respond to parental choice, and to create a
caring community all within the context of considerable national
economic stringency. At a time when all schools are seeking to
adapt to a changing situation, Church schools are necessarily
encouraged to adapt to a very different climate.[18]

Although fully-integrated local ecumenical partnerships in which
Catholics and Anglicans share are comparatively rare because of the
problems of ministry, local covenants exist in many areas where co-
operation between the two denominations is extremely close. In
many areas where Roman Catholic churches do not exist Anglican
incumbents have been happy to allow local Roman Catholic priests
to use parish churches for mass. The presence of both Anglicans and
Roman Catholics within the Ecumenical Society of the Blessed
Virgin Mary has allowed both traditions to examine the Marian
strain in spirituality in greater depth. Donald Allchin for the
Anglicans and Edward Yarnold for the Roman Catholics have
written important articles where the theological and devotional
aspects of Marian devotion have been opened up for both traditions.

> The Immaculate Conception means that it is of faith that God's
> grace requires human co-operation, provides the conditions
> which make the response possible and fruitful, and results in
> sanctification, so that the holiness of the Church will be verifiable
> in the lives of its members, and will overflow from member to
> member; the Assumption means that all that is truly of value in
> human existence continues after death, when it is transformed in
> heaven.[19]

At the level of the 'domestic church' interchurch families have made
sure that the conversations between Catholics and Anglicans do not
remain solely at the intellectual level. Real issues raise theological
problems such as the presence and communication of an Anglican
partner at a daughter's first communion, the presence of the

Anglican priest at a child's baptism in the Catholic church, and the question whether a young person can be confirmed into two church traditions.

Some issues between Catholics and Anglicans will be helped as students in training for the priesthood understand each other's traditions by close involvement during the training process. Here we need only mention that all the Roman Catholic seminaries in England have regular interchange with Anglican students. Perhaps the principal ones to be mentioned because they have been operating for longest are the presence each year of two Anglican students for a semester at the English College in Rome and the month spent together on the eucharist between the final year students of St Mary's, Oscott, and the final year students of The Queen's College at Birmingham.

12

What of Methodists and Catholics?

The Methodist movement arose in the eighteenth century when the members of the English Protestant churches had little contact with Roman Catholics. John Wesley, the leader of the movement, had his London headquarters within a stone's throw of the local Catholic church which was visited regularly by the leader of the London Catholics, Bishop Richard Challoner. As far as we understand they never met but there was a small book in circulation by Challoner from 1760 called *A Caveat Against the Methodists*. In the book Challoner claimed that these Methodists were neither the people of God nor true Gospel Christians, their ministers were not real ministers nor proper teachers of Christianity and that the Methodist Rule of Faith was not the truth faith.

Challoner set out his *Caveat* in six major headings:

I.   The Methodists are not the People of God: they are not true Gospel Christians: nor is their new raised Society the true Church of Christ, nor any Part of it.

II.   The Methodist Teachers are not the true Ministers of Christ: nor are they called or sent by him.

III.   The Methodist Teachers have not the Marks by which the Scriptures would have us know the true Ministers of Christ; nor do their Fruits any ways resemble those of the first Teachers of Christianity.

IV.   The Methodist Rule of Faith is not the Rule of true Christian Faith.

V.   The 'Methodists' pretended Assurance of their own Justification, and their eternal Salvation, is no true Christian Faith; but a mere Illusion and groundless Presumption.

VI.   The true Scripture Doctrine concerning Justification.

Challoner was critical of their doctrine of assurance and set out
the truly Catholic understanding of justification. Wesley only briefly
answered the first two points that Challoner set out. If they had met
they would probably have had a fascinating dialogue with each other
and would have understood quickly that they were actually very close
on justification. Challoner thought that his twenty points on
justification from the teaching of the Council of Trent would totally
contradict the viewpoint of John Wesley. In fact when Wesley's
writings are examined in detail it is clear that on seventeen of the
twenty points they shared the same beliefs. Earlier in 1756 Wesley
had published a reply to the Roman Catechism which he drew from a
work by Bishop John Williams of Chichester of 1686. In it there are
the usual mistakes made in that period about Catholic doctrine; they
break the commandment about idolatry, they worship the Virgin
Mary, Rome had added extra doctrines to the Christian gospel such
as purgatory, the primacy of the Bishop of Rome, indulgences and
the veneration of saints.

> . . . All Romanists, as such, do add to those things which are
> contained in the Book of Life. For in the Bull of Pius IV,
> subjoined to those Canons and Decrees, I find all the additions
> following:
> 1. Seven Sacraments; 2. Transubstantiation; 3. Communion
> in one kind only; 4. Purgatory; 5. Praying to saints; 6. Venera-
> tion of relics; 7. Worship of images; 8. Indulgences; 9. The
> priority and universality of the Roman Church; 10. The
> supremacy of the Bishop of Rome. All these things therefore do
> the Romanists add to those which are written in the Book of
> Life. [1]

All this would have been expected of Wesley as an eighteenth-
century member of the Church of England. What was unexpected
was his conciliatory view of some aspects of Roman Catholicism and
of some persons of the Catholic faith. For example, in his 'Christian
Library', a selection from books of some spiritual worth compiled
for his preachers from 1749 onwards, he includes some Roman
Catholic authors such as Pascal, Fénélon, Molinos, Antoinette
Bourignon, Brother Lawrence and Juan of Avila. The Catholic
proportion is as high as 5% of the total work of fifty volumes, a very

high percentage at a time when Catholic writers were hardly acknowledged. His understanding was that where Catholics wrote of the life of holiness without which no one would see the Lord, they were worth reading. In similar vein, when Charles Wesley's son, Samuel, decided to become a Catholic, John wrote very feelingly to his nephew: 'Whether Bellarmine or Luther be right, you are certainly wrong, if you are not born of the Spirit.'

The spiritual life was all, whether from Protestant or Catholic sources. In his *Letter to a Roman Catholic* of 18 July 1749, we see Wesley at his ecumenical best. The letter was written in the wake of the Cork Riots to remind the Roman Catholic recipient of what Protestant and Catholic shared. John Wesley sets out the essential shared faith, which interestingly includes a belief in the perpetual virginity of the Virgin Mary, and asks whether the Catholic believes either of them shall go to hell for believing less or more. This, he says, is true primitive Christianity. Towards the end of the letter are these words:

> O brethren, let us not still fall out by the way! I hope to see you in heaven. And if I practise the religion above described, you dare not say I shall go to hell. You cannot think so. None can persuade you to it. Your own conscience tells you the contrary. Then, if we cannot as yet think alike in all things, at least we may love alike.

Wesley finally asks that they may resolve not to hurt one another, nor speak harshly of each other, nor harbour unkind thoughts of each other, but help each other on in the ways of the Kingdom.

The history of Catholics and Methodists in the nineteenth century followed the Wesley of the *Reply to the Catholic Catechism* rather than the Wesley of the *Letter to a Roman Catholic*. A good example was a book written in 1842 by Charles Elliott, an American minister, called *A Delineation of Romanism*. The book is as large as a family Bible and ploughs relentlessly through all the issues between Catholics and Protestants in double columned spacing for some 822 pages and a supplement. The distrust felt by Methodists of Catholic ways during the century was not made less by the movement of some Anglicans such as Ward, Newman, Manning and the Wilberforces to Rome. The Oxford Movement and its response to Methodism seems to have moved the Methodists away from Anglicanism and Catholicism and towards the Free Churches. In the twentieth century the movement of Methodism towards Catholicism seemed forever impossible when Pius XI issued his encyclical *Mortalium Animos* in 1928:

> The union of Christians cannot be fostered otherwise than by promoting the return of the dissidents to the one true Church of Christ, which in the past they have so unfortunately abandoned.

Methodists, like Anglicans, Baptists, Congregationalists, and the Orthodox as well, were the 'dissidents' who were asked to return to Rome.

Even before the advent of John XXIII and Vatican II there had been the hint of a new dawn upon the ecumenical horizon. In England in the 1940s Cardinal Hinsley had in his broadcasts and in his attitude generally shown that English Catholicism was not entirely absorbed with its own life. On the continent Hans Küng had done his doctorate on justification and had shown that he and the Protestant theologian Karl Barth were not aliens from different planets. Yves Congar, the great Dominican theologian, had done sterling work on some of the main doctrinal diffrences between Protestants and Catholics as had George Tavard the Augustinian theologian. It is significant that all three of these were at the Second Vatican Council when the documents were drafted which had a direct effect on the ecumenical movement in the Catholic Church. The Dogmatic Constitution on the Church, *Lumen Gentium* (1964), described the Church as a pilgrim people on a journey towards heaven. The Catholic Church was no longer described as *the* Church but the Church was stated to 'subsist in' the Catholic Church. Thus there was room in the words of *Lumen Gentium* for other ecclesial communities which, although deficient in Catholic eyes, had many of the elements necessary for being 'church'. If this seems a bit thin and grudging now, it shows how far ecumenical thinking has moved even since the Second Vatican Council. The Decree on Ecumenism, *Unitatis redintegratio* (1964), was open to calling other ecclesial communities 'separated brethren' which, even though it now sounds sexist, was a remarkable advance on previous official Roman Catholic thinking. Suddenly we were far from *Mortalium Animos*.

In the wake of the Council the World Methodist Conference in London in 1966 was asked to inaugurate a dialogue between the World Methodist Council, the executive body of World Methodism, and the Roman Catholic Church. The dialogue began in 1967 and has reported at the five-yearly meetings of the World Methodist Conference at Denver 1971, Dublin 1976, Honolulu 1981, Nairobi 1986 and Singapore 1991.[2] The Denver Report introduced the dialogue with the note that there was no formal history of separation between the two churches and grounds of affinity in the central place given to holiness and the use of the hymns of Charles Wesley. Agreement was seen in the place of Jesus Christ as God's supreme and final authority, the Bible as God's living Word to us, a theistic world view, and the importance of spirituality in both churches. On the eucharist there was agreement on the presence of Christ under these headings:

1. Both churches affirm the presence of Christ in the eucharist.
2. The presence does not depend on the experience of the communicant.
3. Only by faith do we become aware of the presence of Christ.
4. It is a distinctive mode of the presence of Christ in the worship of the Church.
5. Christ in his fullness is present in the sacrament, human and divine, crucified and risen.
6. Christ's presence is mediated through the elements of bread and wine over which the words of institution have been said.
7. Bread and wine are not the same outside the eucharist as within it.

The differences on the eucharist were then tabled:

1. The presence of Christ in the eucharist for Methodists is no different from his presence in other means of grace such as preaching.
2. For some Methodists the preaching of the Word provides a more effective means of grace than the eucharist.

3. Roman Catholic eucharistic faith is based on the transformation of the elements, i.e. on transubstantiation.
4. The worship of the elements does not occur in Methodism.

A few paragraphs of agreement on the ministry were also included where the following were points of main importance:

1. The minister acts in the name of Jesus Christ.
2. The Holy Spirit calls people to ministry.
3. The ministry means full time service for Christ for life. Its functions include the celebration of the sacraments, the preaching of the Word, teaching and pastoral care.
4. The ministry means that human beings become agents of Christ for bringing God into the lives and conditions of people. This is an extension of the incarnational and sacramental principle.

Important questions about ministry were then asked that would be taken up at Dublin in 1976. The Dublin Report offered clarifications of the 1971 Report about the eucharist. The first was about Christ's presence in both the eucharist and in preaching:

> We both affirm that wherever Christ is present, He is present in all his fullness.

Methodists were prepared to accept the phrase 'become his body and his blood' only in the sense that bread and wine acquired an additional significance as effectual signs, not in the Catholic sense of a transformation of the elements. The Report then talked of sacrifice and how both churches would understand it but then added the significant addition that Roman Catholics talked of the sacrifice of the mass offered through her history, the making present in a sacramental way the sacrifice of Christ. The clarifications on ministry were as follows:

1. There is no problem for Methodists in a threefold ministry as the symbol of the Church's continuity with the past but it is not to be regarded as essential since British Methodism had only a presbyteral order.
2. Oversight (episcope) is not only exercised through individual bishops but also in other ways such as a Methodist Conference.

3. Priesthood is used in the Roman Catholic tradition in the sense of the ordained, in the Methodist tradition as the priesthood of all God's people.
4. The central act of the minister is presiding at the eucharist.
5. Ordination is considered indelible in the Catholic tradition, in Methodism it is not repeated if a minister returns after resignation.
6. Lay presidency at the eucharist is rare but not excluded in the Methodist Church.
7. There is no theological objection to the ordination of women in the Methodist Church.

The Honolulu Report of 1981 was a major agreement on the Holy Spirit in the church and was important mainly for two points which looked forward to Nairobi 1986 and to Singapore 1991.

The old oppositions of Scripture and tradition have given way to an understanding which we share, that Scripture in witness to the living Tradition from which it arose has a normative role for the total tradition of the Church as it lives and is guided still by the Holy Spirit.

The papal authority, no less than any other within the Church, is a manifestation of the continuing presence of the Spirit of love within the Church or it is nothing.[3]

The Nairobi Report stated the goal of the Roman Catholic –Methodist conversations:

In obedience to Him who will bring about this unity we are committed to a vision that includes the goal of full communion in faith, mission and sacramental life.[4]

The commission gave some attention to the important New Testament word *koinonia*, a word that was later to be the basis of an ARCIC II report in 1991, a word meaning fellowship with God in Christ as well as fellowship among believers at all levels.

We have found that *koinonia*, both as a concept and an experience, is more important than any particular model of Church union that we are yet able to propose. *Koinonia* is so rich a term that it is better

to keep its original Greek form than bring together several English
words to convey its meaning. For believers it involves both
communion and community. It includes participation in God
through Christ in the Spirit by which believers become adopted
children of the same Father and members of the one Body of
Christ sharing in the same Spirit. And it includes deep fellowship
among participants, a fellowship which is both visible and
invisible, finding expression in faith and order, in prayer and
sacrament, in mission and service. Many different gifts have been
developed in our traditions, even in separation. Although we
already share some of our riches with one another, we look
forward to a greater sharing as we come closer together in full
unity (cf. Vatican II, Decree on Ecumenism, *Unitatis redintegratio*, no. 4).[5]

But the section that was of most interest proved to be that on the
Petrine office in the Church. After a long section on the references
to St Peter in the New Testament, the Petrine ministry was allowed
to be the result of a development in the life of the Catholic Church, a
part of the tradition:

> From this survey it will be seen that the primacy of the Bishop of
> Rome is not established from the Scriptures in isolation from the
> living Tradition.[6]

But the breakthrough paragraph was the one suggested by Revd
Raymond George, a British Methodist:

> Methodists accept that whatever is properly required for the unity
> of the whole of Christ's Church must by that very fact be God's
> will for his Church. A universal primacy might well serve as focus
> of and ministry for the unity of the whole Church.[7]

This needs no comment, perhaps, but the concept of infallibility did
raise difficulties for Methodists. A way forward was however
provided by the understanding of assurance in the Methodist
tradition. According to the Methodist doctrine of assurance,
believers receive from the Holy Spirit an assurance of their
redemption through Christ so that they can cry, Abba, Father. What

God gives to individuals he might also give to the whole Church by the gift of infallibility, so as to exclude all doubt.

The Singapore Report 1991 centred on the Apostolic Faith and Ministry within the Apostolic Tradition. An important sentence sets the context for the discussion:

> The Saviour rescues us from loneliness and sets us within the infinitely diverse security of his friends.[8]

The Report put the concept of Tradition in this way:

> The Church is sustained by a conversation, initiated by the Lord.

As to the relation of this Tradition to Scripture, the Report said:

> Scripture was written within Tradition, yet Scripture is normative for Tradition.[9]

On ministry within this Tradition of faith, the Report spoke of the normative nature of the threefold ministry but that other gifts for ministry have been bestowed afresh at times of crisis and opportunity; this safeguards the unique position of the Methodist ministry in England which arose once against the Anglican ministry of the eighteenth century:

> Previous paragraphs make it clear that Methodists and Catholics share a fundamentally important perspective on ministry, affirming that the ordained ministry is essentially pastoral in nature. Ordained ministers have the special responsibility of exercising and holding together the functions of proclaiming the Gospel, calling people to faith, feeding the flock with the word and sacrament and making Christ known through the ministry of servanthood to the world.[10]

It was in this way acknowledged by both sides that Christian communities go through periods of dormancy and decline.

One interesting point when English Methodists and Catholics talk together is how much they find in common, perhaps even more than either of them find with any other denominations. This is partly because they seem to come from similar sociological backgrounds which have never been the dominant Christian group in England. They also share an enormous personal devotion to Jesus Christ which feels similar even though its theological expression is very different. Both have shared the experience of making converts in England, usually from people on the fringes of the church.

The British Roman Catholic/Methodist Committee has been important as a reference point for the international commission and has done much work in its own right. Recent work that has been published includes a paper on Roman Catholic–Methodist marriages, a consensus paper on Justification and a paper *Can the Roman Catholic and Methodist Churches be Reconciled?* The most recent offering is a discussion paper on the place of the Virgin Mary in both the two churches.[11] The sense of unity experienced by the members of this committee has been perhaps a main reason for its successful perusal of many controversial questions in its nearly thirty years of existence. The recent papal encyclical *Ut Unum Sint* will be a great encouragement to the partners on both sides of this continuing dialogue.

13

We Are All Members One of Another

Disunity has always been a scandal but it was not always openly admitted to be so. With the modern missionary movement which began for England in the late eighteenth century with the Particular Baptist Missionary Society under William Carey, a new era opened up. The scandal of having different kinds of Christians in Calcutta proclaiming the same gospel and going their separate ways could not continue. Carey suggested in 1810 a meeting of all the Protestant missionary societies at Cape Town to discuss the issues. This speculative hope did not materialize and it was only one hundred years later at Edinburgh in 1910 that the birth of the ecumenical movement came about. One of the hopes of this famous missionary conference was the planting of one united church of Christ in each missionary area.

What might be possible in Africa or Asia would seem impossible in England with its history of conflicts between the churches. Yet curiously it is in England that some of the most exciting work of ecumenism has been done. This may well have come about because in the twentieth century no one church could be said to be totally dominant. It is well known, for example, that by 1900 the number of members of the Church of England was far higher than the number of nonconformists. But if Roman Catholics were included in these nonconformist figures then the 'non Anglican' Christians were greater in number.

Accurate numbers are hard to find but the following figures for 1900 seem to be trustworthy:

Church of England electoral rolls	2.8 million
Baptized Roman Catholics, England & Wales	1.57 million
Methodist members in England	0.73 million
Baptist members in England	0.24 million
Estimated Congregationalist members in England	0.35 million
Presbyterian members in England	0.08 million [1]

Thus 'nonconformity' reached about three million in 1900, a little above the Church of England figures.

There was even a hope that nonconformity might be the major group influence on Christianity in England in the early twentieth century. The First World War put a stop to this and many other optimisms. The decline of nonconformity since the First World War has been close to catastrophic.

> It is probable that Nonconformity reached its height of political power, was most representative of the temper of the English people, round the beginning of this century. . . . But in the generation that has passed since the great Liberal landslide of 1906, one of the greatest changes in the English religious and social landscapes has been the decline of Nonconformity.[2]

But this does not imply that churches only look at unity schemes if they are declining and that the Free Churches of England would not have looked for unity with other churches had they felt themselves viable. This would be to overlook the major work that has been done since the nineteenth century on the matter and theology of Christian unity. That the Orthodox Churches have taken part since the 1920s, and were part of the World Council of Churches at Amsterdam, with the Russian Orthodox Churches joining the WCC in 1961, shows that unity has not just been a case of weak Protestants propping each other up. Unity is somehow seen to be written into the creed of the whole church. The arrival of the Roman Catholic Church on the world ecumenical scene after the Second Vatican Council has also indicated that ecumenism has become a major item on the agenda in Rome. The initial stumbling attempts at ecumenism in England in the forties, fifties and sixties have proved to be a sign or first fruits of a larger outbreak of the unity resolve throughout the major world churches.

Methodist unity   In England the Methodist Church was the result of a long process of discussion and voting before it came about in 1932. The three groups of Wesleyan, Primitive and United Methodists represented certain distinct strands and emphases of Methodism. The Wesleyan was formal, often using the liturgy for Morning Prayer and the eucharistic service of the Church of England, and its ministers believed themselves called of God to be pastors and not to be representatives of the people. The Primitive strand hardly picked up a book in chapel, except it be a Bible or a hymn book. Their emphasis was a gospel proclamation to the mainly working-class areas where they were set. Democratic rights within the groups were important and ministers were less dominant than in the Wesleyan tradition. The United Methodists, as their name indicates, were a group united from the Bible Christian, New Connexion and Free Methodists. They had very little in the way of liturgy and were concerned about what they perceived to be the dominance of the ministry in the Wesleyan areas. The main theological problems to be settled before unity across the three strands were the two which came from the Wesleyan end; what role would the ministers have in a united church, and what would be the status given to the works of John Wesley in Methodist doctrinal standards? Although the United Methodists and the Primitive Methodists voted overwhelmingly for the reunion it was passed in the Wesleyan Conference by the smallest possible margin, the 75% required in the ministerial session being just achieved. With the publication of the new Methodist Hymn Book in 1933 and the Book of Offices in 1936 the new Methodist Church was given some strong meat that would last it for over forty years, until a new Methodist Service Book was produced in 1975 and a new hymn book, *Hymns and Psalms*, in 1983.

After a historical outline of all previous books, the preface to the 1933 Methodist Hymn Book continues:

This hymn-book is issued for the use of *all* British Methodists, and for not a few Methodists 'beyond the seas' as well. It is the first such book since Wesley's final collection of a hundred and fifty years ago. Its publication, therefore, may rightly be called an historic event in Methodism. Wesley's historic preface for its predecessor of 1780 is appended in full.

This collection, like that of 1780, is primarily evangelical. It contains a large number of hymns which have proved their power both to deepen the spiritual life of believers and to inspire saving faith in Christ. Among their writers Charles Wesley holds a dominant place. The claims of poetry have always been in mind, but those of religion have been paramount, and not a few hymns have been selected chiefly because they are dear to the people of God. For the one aim of every true hymn-book must be to 'raise or quicken the spirit of devotion'.

This hymn-book, like its predecessors, is intended for use in private devotion as well as in public worship. A few hymns have therefore been included that are especially suitable for select gatherings or for solitary communion with God. Most good hymns, however, may be used either in public or private worship, and it is confidently hoped that this book will enrich both.

In the manifold ministries of Divine worship, song is specifically the people's part, and in Methodism, in particular, the whole congregation has always been called to sing the hymns. We hope that none of our people will consent to be cut off from any part of their heritage of song. In many a hymn that may not at first attract, they will find 'hid treasure' if only they will seek it.

Several interesting points arose from this union. The first was that the majority of the new Presidents, Vice-Presidents and Secretaries in the first year of the reunion came from the dominant Wesleyan group. The second is that the reunion of three churches should have made some chapels redundant. Sadly this nettle was not grasped at the time and although different circuits of churches were amalgamated there were still two (or three) chapels open in the same area, sometimes in the same street. The hymn book, although greatly loved, was inevitably a compromise and contained not only evangelical chorus types of hymns (Blessed Assurance, What a Friend We Have in Jesus, When We Walk with the Lord, etc.) but even those that would not have looked amiss in the Catholic Westminster Hymnal (there were translations of the *Stabat Mater* and the *Dies Irae* as well as hymns by F. W. Faber, founder of the London Oratory).

There was clearly always going to be a tendency for the different groups to look for 'our' hymns rather than to try 'their' hymns. The reactions to the Book of Offices varied; some churches and chapels took to it as if it had dropped from God in heaven, others regarded it as 'that infernal new book'. Over sixty years after Methodist union the cracks still show here and there. Methodist union seems to show that:

1. When smaller groups join a larger one, the larger group after

the unity settlement must show its commitment by being less than dominant in the united church.

2. The principle, 'death and resurrection', must be applied and realized by local people who may have to ask the fundamental question, 'Is our building, our minister, our organization, needed for the mission of God in our area?'

3. It is not possible to impose a liturgical style on those who are not used to it. Before the use of new forms major teaching and preaching have to take place. The pill has to be sugar-coated.

4. Loss of identity could be seen as ultimately threatening. Some may have been lost to the Methodist Church because it was not perceived what a simple statement such as, 'I am a Primitive Methodist' might fully imply. Take away a name and you may take away all identity. Some of the above must be borne in mind for future reunions in England.

Local Ecumenical Projects (Partnerships)   The hopes of future Anglican–Methodist unity had caused Christians in some areas to anticipate future unity in some ways, for example in sharing buildings, in planning only church building in new areas, sometimes in making ministers cross their usual pastoral boundaries and care for members from other churches. By 1964 at the Nottingham Conference on Faith and Order these experiments were officially designated 'Areas of Ecumenical Experiment'.

> Among other resolutions the Nottingham Faith and Order Conference called on the churches to:
>   . . . designate areas of ecumenical experiment, at the request of local congregations, or in new towns and housing areas. In such areas there should be experiments in ecumenical group ministries, in the sharing of buildings and equipment, and in the development of mission.

> The conference's 'Section on Ministry' expanded what it meant by this in the following words:
>   Some experiments are already in being in the field of *group ministry* (an ecumenical group of ordained men) and of *team ministry* (a group of full-time workers, ordained and non-ordained, men and women, which might be denominational or

ecumenical). Many more are required to provide a new, common strategy in downtown areas and on new estates, with the co-operation of several churches.[3]

This title was later revised to the more familiar 'Local Ecumenical Project'. By about 1984 there were about four hundred of these projects, usually consisting of one of four types:

1. The simplest form was where two or more congregations shared a church building under a statutory agreement. There was no necessary commitment to do more than offer certain times for services to the other church group, but at least it was a start. A Sharing of Church Buildings Act was passed by Parliament in 1969.

2. At the local level, with the Roman Catholics being increasingly involved, official guidelines were drawn up whereby Catholics could share with other churches in a Local Covenant. This entailed a formal signing of a commitment at the grass roots level, to do together what could in conscience be done, but with no sharing in sacraments or pastoral care.

3. Ministries could be shared in an LEP with the agreement of the churches signatory to the agreement. This did not necessarily mean that all ministers would be considered to have equal rights and responsibilities, though it often did. A lot of sensitivity is needed when ministers move in LEPs. Consultation with the partners in the LEP is essential and not merely done for politeness.

4. Where an LEP had an agreement to recognize each other's church's members, the LEP was probably as fully committed as it could be. At church membership and confirmation services in such places, for example, the new members were confirmed into all the churches (e.g. Anglican, Methodist, URC, Baptist). The problem of course when moving from such an ecumenical church was, 'to whom do I belong?' Some members of LEPs found themselves having to tell their new areas that they belonged to more than one church. Such things were not supposed to happen.

A lot of work has been done in LEPs since 1984 and in some ways they constitute a sharp end of ecumenism, the place where not only problems are raised but where the solutions to ecumenical problems are being worked out week by week. Some church leaders abhor them as they take up so much time; they are seen too to be like a burr under the horse's saddle. It is of interest that most mainline churches never receive any kind of inspection; perhaps it is best that many do not. LEPs by their very constitutions have to be inspected every five years. Among the important questions is the one which asks what effect has the LEP had on outreach to the neighbourhood and in offering the Christian proclamation to others. One wonders why all churches don't draft these questions into their standing orders. Let me give two illustrations from my own experience.

In this particular LEP there are three denominations involved, Roman Catholic, Methodists and the Church of England. It came about from 1967 because the local council and the Council of Churches wanted an interdenominational church in a new housing area. The church and community centre was built by 1974 with money coming mainly from the local corporation and about 25% from the three churches. The building is held by the three denominations on a Sharing Agreement. A full-time community worker is salaried by the community. The centre is open for community use during the week but the churches have exclusive Sunday use. The churches have preferred involvement in established community structures to setting up their own organizations. Worship is separately denominational in a tight Sunday timetable but a 'Joint Eucharist' has been approved by all three denominations for monthly and other special occasions. Pastoral care by the ministers is closely co-operative and joint marriage preparation and follow-up are used. The people share a fulfilling and thrilling ecumenical venture.

The second dates from the summer of 1976, when the local Anglican church began to suffer from the movement of the clay in its foundations. The vicar wondered whether any local church could accommodate his people and an approach to the Methodist church was positive. Eventually a Sharing Agreement was signed and the Anglicans had their Sunday service at 9.15 am followed by the Methodists at 11.00 am. Joint services began to be held on special occasions such as Harvest, Christmas and Easter. Some Methodists found the Anglican services too 'high', with incense and ceremonial. Some Anglicans found the Methodists too noisy when they were trying to meditate. After several years of living in parallel the decision was made to hold all services at the same time, with alternating

Methodist and Church of England services. The ministers appointed to the church share pastoral care and the preparation of marriages and confirmation candidates.

Since 1994 the phrase 'Local Ecumenical Partnerships' has been the preferred title since 'project' implies something short term whereas 'partnership' suggests long term commitment. These local partnerships are usually overseen by sponsoring bodies at the intermediate level of 'county' level. At present about fifty or more of these bodies exist, either at the level of a large new town (e.g. Telford) or in a large metropolitan area (e.g. Manchester) or at county level (e.g. Norfolk).

The most recent figures for Local Ecumenical Partnerships indicate some 766 of these. In some areas LEPs are very abundant, for example in the Milton Keynes and Wiltshire areas, in other places LEPs are almost a rarity. Clearly Sponsoring Bodies who regulate and encourage LEPs throughout England have worked at different paces in different areas, but the growth of these partnerships has been a uniquely English phenomenon concerning which the English churches can be justly proud. The denominational league table in 1992 looked like this:

1. United Reformed Church   396 LEPs,   23% of all churches
2. Baptist Union   165 LEPs,   10% of all churches
3. Methodist Church   579 LEPs,   8% of all churches
4. Roman Catholic Church   174 LEPs,   6% of all churches
5. Church of England   373 LEPs,   2% of all churches

These figures are very approximate and not too much should be made of them, but they are interesting. Of the smaller denominations, with far fewer churches, the Moravians lead with 7% from the Congregational Federation with 2%, while the Society of Friends and the Salvation Army have about 1%. Whether the percentages show the ecumenical commitment of the denominations or not, we have to leave the reader to judge.

Ecumenical training   Almost all training for ministry in England now has an ecumenical component. All people who are trained nonresidentially on courses train alongside people of other denominations. In all there are thirteen such courses where candidates for ordination in the Church of England, the Methodist Church and the United Reformed Church may train together, sometimes with other denominations too such as the Baptists and Pentecostals. They are: the Carlisle Diocesan Training Institute; the East Anglian Ministerial Training Course; the East Midlands Ministry Training Course; the North East Ordination Course, the Northern Ordination Course; the North Thames Ministerial Training Course; the South East Institute of Theological Education; the South West Ministry Training Course; the Southern Dioceses Ministerial Training Course; the Urban Theology Unit, Sheffield; the West of England Ministerial Training Course; the West Midlands Ministerial Training Course and the College of Ripon and York, St John. The usual commitment is for one week night, about fifteen hours weekly of academic work alongside this, and several weekends along with a residential week. Such a course usually lasts for three years after which people go into their specific form of ministry, some full-time, others part-time, some stipendiary and others non-stipendiary. The ecumenical component is ensured by having different lecturers and in experiencing differing denominational worship. Thus an Anglican may have been taught Church History by a Methodist for three years, and a Methodist taught Liturgy by an Anglican. Methodists and URCs will have experienced an Anglican High Mass, while URCs and Anglicans will have experienced the Methodist Covenant Service. URCs will have offered the Methodists and Anglicans a unique style of eucharist as well as an excellent new hymnbook, *Rejoice and Sing*. From time to time students will have had opportunities to preach and lead worship in the churches of other traditions than their own.

Residential theological training is mainly denominational in this country. Part of the reason for this is that within denominations 'parties' exist which are concerned for the survival of their type of Christianity. Thus evangelical students within the Church of England are more likely to choose Oakhill in North London or Ridley Hall in Cambridge than Westcott House, Cambridge or Mirfield in Yorkshire, where more Catholic Anglicans find themselves. Similar comments could be made about Baptist, URC and Methodist colleges, though in many cases students do not have a choice in which college they attend. Where colleges of different denominations are close to each other federations have come to exist, for example between the Anglicans, Methodists and United Reformed at Cambridge, and between the Baptists, Methodists, Unitarians and United Reformed at Manchester. Sadly, as yet no Catholic seminary is officially part of an ecumenical group in England. The only college which has a total united constitution is The Queen's College at Birmingham. In 1970 the Anglican college at Edgbaston and the Methodist college at Handsworth came together under the principalship of Dr John Habgood. Since that date some thirty or so Anglicans have been trained each year alongside some thirty or so Methodists, with complete sharing of tutors, worship and residential facilities. Queen's is now also officially registered as a college for United Reformed students and about half a dozen each year train alongside Anglicans and Methodists. Students training for the presbyterate are the larger percentage, but a few students are trained for the Methodist Diaconal Order and for the permanent diaconate within the Church of England. The constituency of candidates for the presbyteral ministry for 1994/5 was as follows:

Church of England	26
Methodist Church	25
United Reformed Church	9

In addition, there were:

Candidates for diaconal ministry	2
Access to Black Theology students	7
Students from overseas	2

In addition to candidates for full-time ministerial occupations the Methodist Church has undertaken at Queen's a year's empowerment programme for black lay people in connection with Bournville College of Further Education. This will enable the black students to qualify for admission to university courses. The Queen's College is unique in having an annual course with the Roman Catholic seminary, St Mary's, Oscott. During the course final year students live at Queen's and Oscott and take part in a month's course on the eucharist, a period that puts both sets of students in touch with the theology and practice of the other denominations.

It was in 1976 that another, and still unique venture was inaugurated. The Rector of Oscott, Monsignor Francis Thomas, now Bishop of Northampton, and the Principal of Queen's, the Revd Dr Anthony Bird, were both warmly supportive, but it was Father Denis Egan and the Revd Dr Raymond Hammer who had the idea of a month's joint course late in each autumn for the final year students, a fortnight to be spent at Queen's and a fortnight at Oscott . . . From 1978, the colleges have together confronted the Eucharist, historically, the most divisive of subjects.

The time is divided between lectures, groups and the sharing of worship and life. The lectures cover the whole range of Eucharistic faith and practice from the Upper Room to the divided observances of the sundered Church today. No controversies are ignored; no theories omitted, not least those emanating from the modern philosophy of signs and symbols and Dom Odo Casel's understanding of the Christian Mystery, even though these are suspect to the official pronouncements of Rome and are not accepted as alternatives to transubstantiation. The richness of Anglican and Protestant understanding is appreciated and the possibility of convergence is clearly seen. This matter should unite Christians rather than tear them apart.

Worship is obligatory, whatever the service, but there is no breach of communion rules. Some of the Queen's students, Methodists and evangelicals for the most part, resent the inability to meet at the altar – though many of those who do would prefer to speak of the Lord's table. Those who have been involved in Christian life only since Vatican II, cannot remember the old days and are not therefore amazed at the way we have been led.[4]

Ecumenical training for ministry is a fairly obvious way of doing ecumenism, and it is sad that only in Birmingham has it been taken fully into the system of the sponsoring churches. Because Queen's came about when Anglican–Methodist unity was a distinct possibility, with the failure of the talks in 1969 and 1972 there was not much enthusiasm for further efforts at ecumenical education. Enthusiasm for the Covenant proposals was punctured in 1982 and the chance to unite other colleges probably could not be taken up. With the 'Not Strangers But Pilgrims' ventures which led to the

Swanwick Conference in 1987 perhaps a new period might be said to have begun. The 1987 Swanwick Declaration had a section which quite deliberately put ecumenical theological training high on its list of priorities: 'Formation for the ordained ministry and post-ordination training should be strongly ecumenical and further schemes of joint training should be encouraged.'[5] As yet this paragraph has barely been noticed by the ecumenical bodies which were set up after Swanwick. One suspects that the problem is that ecumenism is not just something that needs doing between the churches but needs doing within individual denominations first. It is difficult to unite with a group that is internally divided.

The United Reformed Church   In 1972 the Presbyterian Church of England and the Congregational Union united to become the United Reformed Church with about two hundred thousand members. The few churches that remained outside the union were called the Congregational Federation with about ten thousand members at present. Uniquely, the new United Reformed Church made it clear that it considered itself an intermediate entity with a desire to cease existence in the event of further unity in England. The eldership of the Presbyterian tradition was married to a Congregational polity. This meant that in local churches regular meetings of members would be responsible for key decisions on witness and service while lay elders were elected and ordained to form local leadership and to share in the pastoral care of members. In 1981 the Re-formed Association of Churches of Christ in England came into the URC. Since the Churches of Christ were a group that insisted on believer's baptism as the means of entry into the church, a unique situation now exists where within the same church two baptismal policies exist side by side. Members of the URC often say that they feel like a young church because of their need to explore new ways of being the church.

Congregational and Presbyterian churches came together in 1972 and were joined by the Re-formed Association of Churches of Christ in 1981. These acts of union were not without pain. We said farewell to some old friends who could not join us in the enterprise. There are those among us who still feel that they have lost something precious in a particular tradition. But for many this has been a time of joy, learning and enlargement, with horizons being widened. It is a young church and it often *feels* a young church. It is, perhaps, the reality of change and the constant exploration of new ways of being the church which have contributed most to the feeling that the URC is young and alive. There is a tension created, on the one hand, by the need to settle down and realize our own potential and establish our identity, and, on the other hand, the call to press forward into new exploration of how the whole church may be healed of its divisions. It is a healthy tension to live with, for it reflects the 'now' and 'not yet' of the Kingdom. The URC is not a piece of ecclesiastical territory we have won and intend to hold, but rather a bridgehead where we dare not remain and from which we are called to move forward.[6]

The freedom of minority opinion in the URC is something that is jealously safeguarded by the church. That through their Congregational roots they have had about eighty years experience of ordained women's ministry is an indication that they may have much to offer in discussion about the ministry of the whole people of God. As indicated above, the United Reformed Church has about 23% of its local churches involved in local covenants and local ecumenical projects or partnerships, the largest percentage of all the English churches.

Lessons of the Covenant   Soon after the failure of the Methodist –Anglican scheme the United Reformed Church took the initiative of putting Ten Propositions to the Churches in England, asking whether these might form the basis for further talks on unity. These were:

1. We affirm our belief that the visible unity in life and mission of all Christ's people is the will of God.
2. We therefore declare our willingness to join a covenant actively to seek that visible unity.
3. We believe that this search requires action both locally and nationally.

4. We agree to recognize, as from an accepted date, the communicant members in good standing of the other Covenanting Churches as true members of the Body of Christ and welcome them to Holy Communion without condition.

5. We agree that, as from an accepted date, initiation in the Covenanting Churches shall be by mutually acceptable rites.

6. We agree to recognize, as from an accepted date, the ordained ministries of the other Covenanting Churches, as true ministers of word and sacraments in the Holy Catholic Church, and we agree that all subsequent ordinations to the ministries of the Covenanting Churches shall be according to a Common Ordinal which will properly incorporate the episcopal, presbyteral and lay roles in ordination.

7. We agree within the fellowship of the Covenanting Churches, to respect the rights of conscience, and to continue to all our members, such freedom of thought and action as is consistent with the visible unity of the Church.

8. We agree to continue to give every possible encouragement to local ecumenical projects and to develop methods of decision making in common.

9. We agree to explore such further steps as will be necessary to make more clearly visible the unity of Christ's people.

10. We agree to remain in close fellowship and consultation with all the Churches represented on the Churches' Unity Commission.[7]

The Roman Catholic and Baptist Union response was mainly negative though qualified by their offering 'observers' to the eventual Council for Covenanting that emerged. The Council for Covenanting consisted of the Church of England, the Methodist Church, the United Reformed Church, the Moravians and some Baptists. Within two years a report on the Covenant was issued which showed a way forward for the churches to recognize each other, with each other's sacraments and ministries. The Church of England's General Synod rejected the covenant, mainly because of opposition in the House of Clergy where many members were opposed to the ordination of women which obtained in the other churches.

34. What cannot, however, be avoided is a judgment on the

matter of 'women ministers' in this context by the appropriate authority in the Church of England. As we have previously insisted (our para. 5 above), it is not in our view for those who have represented the Church of England in these discussions to attempt to pre-judge the matter or to pre-empt in any way the responsibility of the proper Church of England authority on a matter of this gravity and sensitivity. We are aware of the strong views which our covenanting partners have understandably and consistently held on this matter, but we regret that in the Proposals now submitted to the Churches a decision by the Church of England in favour of the presbyteral and episcopal ministry of duly ordained or recognized and accepted 'women ministers' has been assumed – without question or qualification.[8]

The other churches had accepted the Covenant proposals despite the large changes it would have meant in their traditions. The rejection of the Covenant was seen by many as fear of change and desire for the *status quo*. Derek Palmer quotes Rupert Davies:

> Some have argued that the rejections were the will of God, eccentrically disclosed to a minority of Anglican clergy, a few bishops, and less than a quarter of the Methodist Conference. This view is unsustainable in the light of the dire circumstances for all the Churches involved.[9]

Rupert Davies in 1992 had indicated four ecumenical lessons he had learned:

1. Our churches have an ingrained desire to keep themselves as they are. Only if a prophetic person gives an exciting vision of the future do new things begin to happen.
2. Similarly, if an effort towards unity fails or falters they quickly relapse into preoccupation with their own denominational affairs.
3. Ecumenical enthusiasm must not be mistaken for ecumenical understanding. Church members often express a great desire for unity, and then withdraw when the going gets rough.
4. Ecumenism is not based on convenience, but on belief in the Church as one body engaged in mission. Anything less simply results in 'ecumenism on the cheap.'[10]

But while 1982 saw the failure of the Covenant, it saw also the publication of the Final Report of ARCIC and a memorable visit to England by Pope John Paul II. Increasingly Roman Catholics were involved in Local Ecumenical Projects such as that at Thamesmead in South East London, and local covenants were being signed. By the time that the new ecumenical instruments were being thought through, the Roman Catholics were at the centre of the English ecumenical scene.

Ecumenical apologetics   Since the death of C. S. Lewis there has not been any one person who has been able to command respect from all churches as far as the task of apologetics is concerned. By apologetics is usually meant giving reasons for one's Christian faith and hope. Lewis was able to do this in *Mere Christianity*, a book which is still in print although over forty years old. The need for the task to be attempted was made clear at the 1991 Forum of Churches Together in England (see below p. 164), and it was also indicated that the apologetic task would have to be attempted as a preliminary to evangelism.

During his time of service at the Church of England Board for Mission and Unity, Canon Derek Palmer was responsible for creating the Christian Enquiry Agency. The Agency is an inter-denominational organization based at the Inter-Church House in Waterloo which works with all the major denominations in England. It receives enquiries every day from people who want to know more about the Christian faith. Interestingly in 1991 it had some two thousand enquiries, the largest single group being men between twenty-one and forty. CEA places advertisements in newspapers as well as distributing enquiry cards for display. Libraries, prisons, community centres, and hospitals have them, as do some churches and cathedrals. Those who enquire are sent a free copy of St Luke's Gospel and a letter. If further help is requested they are put in contact with a local Christian community of their choice. Two of their newer initiatives have been the production of bookmarks available to libraries from June 1994 which can be returned post free by enquirers, and the circulation of beer mats with the slogan, 'Life isn't all beer and skittles' and a brief Christian message. It would be good to be able to report that all churches which are regularly visited by tourists have a stock of Christian Enquiry Agency material available. The sad fact is that not many do stock them. Could we be missing out on an evangelical opportunity in many places?

14

The New Ecumenical Scene:
Not Strangers But Pilgrims, and after

Derek Palmer has written the clearest account of the Inter-Church Process that became *Not Strangers But Pilgrims* from the enviable position of one who was at the centre of the events. To his book *Strangers No Longer* the largest debt is due for this section. The new thinking came about because the churches in England were conscious of five difficulties and opportunities:

1. The failure of the unity talks in England. This has been covered in outline above.

2. The growing understanding among the churches that Britain had become a mission field. Almost all the English churches had experienced decreases in membership during the previous decades to the extent that only about 12% of the population were active church members by 1982; in some areas such as certain parts of cities the percentage was as low as 1%. New ecumenical thinking would need to be as much about evangelism as about ecumenism.

3. The failure of the churches to welcome black people who had arrived in England from 1948. This had led in some places to the creation of black-led churches, often of a pentecostal nature, in other places to a total alienation of black people from organized Christianity.

4. The increasing number of people of other faiths in England and the failure of the churches to relate to people in their neighbourhoods at the level of real inter-faith dialogue.

5. The growing number of new 'House Churches', often created by disenchantment with existing denominational groups. The main ingredients of such groups were direct experience of the supernatural with conversions, healings and an infectious enthusiasm that

made existing churches look dull and staid, not open to the Spirit. Statistics were hard to come by in 1982 but rough figures were given of between fifty thousand and one hundred thousand members, so that some estimated that they were close to the size of the Baptist Union or United Reformed Church.

In May 1985 leaders of the churches in England, Wales and Scotland met at Lambeth Palace and launched a 'three year Inter-Church Process of prayer, reflection and debate together on the nature and purpose of the Church in the light of its mission'. It was recognized that wide consultation would be needed at the local level since 'unity from above' had not worked in England in particular or in Britain as a whole. Three publications were projected for the perusal of the future conferences at Nottingham, Bangor and St Andrews. One would attempt to look at the churches from outside; from people outside Britain, from outside the British churches. When *Observations* was published in 1986 it included comments from young people, theological colleges, the Association of Interchurch Families, the House Churches, the Evangelical Alliance and from third world churches.

> The Church would also be seen as a community of God's people rather than simply a congregation of God's people. As a community there would be an interaction of life together (Acts 2.42–47), as opposed to church being a place or an event that Christians attended. In these terms church would be seen as anything that Christians did together, worship, eat meals, play games or work. As a community of God's people the church is seen as what the believers are rather than what they do or an event to which they attend. Christians cannot go to church, they are the church. It would also mean that there would not be a distinction between church and para-church.[1]

It was a pity that few secular agencies seem to have responded to this appeal from the church to be 'seen as others see us'. *Reflections* was a book from inside the churches, with responses from the thirty-two participating churches in the Process. Churches were asked to offer an answer to, 'In your tradition and experience, how do you understand the nature and purpose of your church in relation to other Christian denominations as we share in God's mission to the world?' Each church offered its own answer complete with up-to-date statistics of membership and numbers of ministers and churches. Vincent Nichols emphasizes in his introduction that the statements are provisional responses rather than formal statements by Synods, but nevertheless are recognizable expressions of the self-understanding of each church.

> This present volume, however, brings together the statements put forward by the participating Churches at national level in response to the question which is central to the whole process *Not Strangers But Pilgrims*:
>
>> In your tradition and experience, how do you understand the nature and purpose of your Church (or Churches when the national body is a federation of local Churches) in relation to other Christian denominations and as we share in God's mission to the world?
>
> . . . The responses were to be provisional responses, drawn up by whatever means each Church chooses for the purpose of this process. 'It is not intended to seek statements formally approved by general Assemblies and Synods. Nevertheless they should be responses which members of that church would recognize as an expression of its self-understanding' (Introductory Document, *Not Strangers But Pilgrims*, p. 9).[2]

Reflections is thus a unique collection, not available elsewhere, of the understandings churches have of themselves and of their relations with each other. The most important and underestimated volume was *Views from the Pews*. During Lent 1986 local ecumenical groups, other groups and individuals were encouraged to take part in a course called *What on Earth is the Church For?* The course was based on a booklet by Martin Reardon of which well over 120,000 copies were sold. The booklet was published by the British Council of Churches and the Catholic Truth Society, an example of ecumenical co-operation in publishing. In addition to the booklet some fifty-seven local radio stations, BBC and Independent, put out local programmes. The estimate is that an astounding one million people were reached by the course. The previous ecumenical course, *People Next Door*, from some twenty years before had reached seventy thousand people. Local radio made Lent '86 a real success in terms of numbers reached. Response sheets for the questions were freely circulated. The questions were: Why believe in God? What did Jesus come for? Why did the church begin? Why different churches? What now? The response to the Lent '86 course was overwhelming with a large number of replies received. Trumedia Study Oxford Ltd used Judy Turner-Smith to analyse a percentage sample of ten thousand replies. *Views from the Pews* gives an analysis of the opinions of the largest cross-section of people ever to be asked about the Church in Britain. The main headlines which came out in response to the five questions were:

1. *Grass-roots find a voice.* People became aware of the differences between the churches in the spirit of open fellowship. Groups often indicated that they were inhibited by the presence of local priests or ministers and felt frustrated by barriers erected by the churches' leaders.

2. *Jesus hidden by jargon.* The answers revealed that people in the churches needed more teaching, not only about other denominations but about prayer and theology. But theology needs to be offered without all the technical language of justification, grace, redemption etc. which causes Jesus to be hidden by jargon.

3. *Afraid to share.* Groups rather than individuals had this concern. When people have a faith that they want to share with others they often feel inhibited by lack of words and this discourages them. Simple ways of sharing faith informally are called for.

4. *Enjoying our differences.* Answers indicated that a vast number were wrong in what they thought other Christians believed. The surprise for many was the common ground shared by Christians. Yet to be different in details is not to be wrong. The discovery of diversity was felt to be enriching and enjoyable.

5. *Time to become one.* While people recognized the problems in the way of unity, uniformity was definitely not wanted. Yet proper attention was needed to do jointly: worship including the eucharist; meetings for teaching and fellowship; evangelism; use of resources especially in youth work; action in the community. The responses indicated a large measure of frustration where the priorities of the clergy and laity did not coincide in matters of unity. Lay people felt strongly that a divided church was no example to a divided world.

Several insights are still very relevant from *Views from the Pews* some ten years on. Sadly, they have not always been heard by the churches. The call for joint holy communion has been strongly voiced.

> We think that Christ must wring his hands in anguish at the way we have allowed the Eucharist, Mass or Communion to become such a divisive exercise – who can and who can't; who may and who must. Shame on us. It was a simple meal and a simple straightforward message for all generations and men have made it impossible for all His sheep to share.[3]

At the Nottingham 1987 conference a man suggested provocatively to the Roman Catholics, 'If you have the best cooks, let us taste your food.' Church leaders and theologians, even local clergy, are recognized in some answers as being the chief obstacles to Christian unity. Fascinatingly, Lent '86 seemed to show that a lot of Christians were waiting to do the work of explaining their gospel to those around them and were only waiting to find out appropriate ways of doing it.

Three national conferences took place at Nottingham, Bangor and St Andrews which agreed that new ways of working ecumenically were necessary. The Hayes Conference Centre at Swanwick, where an inter-national conference took place from 31 August to 4 September 1987, became the focus for decisions about the future working of the churches in Britain and Ireland. The group experience and the worship at Swanwick proved to be vitally important. The work in the groups brought home to individuals that they were indeed strangers no longer but fellow pilgrims, while the worship proved to be less divisive than had been the case at Nottingham. Non-Catholics received a blessing at the Roman Catholic eucharist conducted by Cardinal Hume and Catholics accepted a blessing at the Covenanted Churches of Wales eucharist. Memorable services took place which included an important session, at which I was present, led by Bishop Graham Chadwick called 'The Healing of Ecumenical Memories'. As Graham Chadwick unfolded his theme, we were asked to remember the times when we had been offended by other people from other churches. I remembered Father Michael, who, when I told him that I was now going to the Methodist church, retorted 'that's not a church'. I did not have the ecclesiology to answer him or even the history to remind him of what *Apostolicae Curae* had made of his orders, so I kept quiet. Bishop Chadwick's meditation enabled me to forgive Father Michael and offer the incident to God. As I looked around the chapel at Swanwick there were many with tears in their eyes. The exercise ought to be repeated in all areas of the country.

At a black pentecostal celebration the most unlikely people seemed able to raise their hands in praise to God. After denominational groups had met to decide where the Swanwick Conference had brought them, a plenary session was held at which some of these denominational positions were shared. The crucial moment came when Cardinal Hume asked to speak on behalf of the hierarchies of England, Wales and Scotland.

> Knowing that he had arrived on the Monday uncertain as to what lead he should give, the clarity and power of his words were quite overwhelming. He seemed to catch the mood of everyone in the hall and raise expectations to new levels. It was an astonishing moment which no one present in the hall will forget.[4]

He affirmed that Catholics were in favour of full engagement in the new process and its possible outcome:

> I hope that our Roman Catholic delegates . . . will recommend to members of our Church that we move now quite deliberately from a situation of co-operation to one of commitment to each other. This commitment, then, should be official policy at every level. But we should have a view in moving, in God's time, to full communion, or communion that is both visible and organic . . . In full communion we recognize, of course, that there will not be uniformity but legitimate diversity.

With these words the Roman Catholics of Britain may be said to have come to the centre of the ecumenical movement in our island. The change of situation is clear: from co-operation to commitment. The future goal of ecumenism in Roman Catholic thinking is made clear: visible unity. And if ever there were doubts about the shape and style of a future church in Catholic thinking: legitimate diversity and not dull uniformity was the offer of the Cardinal. The prospects after 3 September 1987 were exciting. Other leaders of the churches

offered similar commitments, the most memorable being that of
Archbishop Robert Runcie who remembered a mistake made by a
curate in a grace. It seemed appropriate after the gracious words of
the Cardinal: 'Lord, make us needful of the minds of others.' With
these resolutions the scene was set for the final Swanwick Declaration:

> It is our conviction that, as a matter of policy at all levels and in all
> places, our Churches must now move from co-operation to clear
> commitment to each other, in search of the unity for which Christ
> prayed, and in common evangelism and service of the world.

Ecumenical euphoria can be short lived when faced with local
reality. A member of staff at a theological college returned from
Swanwick and was asked by a colleague where he had been. To the
answer 'Swanwick, the Inter-Church Process' the reply he got was
'what's that?' The Swanwick Report[5] published in November 1987
set out the flow-chart for the future which would be inaugurated in
September 1990. It envisaged new national bodies: Churches
Together in England (CTE), Action of Churches Together in
Scotland (ACTS), Churches Together in Wales (CYTUN), and
the inter-national Council of Churches for Britain and Ireland
(CCBI). The new instruments encouraged a new way of thinking, a
shift from the idea of ecumenism as an extra, absorbing energy, to
ecumenism as an essential ingredient of all that the churches would
do, releasing energy through the sharing of resources. Some
criticized the British Council of Churches in that it had encouraged
a mentality of 'those over there' over against 'us', 'us' being the local
churches. The new ecumenical bodies would help churches to
consult and establish their own priorities and make their own
decisions; only then would the ecumenical body or one denomination or agency be empowered to act on behalf of everyone. Suppose,
for example, that the churches in England decided at a consultation
that research was needed into the reaction of young people to the
Christian faith. Churches Together in England could be asked to
create a group to do this or an organization with expertise, say the
Division of Education and Youth of the Methodist Church, could be
asked to do the work on behalf of all the churches. Whether this kind
of co-operation will happen increasingly in the future will be the

measure of the success of the new instruments. There are hopeful signs that major work is now being done ecumenically which was being done by individual churches on their own only five or ten years ago.

The Association of Interchurch Families When a member of the Baptist Church marries a member of the United Reformed Church choices have to be made. Where will the ceremony take place? Will both ministers be invited to take part? To which church will the couple go after the wedding? It is of course possible for the couple to remain members of their respective churches and, because of the discipline surrounding the Lord's Supper, there is no problem in them receiving the bread and wine together at one of their churches. When a United Reformed member marries a Roman Catholic, however, things are very different. It is most likely that the marriage will take place in the Catholic church and although in these ecumenical times the United Reformed minister may be asked to take a part in the service, usually there will be no opportunity for the man and wife to take communion together either at this service or at any future ones. If both the Catholic and the URC decide to remain faithful to their church-in-law denominational loyalties, there are some important questions that will arise. For example, when children are born to them, where will the children be baptized, in the United Reformed Church or in the Catholic Church? Will the children of parents belonging to two different denominations be members of both churches? When it comes to important occasions such as first communion, will the URC person be able to communicate with the child and the spouse? At confirmation does the child have to decide to belong to one of the churches or may he/she be confirmed in both churches?

In 1968 Ruth and Martin Reardon had begun to meet problems such as this and felt that an association for mutual support of such families would be useful. Ruth was a Roman Catholic while Martin was a priest in the Church of England. What became known as the Association of Interchurch Families began as it were on their kitchen table and has spread worldwide from England into the rest of Europe, to Canada and the USA, to Asia (India and Singapore), and Australasia. The AIF has become part of the wider ecumenical movement, not least because of its questions to ARCIC and through Martin's work as General Secretary of Churches Together in England. A publication, *Churches Together in Marriage,* was issued at the time of the silver jubilee of the Association in 1994. At present Ruth runs the Association office which is Inter-Church House in Waterloo, in the same building as CTE and CCBI.

Interchurch families are at the sharp end of the unity movement and in themselves are a very intimate Local Ecumenical Project or Partnership. The sharp end means that such couples have to encounter the scandal of a divided church for themselves. The issues of marriage, baptism, first communion, intercommunion and confirmation across two church allegiances are felt very clearly. What happens when local Catholic priests are less than sympathetic and suggest that Catholics should stick to marrying Catholics? What if the local minister would not be seen dead in a Roman Catholic church? Will the bishop be open to the possibility of the non-Catholic spouse communicating at the son's/daughter's first communion? Do Catholic priests know the Directory of Ecumenical Norms of 1993 and how they might be applied? The Association has as part of its task the work to educate clergy and church leaders generally in the way that interchurch families can enrich the local ecumenical scene. It also has the tasks of being a place for research into family life, of encouraging churches to prepare couples for marriage ecumenically, of helping the children of interchurch families to be articulate about their predicament as well as being a place for the spread of information to those contemplating interchurch marriage.

Speaking to interchurch families at York in 1982, Pope John Paul II said to them: 'You live in your marriage the hopes and difficulties of the path to Christian unity.' Interchurch families are very conscious of the difficulties, but they feel that they are living the hopes as well, and they want to be able to express the hopes which they experience. This is why they are raising questions, very difficult questions for the churches: not only questions of eucharistic hospitality but underlying questions of double belonging, of dual membership, especially for the children of such families. How can the churches help us to express what is a reality for us: that we are members of one domestic church attached to the one Church of Christ through two different churches, that our children are initiated into the one Church of Christ first and foremost through our one domestic church which draws on two distinct traditions?[6]

The new papal encyclical *Ut Unum Sint* has given new hope to interchurch families. In it Pope John Paul notes that it is 'a source of joy' that Catholic ministers are able, in certain particular cases, to administer the various sacraments to those who are not in full communion with the Catholic Church (46). Through the work of Ruth Reardon the Association has built up a remarkable store of expertise and theological wisdom in ecumenical encounters. It is Ruth's hope that the Association will not be needed ten years hence; the English churches and Rome will have taken unity so seriously that the Association of Interchurch Families will be redundant.

The Society for Ecumenical Studies   That there existed no group for the study of the academic ecumenical scene in England has often seemed strange to academics from continental Europe. They would have noted societies for New Testament and Old Testament studies, as well as for the discipline of Theology, Church History and Pastoral Theology, but would have noted an absence in the area of Ecumenical Theology. Perhaps the English attitude to ecumenical affairs has often been to sort matters out pragmatically and think of a theology afterwards. Some would say that LEPs have happened and sometime after theological reasons have been put together to justify them. The Society for Ecumenical Studies was launched in October 1994 at a meeting in London. It is obviously too early to see what effect the Society will have on the English scene but the importance of having a list of competent academic ecumenists will be obvious. So far the Society has produced regular newsletters and had several meetings. The topics have included days on the Leuenberg and Porvoo agreements, the Anglican–Reformed –Lutheran conversations, baptismal practice and recognition, the question of the extent of legitimate diversity, and the subject of *koinonia*. Under the able secretaryship of Dr David Carter the Society has an exciting future. At its opening meeting it was hoped that the Society would be able to help in fostering and pioneering ecumenism as widely as possible, in a spirit that would be rooted in practical experience and be capable of setting the highest theological standards.

The Ecumenical Society of the Blessed Virgin Mary   That anything concerned with Mary should have 'ecumenical' attached to it has seemed nonsensical to many Protestants. Mary belongs to the more Catholic parts of the church and has no place in Protestantism. This attitude is unfortunate for many reasons, not least because the early reformers, in particular Luther, preached regularly on Mary and particularly on those New Testament passages that were concerned with her relationship with Christ, with her faith and witness. In April 1967 a group of friends from several different Christian churches met to give some form to a need that they felt. This need was to promote the study of the place of Mary in the church and to promote ecumenical devotion:

> The Society, founded in 1967 by H. Martin Gillett and others, exists to advance the study of the place of the Blessed Virgin Mary in the Church under Christ, and of related theological questions; and in the light of such study to promote ecumenical devotion (Constitution, Art. 2).

Martin Gillett, a Roman Catholic lay person, dedicated the remaining years of his life to what became 'The Ecumenical Society of the Blessed Virgin Mary'. Members and supporters have come from all areas of church life and branches have been formed in Europe and the United States, members being found even further afield.

In his book *Heart Speaks to Heart* John Newton refers to his own involvement as a Methodist with the ESBVM. He describes his background ignorance and the way in which his theological tutor would refer him to Giovanni Miegge's *The Virgin Mary*, a Protestant reaction to Mariology written before Vatican II. The surprise of Catholics and Methodists at the Methodist Neville Ward's book published in 1971 on the rosary as a method of devotion, *Five for Sorrow, Ten for Joy*, is then registered, with Ward's 'in Methodism the silence about the Mother of Jesus is positively deafening'.

... in Methodism the silence about the Mother of Jesus is positively deafening. It is so complete that during a ministry of over thirty years I have begun to wonder what anxiety is behind this surprising mental hang-up. This wonder has increased as I have learned how much she means in the public and private praying of both the Roman Catholic and the Orthodox Churches and, incidentally but importantly, as I begin to discover among our own people signs of shy but nervous interest in her mysterious being.[7]

Gillett had asked John Newton to take the place of the deceased Marcus Ward on the ESBVM Council. His importunity brought John, then Superintendent of the West London Mission, into the ESBVM. The Society, Newton discovered, was not interested in extravagant devotion to Mary but in grasping the nettle of one of the most divisive issues in the history of the church since the Reformation. The Society was interested in the study of Mary, but always in subordination to her Son and never as an end in herself. This attitude was in contrast with extravagant Marian understandings which had so often marred Marian devotion in the eyes of Protestants. Bleeding Madonnas, crowned and lit Marys were not what the Society was about. Just a few years previously the Second Vatican Council had refused to formulate a special document on Mary but had opted to put Mary within the Dogmatic Constitution on the Church. The contents of chapter 8 in *Lumen Gentium* are an attempt to place Mary within the Christian scheme of salvation, while avoiding much of that extravagant devotional emphasis that seems so alien to Protestant Christians in Northern Europe.

II   The Role of the Blessed Virgin in the Economy of Salvation
III   The Blessed Virgin and the Church
IV   Devotion to the Blessed Virgin in the Church
V   Mary, a Sign of Sure Hope and of Solace for God's People in Pilgrimage

The Ecumenical Society of the Blessed Virgin Mary has done a great deal for ecumenism in England. It regularly publishes articles about Mary and her place in the Catholic, Orthodox and Protestant traditions. These articles have done a useful work in making devotion to Mary as Mother of God more acceptable and doctrinally digestible to Protestants. Perhaps a few chapter headings from a book reporting an international conference of 1986 will make this clearer: Mary, model for Church; Mary's place in *Lumen Gentium*; New Testament Charisms of the Blessed Virgin Mary; Our Lord's Relationship with his Mother; Mary in Recent Ecumenical Documents; Visions of the Virgin; Mary as a human person; Thoughts on the future development of the Ecumenical Society of the Blessed Virgin Mary.

It may be of interest to English readers to remind them how abundant before the Reformation were churches designated 'St Mary's' and to ask how many non-Roman Catholic churches after the Reformation were similarly designated. Many believe that there are none and though that is difficult to prove, it may indicate something of the strongly adverse reaction to the veneration of Mary by English churches after the Reformation. When Henry VIII was concerned about the succession to the crown and desperately desired a boy to be born of Katherine of Aragon, he took himself more than once to the shrine at Walsingham to petition there at the shrine of Mary. Walsingham was one of the first shrines to be destroyed at the hands of Henry's agents in 1536. Did a king's revenge take Mary away from the English?

15

Do the Reformation Controversies Still Divide?

Martin Luther made an initial protest about indulgences when he demanded a disputation about them which he nailed to the door of the Castle Church at Wittenberg on 31 October 1517. This issue was about how people could find some security for themselves and their loved ones after death. The church taught that, grave sinners apart, most people went after death to the intermediate place called purgatory, there to be purified from their sins for a time until they were suitable for heaven. To many modern Protestants it seems a strange doctrine but it is in fact an optimistic one, for who at his/her death feels ready to come face to face with God? Time in purgatory would depend on how much evil had to be removed from the soul of the individual. But the church had a treasury of merits available. The saints and the Virgin Mary had been far holier than they need have been to merit the life of heaven. Their merits created a kind of bank deposit that could be made available for people in purgatory. The merits of Christ himself of course made the store of merit an infinite unfailing deposit. All this could be used at the behest of the pope, who had the key to the deposit. When the old St Peter's was being demolished and rebuilt the popes of the time, Julius II and Leo X, proclaimed special indulgences which could be bought for people in purgatory. Half the money would go to the rebuilding of St Peter's and the rest to pay debts. In Germany, Albert the Archbishop of Mainz was allowed to offer an indulgence whereby half would go to St Peter's and half to the banking house of Fugger to whom he owed money for buying his episcopal sees. One of his salesmen, Johannes Tetzel by name, a Dominican, conveniently forgot that indulgences were offered only under certain terms, one important term to the buyer being the stipulation 'provided penitent'. Tetzel is said to have offered to sell indulgences with the motto

> As soon as the coin in the coffer rings
> Then the soul from purgatory springs.

Tetzel was clearly out of line; nobody knew how soon anybody could spring out of purgatory and the offer of heaven for a money payment alone was out of order. If the pope was a steward of the resources of the merits of Christ and the saints then here was a sign that a stewardship campaign had gone wrong.

Luther asked why the pope could not release souls from purgatory out of love rather than for a payment to St Peter's. No. 82 of the Ninety-Five Theses reads:

> For example: Why does not the Pope empty purgatory for the sake of most holy love and the supreme need of souls? This would be the most righteous of reasons, if he can redeem innumerable souls for sordid money with which to build a basilica, the most trivial of reasons.

But the point at issue soon began to be seen as, how can a person be sure of salvation? Luther suggested that the search to achieve merit for oneself or one's loved ones was contradicted by the gospel, particularly as interpreted by the apostle Paul. Paul's understanding was taken up by Luther as justification by faith and not justification by merit (or even the merits of the saints that were passed down by the church) or justification by works as it has often been called. Sometimes this 'justification by faith' became 'justification by faith alone' (in Latin *sola fide*). To some later Protestants, such as John Wesley, it did seem as if the search for Christian holiness was neglected by the Reformer. Luther for his part seems to have assumed that to be put right with God according to one's faith would lead automatically to a life full of good works. Recent statements from Rome about indulgences seem to have been barely noticed by the Catholic faithful at large and it could be that the doctrine is no longer truly significant in the Protestant–Catholic divide. The question of justification (being put right with God) and that of sanctification (being made holy by the work of God) could be said to be the crunch issue between Protestants and Catholics. ARCIC II in *Salvation and the Church* of 1987 put it thus:

> ... Protestants took Catholics to be emphasizing sanctification in such a way that the absolute gratuitousness of salvation was threatened. On the other side, Catholics feared that Protestants were so stressing the justifying action of God that sanctification and human responsibility were gravely depreciated.[1]

ARCIC II sees justification and sanctification as two sides of the same act of God:

> By pronouncing us righteous, God also makes us righteous. He imparts a righteousness which is his and becomes ours.[2]

The Lutheran–Roman Catholic dialogue in 1980 had the following statement:

> A broad consensus emerges in the doctrine of justification, which was decisively important for the Reformation: it is solely by grace and by faith in Christ's saving work and not because of any merit in us that we are accepted by God and receive the Holy Spirit who renews our hearts and equips us for and calls us to good works.[3]

In 1519 Luther had a major confrontation with John Eck at Leipzig. Eck forced Luther into making the statement that councils had sometimes erred, in particular the Council of Constance of 1415 which condemned John Hus. Some Anglican theologians similarly, while echoing Luther's thoughts on Constance, began to recognize the first four councils only as truly indicative of the true doctrine of the church. Most seem to have regarded Nicaea II of AD787, the seventh council, as doubtful because of its approbation of the veneration of images. Its Definition on Sacred Images reads:

> For, the more frequently one contemplates these pictorial representations, the more gladly will he be led to remember the original subject whom they represent, the more too will he be drawn to it and inclined to give it ... a respectful veneration (*proskunêsis, adoratio*), which, however, is not the true adoration (*latria, latreia*) which, according to our faith, is due to God alone.

Within Anglicanism then there was approval of four, five, six or seven councils, but no consensus. ARCIC I claimed the following for the authority of councils:

> This binding authority does not belong to every conciliar decree, but only to those which formulate the central truths of salvation. This authority is ascribed in both our traditions to decisions of the ecumenical councils of the first centuries.[4]

There is no indication offered here of which councils are meant although clearly at the least Nicaea I, Constantinople I, Ephesus and Chalcedon are meant. A clarification of the authority of the ecumenical councils is obviously an issue that will still have to be tackled.

Because Luther was eventually excommunicated by Pope Leo X the issue of the priority of papal authority over the gospel was one that would have to be looked at. The awful wood-cuts that were issued in the Reformation period showed that the papacy quickly became a major target for the propagandists of the Reformation. One shows a contrast between Christ and Antichrist. On the left Christ is seated being beaten with rods, having a crown of thorns pressed down on his head and receiving the jeers of the soldiers. On the right the pope is receiving the adulation of monks and bishops while two prelates are crowning him with his papal tiara. In the background the papal forces are fighting their Italian war with guns and cannon.

Luther was at times over hasty in his condemnation of the papacy; phrases such as 'antiChrist' became common. The Anglican Thirty-Nine Articles were concerned for the Bishop of Rome only in so far as his legal rights extended in England, Article XXXVII, 'Of the Civil Magistrates', stating that: 'The Bishop of Rome hath no jurisdiction in this Realm of England.'

By the time of ARCIC I and the 1986 Nairobi Report of the Methodist–Catholic conversations, there is a sea change in thoughts about the papacy. After ARCIC had stated that historically the see of Rome eventually became the principal centre in matters concerning the universal Church, the statement goes on:

> The importance of the bishop of Rome among his brother

bishops, as explained by analogy with the position of Peter among the apostles, was interpreted as Christ's will for his Church.[5]

A similar position was taken at Nairobi 1986:

> Methodists accept that whatever is properly required for the unity of the whole of Christ's Church must by that very fact be God's will for his Church. A universal primacy might well serve as focus of and ministry for the unity of the whole Church.[6]

Both ARCIC I and the Nairobi Report were hesitant about a papal primacy without any restrictions, and indeed about infallibility:

> We also recognize that the ascription to the bishop of Rome of infallibility under certain conditions has tended to lend exaggerated importance to all his statements.[7]

While Methodists offered the doctrine of assurance as a possible way into an understanding of infallibility, the general theme of the dialogues has been to allow the understanding of the papal office to wait until practical steps to unity have been taken:

> We suggest that some difficulties will not be wholly resolved until a practical initiative has been taken and our two Churches have lived together more visibly in the one *'koinonia'*.[8]

In 1529 Luther joined a colloquy at Marburg of reformers who hoped to make a joint statement of faith in order to unite the reformers. Most items were agreed by both the Lutheran group and the other group which contained such reformers as Zwingli of Zurich, Bucer of Strasbourg and Oecolampadius of Basle. Luther stood firm against the majority of the others over the doctrine of the eucharist. He took his stance on the words of institution, 'this is my body'. He wrote the words on the table in Latin, *hoc est corpus meum*, and underlined the *est*, thus showing against many of the other reformers that he believed the scriptural account in a literal sense.

> It is precisely the same devil who now assails us through the fanatics by blaspheming the holy and venerable sacrament of our Lord Jesus Christ, out of which they would like to make mere bread and wine as a symbol or memorial sign of Christians, in whatever way their dream or fancy dictates. They will not grant

that the Lord's body and blood are present, even though the plain, clear words stand right there: 'Eat, this is my body. Yet these words stand firm and invulnerable against them . . . Now, here stands the text, stating clearly and lucidly that Christ gives his body to eat when he distributes the bread. On this we take our stand, and we also believe and teach that in the Supper we eat and take to ourselves Christ's body truly and physically.[9]

Many of the others, Zwingli and Oecolampadius in particular, took the *est* or 'is' to mean *significat* or 'signifies'. This attitude to the eucharist has often been called 'memorialist' and if the Catholic and Lutheran doctrine can be called 'the real presence' then this other doctrine could be called 'the real absence'. Luther refused to accept the doctrine of transubstantiation that Catholics held, that while the outward appearances of bread and wine remain the substance of the bread and wine become the body and blood of Christ. In fact Luther's understanding was even more carnal than that held by Catholic theology, a deliberate hanging on to the words of scripture, 'this *is* my body'.

Modern eucharistic agreement has been centred around the idea of *anamnesis*, the Greek word for remembrance. It has been shown that the term means in some sense, 'to bring back into the present'. Thus anything short of a doctrine of 'the real presence' is excluded from most agreements on the eucharist. A few examples will suffice:

> In the sacrament of the Lord's Supper Jesus Christ, true God and true man, is present wholly and entirely, in his body and blood, under the signs of bread and wine.[10]

> Communion with Christ in the eucharist presupposes his true presence, effectually signified by the bread and wine which, in this mystery, become his body and blood . . .[11]

> Both Catholics and Methodists affirm as the primary fact the presence of Christ in the Eucharist, the Mass, or the Lord's Supper.[12]

Although it is often said that Luther was so concerned to make scripture the prime source for doctrine that he took a 'Scripture only' position, *sola scriptura*, this has been manifestly discounted by twentieth-century research. Luther clearly believed that the church before the sixteenth century had had authority to decide on such things as the baptism of infants, the canon of the New Testament, the doctrine of Christ as both human and divine, etc.

Luther wrote against the Anabaptists who affirmed that in the scriptures baptism was given only to adults on profession of faith:

> So whoever bases baptism on the faith of the one to be baptized can never baptize anyone. Even if you baptized a person a hundred times a day you would not know at all if he believes . . . Since our baptizing has been thus from the beginning of Christianity and the custom has been to baptize children, and since no one can prove that they do not have faith, we should not make changes and build on such weak arguments.[13]

Luther's view of the ministry took the form of the affirmation of the priesthood of all baptized Christians, the so-called 'priesthood of all believers', a term incidentally that Luther never used. The reformers generally were critical of the ministry solely as a sacrificial priesthood as this seemed to endanger the once-for-all work of Christ as high priest.

> During a Faith and Order conference in Ireland, a famous Roman Catholic theologian was speaking when a stranger walked in. The other delegates thought he was a member of the conference since, despite his somewhat scruffy appearance, he seemed quite confident. After listening for a while, he made a suggestion to the delegates: 'Go on talking about these things, we need it. But don't use long words. Remember, he was only a carpenter.' The man left the room and was never seen or heard of again. But the atmosphere of the meeting was subtly changed.[14]

If a consensus on the eucharist has emerged between Catholics and Protestants, there is perhaps still a long way to go in the matter of the nature of the church. In the Augsburg Confession of the Lutherans in 1530 the church was defined as the congregation of the faithful in which the gospel is rightly preached and the sacraments duly administered. This definition found its way as number XIX of the Thirty-Nine Articles of the Church of England. Luther believed that 'the church' meant the invisible church of all faithful believers throughout the world. This 'invisible' definition of 'church', while helpful because it did not precisely define who was and who was not a true member of it, still creates a problem between Catholics and Protestants. Catholics prefer their own understanding of a wholly visible church to which you either do or do not belong. Ecumenical dialogue has helped to decrease the gap between the two sides on this. Both Methodist–Roman Catholic and Anglican–Roman Catholic dialogues have centred on the use of the word *koinonia* as the pivotal work for discussion of what 'church' actually implies. ARCIC II in *Church as Communion* in 1991 described what being in communion actually means in practice:

> For a local community to be a *communion* means that it is a gathering of the baptized brought together by the apostolic preaching, conferring the one faith, celebrating the one eucharist, and led by an apostolic ministry.[15]

Thus ARCIC II suggests that the essential constituents of 'church' are baptism and eucharist, apostolic preaching and apostolic ministry, and the confession of one faith. ARCIC I clearly believed that it had brought Anglicans and Catholics very close on many of these items, with perhaps the exceptions of full acceptance of developed Catholic faith (as seen for example in the definitions about Mary), and a total acceptance of all the implications of the developed apostolic ministry of the Bishop of Rome. The Methodist–Roman Catholic dialogue, commenting upon the meaning of *koinonia*, was concerned to keep 'fellowship' to signify both its visible and its invisible aspects:

> And it includes deep fellowship among participants, a fellowship which is both visible and invisible, finding expression in faith and order, in prayer and sacrament, in mission and service.[16]

Presumably 'invisible' in the Methodist–Roman Catholic context means those situations in which both sides find themselves in a spiritual unity despite the fact of their division into different ecclesial communities. ARCIC II was severe on those who desire only invisible spiritual unity:

> But it is inadequate to speak only of an invisible spiritual unity as

the fulfilment of Christ's will for the Church; the profound communion fashioned by the Spirit requires visible expression.[17]

The Lutheran–Roman Catholic dialogue made the same point:

> We want to stress the fact that the unity we seek should be an outward, visible unity which is becoming historically manifest in the life of the churches.[18]

Over against this 'visible unity' understanding has to be set the contrary understanding that does not wish unity to take visible form. We use the statement on the Nature of the Church offered by the Independent Methodist Churches offered to the Inter-Church Process booklet called *Reflections* in 1986:

> It pictures the Church globally, not confined within denominational boundaries, but embracing all who share a common faith in Christ . . . The standpoint which the denomination takes in relation to church of other communions is, therefore, one which recognizes a spiritual oneness with all who acknowledge and trust the same Saviour and Lord . . . It is only right to point out that not all Independent Methodists see the need for spiritual unity to be translated into organic forms of union.[19]

This position is far from unique in English church organizations but it will be clear how far away it is from the attitude of the major bilateral dialogues. The 'spiritual unity' plea has been seen by many to be at least a failure to understand the fuller implications of a gospel of reconciliation. It feels as if Reformation positions have been allowed to harden in some denominations while the major Reformation churches have moved away from them in their dialogue with Rome and others.

16

Ecumenical Convergence
in Spirituality

Spirituality is a word that has been coined only fairly recently. In the English language it meant for a long time the ordained members of the church, most principally the bishops of the church. Perhaps the reason for its late arrival may be its closeness to the word 'spiritualism', which refers to the beliefs and practices whose purposes are to establish contact with the dead. The modern meaning of 'spirituality' does not seem to have been completely clarified, though it has often been noted that Catholic writers, principally Bishop Richard Challoner in eighteenth-century England, used the term to indicate the life of devotion or piety. Although this way of looking at the term might indicate that piety and normal life were essentially compartmentalized, there have been many writers who have insisted that spirituality impinges on all life. Kenneth Grayston has suggested that spirituality is what we are when we are not specifically trying to be religious or Christian.[1] Gordon Wakefield wrote: 'And spirituality concerns the way in which prayer influences conduct, our behaviour and manner of life, our attitudes to other people.'[2]

It would be true to say that spirituality has become a best selling topic for books. For example a book on, say, the *Life of Wilberforce*, however complete and well presented in its view of the reformer's life, will not sell nearly as many copies as *Wilberforce. His Life and Spirituality*. People are interested in how other people have prayed and are deeply involved in the discovery of how they might begin to pray better.

They are also reading widely and entering into courses where they experience things beyond their tradition. An Anglican, for example, may find herself learning the spirituality of the Orthodox icon and end up prayerfully painting her own icon of some saint. Methodists have found themselves with Delia Smith and understanding the spirituality of Lent, as well as being reminded of what can be cooked during the Lenten fast. Many Roman Catholics believe that the best book on the Rosary is that written from outside their tradition, namely *Five for Sorrow, Ten for Joy* by the Methodist, Neville Ward. Some years ago some Roman Catholics in suburban London were delighted to hear what they felt was the best exposition of Roman Catholic spirituality they had ever heard, and it came from Michael Walker, a Baptist minister in Beckenham. Because there has been such a tremendous appreciation of other traditions it can be truly said that spirituality is even more truly ecumenical than theology and biblical studies have been. This may be because prayer has always been a part of the ecumenical task, especially since Paul Couturier in France began what came to be called the Week of Prayer for Christian Unity.

> Prayer for unity, already so deeply rooted in and spread throughout the body of the Church, shows that Christians do indeed see the importance of ecumenism . . . Moreover, through prayer the quest for unity, far from being limited to a group of specialists, comes to be shared by all the baptized.[3]

Before Couturier's work the Methodist minister Henry Lunn in the 1890s had called British church leaders to discuss reunion. These Grindelwald conferences called for prayer for unity at Pentecost. The call was taken up by the Free Churches and the Anglicans, while Roman Catholics were encouraged by the *Ad Anglos* letter of Leo XIII in 1895 and by his call for prayer for unity. Before the Faith and Order movement got under way, in 1920 there was encouragement in its preliminary meeting for an annual Week of Prayer for the Unity of the Church, a week which would end at Pentecost. An octave for unity from 18–25 January was begun in 1908, started at first by Anglicans, many of whom later converted to Rome. In 1916 Pope Benedict XV extended the octave throughout the Roman Catholic Church. Paul Couturier sought to make the octave less pro-Catholic by the use of his famous formula: 'that God will grant the visible unity of his kingdom such as Christ wishes and through whatever means he wishes'. This open-ended formula, while it has led to the usual questions about 'what Christ wishes', has enabled the World Council of Churches, as it now is, to meet the Roman Catholics half-way. At last, in 1966, it was possible to create a joint WCC–Roman Catholic Group to prepare the material for the worldwide observance of the Week of Prayer for Christian Unity.

The experience of people living in England of the Week of Prayer has been extremely diverse. For some areas it is the only time that local Christians come together, for other areas it is a well-publicized week in which many local members of the churches participate. Some united services have been criticized as offering bland and 'lowest common denominator' worship. Others have used the material available to produce a worthwhile celebration. Many believe that 'special services' are less effective than those services in which local churches do their own thing. Perhaps one can only appreciate Pentecostal worship when one is there for two to three hours and really involved. Possibly the Catholic spirituality of the eucharist is best understood at a mass in the local St Ignatius parish church. It is better than reading about it.

The success of the ecumenical movement in England in giving Christians contact with each other's traditions of spirituality will be obvious. The Orthodox tradition has led us to look at icons in a new way and shown many of a more Protestant viewpoint that veneration of icons is far from the idolatry condemned in the Ten Commandments. Huge success has attended the publication of the works of Timothy Ware on the history and understanding of Orthodoxy. Archbishop Anthony Bloom's books on prayer in the Orthodox tradition have been best sellers for many years. Orthodoxy for many has been a path away from Western spirituality into a more transcendental understanding of the presence of God, in the liturgy as well as in the techniques of prayer. Retreatants can spend hours in the experience of the profound implications of the 'Jesus Prayer': 'Jesus Christ, Son of the living God, have mercy upon me, a sinner.' Orthodoxy has shown that the church has an eternal quality of changelessness and that the church is nothing if it is not a bridge whereby humanity can reach out to the transcendent God.

At the Second Vatican Council the Roman Catholic Church emphasized the vocation of all people to holiness: 'Thus it is evident to everyone that all the faithful of Christ of whatever rank or status are called to the fullness of the Christian life and to the perfection of charity.'[4] This would have pleased John Wesley in the eighteenth century just as much as it would have pleased Francis de Sales in the previous century. Both the Methodist patriarch and the writer of *An Introduction to a Devout and Holy Life* were concerned for the growth in holiness of the ordinary people of God. Vatican II thus indicates a movement away from a 'monastic' form of spirituality to one available for all. Perhaps one of the signs of this has been a lessening of vocations to certain monastic orders and sisterhoods. The recent crisis caused by the lower numbers of men entering the priesthood has been countered in part by the use of eucharistic ministers during the mass and by lay leadership during the service of the word followed by the use of the reserved sacrament. Bringing more people into the sanctuary has lessened the mystery of the separateness of the priest and encouraged increasing numbers of lay people to find their own spirituality from which eucharistic ministry can be fed. This personal spirituality was once fed by the devotional practices of the period up to and including the 1950s; devotion to the Sacred Heart of Jesus, devotion to the Blessed Virgin Mary and Benediction of the Blessed Sacrament. After the Council the main sources of spirituality became the liturgy, the Bible and the retreat movement. By about 1970 the Charismatic Movement had added a new dimension of spirituality to the Roman Catholics in England. In the 1970s new base communities of spiritual life sprang up, some taking their origin from the Latin American churches and their concern with issues of justice and peace, others arising from sources such as the Focalare (fireside) movement of Chiara Lubich. Personal direction in the spiritual life has brought some into the way of finding a 'soul friend' to accompany them on the spiritual journey. Others have used the Spiritual Exercises of St Ignatius Loyola, either on the full thirty day guided retreat or on the 'Nineteenth Annotation', a way of doing the exercises in the world.

Protestants before the 1960s were generally dismissive of spirituality, regarding it as antagonistic to their main task of the uncovering of the meaning of the word. Edwin Hoskyns, Richard Niebuhr and John Oman were just some who were antagonistic to the mystical life. In the 1950s George Macleod, founder of the Iona Community,

talked of the least visited areas of ministers' shelves which contained
books of prayer and books about prayer.

> I have what I call 'bankrupt corner' in my library and I am, if
> negatively, encouraged to discover it on the manse shelves of most
> ministers who have tried to pray. It is a platoon of bantam booklets
> enlisted at intervals to help one to pray better: purchased, as each
> severally went dead on us, on the principle that 'Hope springs
> eternal'. Why do they go dead on us? Because most of them were
> written in terms of a different consciousness. Because most to
> them are conceived in mediaeval terms, we are not really
> conditioned to read what they are really saying.[5]

Bonhoeffer was one of the influential theologians in the 1960s
when his *Letters and Paper from Prison* became well known to a wide
reading public. He had indicated that the pietistic 'religion' which
abounded in Hitler's Germany was in fact antagonistic to the
Christian faith.

> Here is the decisive difference between Christians and all
> religions. Man's religiosity makes him look in his distress to the
> power of God in the world: God is the *deus ex machina*. The Bible
> directs man to God's powerlessness and suffering; only the
> suffering God can help. To that extent we may say that the
> development towards the world's coming of age outlined above,
> which has done away with a false conception of God, opens up a
> way of seeing the God of the Bible, who wins power and space in
> the world by his weakness.[6]

'Religion' had in fact acquiesced in the rise of Nazism and had been
uncritical of the ethos of National Socialism. Because Bonhoeffer
was a Christian martyr his words concerning false religion became
part of the Protestant agenda of English Christianity and caused
many Protestants to shy away from 'spirituality' or 'progress in the
Christian life'.

The influence of the Protestant community of Taizé in France
and the Scottish Iona Community was very important for a new
generation, particularly those who had not been alive during the
Second World War. The hymns and the atmosphere created within
these new communities enabled quite a few younger people to find a

new, and Protestant, spirituality. To some of course it looked like a modified Catholic version of spirituality. When spiritual writers such as Neville Ward and Gordon Wakefield, both Methodists, wrote movingly and helpfully about non-Protestant traditions, some regarded this as an abdication from Protestant spirituality which they felt should be non-structural, informal, and Spirit-dependent. With the rise of the Charismatic movement within the churches it was felt that the essence of this Protestant spirituality had been regained. At last the intellectualist ascendency could be challenged, the hierarchical ministry would have to face the Holy Spirit energizing God's ordinary people in the pews, spontaneous groups would replace the old dry fellowships and new songs could be sung about the new experiences. Again, to some extent, the new Charismatic experience moved the young more than it did established church members.

It is of interest that most of the people who ask for information about retreats are not regular churchgoers. This is just one indication of spiritual thirst in our country. The Ecumenical Spirituality Project has experience of helping churches to find an ecumenical spirituality for today. The National Retreat Association produces a regular listing of retreats available in the magazine *Vision*. The extent of provision of retreats seems to have more than doubled in the last twenty-five years. The making of a retreat means a time to seek God and to be in his presence in quiet prayer and reflection.

> . . . the purpose of retreat is to dispel illusion, to set aside distraction, and to penetrate the crust of superficiality in personal existence, which can deaden sensitivity to the reality of God.[7]

A period of struggle to let go of one's preoccupations is almost certainly a preliminary part of the process. Certainly retreatants learn a lot about themselves during the few days they spend, mainly in silence, with the opportunity to talk to the retreat giver. Organized retreats began in the time of the sixteenth-century Catholic reformation. The main encouragement to the movement was given by the saints of the period; Ignatius Loyola, with the use of his *Spiritual Exercises*, then St Francis de Sales, St Vincent de Paul, Jean-Jacques Olier, and others. Since the mid-nineteenth century the Church of England has used conducted retreats and in the twentieth century all other denominations have discovered their value. While the retreat with talks, silence and daily worship is still the norm, the multiplicity of methods of using retreats has to be listed to see the variants. Recent ones offered have included, in alphabetical order: Calligraphy and Prayer; Contemplative Prayer; Enneagram Workshop; Explore the Artist within; Exploring the Living Psyche; Guilt and Healing; Healing and Holiness; Holistic Spirituality; Ignatian Spirituality; The Inner Child; Inner Healing; Myers-Briggs Workshop; Myths to Love By; Prayer and Clay; Praying the Liturgy; Praying the Scriptures; Quiet Day with St Benedict; Rediscovering God; Retreat for People affected by HIV/AIDS; Sadhana meditation; Sexuality and Spirituality; Shadows and Archetypes through film and literature; Towards a Universal Spirituality; The Way of St Francis; A Weekend with Meister Eckhart. One is tempted to say that all human life is there in so far as it is in movement towards the experience of God. We are perhaps reminded of two quotations from Augustine's *Confessions*:

> For when I seek you, my God, I seek a happy life.

> You have made us for yourself, and restless is our heart until it comes to rest in you.

17

The New Scene: Black and White

The *Not Strangers But Pilgrims* Process which culminated in Swanwick 1987 introduced many white people for the first time to the presence on the ecumenical scene of black churches in Britain. The names of some of the churches that sought involvement in Churches Together in England from 1990 are instructive: Calvary Church of God in Christ, New Testament Assembly, Shiloh United Church of Christ, Wesleyan Holiness Church. All of these churches and groups of churches have grown up since the Second World War in England and are almost entirely black in their constituency. Some represent churches that were already present in West Africa and the West Indies, others have grown up in response to the reaction of white churches to immigration from 1948 and beyond. The Church of England, the Methodist Church and other mainline churches have significant black memberships (about 5% of the Methodist community), most of whom are concentrated in urban areas. It would be fascinating to speculate on what the percentages would have been had the early Afro-Caribbean experience from 1948 in English churches been one of total acceptance. A more typical experience would be something like this: 'When I shook hands with the minister he made it clear that he and the congregation would not welcome me next week.' The early experience of coldness and overt racism revealed to some of the people who arrived in England in the 1950s was perhaps understandable in some work places but was unforgiveable in the churches.

That some black people remained in the mainline churches as an 'invisible' remnant is a tribute to the depth of their Christian forgiveness. That the churches in England have only recently woken up to the fact that black people belong to the body of Christ is a serious indictment against English Christianity. That there is a black

Christian identity that clamours for expression has barely been noticed yet. John Wilkinson in his important book *Church in Black and White* has drawn attention to the distinctive ethos and spirituality of black Christianity and I am grateful to John for much of what follows. He tells how he discovered the dynamic black Christian tradition of people in Aston, Birmingham where he was priest-in-charge:

1. Black Christian faith is rooted in Africa from which people have learned the 'primal vision' of African traditional religion. This means that all of life comes from God and that the spirit world is present to us in all that we do. Someone put it thus, 'Africa *is* religion.'

2. The encounter with Jesus is with the one who gave slaves a sense of dignity, with whom they could identify in their struggle to be human and to be free. Christ has been oppressed as they were oppressed ('Nobody knows the trouble I've seen . . . nobody knows but Jesus').

3. Black Christian faith is a religion where the Spirit is given to help believers express their deepest feelings of joy and sorrow. The Spirit makes free worship and expression possible, producing an atmosphere of liberation where song and dance, personal testimony and open prayer can be experienced.

4. Because of the experience of black people as slaves, the faith is one of liberation. The truth of it comes in the way the poor and the oppressed have been lifted up by God and have been enabled by the experience of liberation to have love even for erstwhile enemies. This is seen in Martin Luther King's 'strength to love' and in the work of Archbishop Desmond Tutu.

5. It has a vision of a new future when all people, regardless of skin colour, will feast in the kingdom of God together. This hope of a new future is not only the hope of all things being right in heaven ('living on the alleluia side' it has been called) but the hope of an end to all oppression this side of the grave.

Wilkinson argues that black Christian faith has never been seriously engaged with by the English churches who have preferred that their black members should conform to the white Christianity. White Christianity of course in its English form is less likely to see all life as coming from God and religion being a totality of all experience.

White Christianity is also less geared to a personal encounter with a liberating Jesus who frees people not only from slavery but from a conventional worship where the whole person is not caught up and where the emotions are demoted to an insignificant place. The identification of black Christianity is clearly a major need for the churches in England. Apart from black members of the mainline denominations other groups exist that are usually described as black-led churches, although some of these groups have significant white membership:

1. African Methodist Episcopal – a black Methodist denomination originating in the USA and with a small number of members in England, about two hundred in 1987.

2. Sabbatarian movements, including Seventh-Day Adventists, white as well as black, but with a free black style of worship as seen in the music of its many choirs which have made a significant impact in radio and television broadcasts.

3. Small groups related to Native Baptist and Revivalists from Jamaica, such as the Mount Zion Spiritual Baptist Church.

4. The Wesleyan Holiness Church which traces its origin in Wesley's doctrine of perfect love or sanctification. It arose in the nineteenth century as a protest against the American Methodist attitude to slavery and the emancipation of women. In 1987 it numbered about 3,100 members in nineteen churches.

5. Trinitarian Pentecostal groups such as the New Testament Church of God, the Church of God of Prophecy and the Calvary Church of God in Christ. These churches emphasize the black contribution to Christianity and represent a field where African religious emphases have been retained.

6. The Oneness Pentecostals are about a third of all black Pentecostals. They believe in baptism into the 'one' name of Jesus Christ as more biblical than the name of the Trinity. The Shiloh United Church of Christ is the largest black-led church in Britain with in 1987 some 18,000 members and forty-six ministers. Each minister is free to serve his or her church as led by the Holy Spirit, there being no set forms or liturgies.

7. The Pentecostal Healing Movement is a small group of churches strongly influenced by the healing traditions of American evangelists.

8. The African Independent Churches include the Aladura International Church, the Celestial Church of Christ and the Cherubim and Seraphim Church, all of which began in Nigeria. African elements and pentecostal elements such as speaking in tongues, healings, dancing and shouting are traditional parts of their worship life. In England the groups are federated under the name of the Council of African and Afro-Caribbean Churches and in 1987 had some 2,500 members and sixty ministers.

9. The Ethiopian Orthodox Church is a small group in England. The interest of Rastafarians in Haile Selassie as the coming black Messiah made the church grow for a while but the church has been critical of its would-be followers and has remained small.

It is notoriously difficult to estimate the number of people in black-led churches like the above, partly because statistics are few and also because there is much movement of membership between them. It is highly likely, however, that there are ten times as many black people in black-led churches as there are in mainline denominations. One guess would be to put the number at 80,000–100,000, almost the same size as the United Reformed Church. Thus black-led churches are a significant part of the English church scene and their significance for the work of the Churches Together in England has to be recognized. Churches Together in England has in its Forum representations of the African Methodist Episcopal Church, the Calvary Church of God in Christ, Cherubim and Seraphim, the New Testament Assembly, the Shiloh United Church of Christ, the Wesleyan Holiness Church and, in addition, the Afro-West Indian Council of Churches, the Black Pastors' Conference, the Council of African and Afro-Caribbean Churches and the West Indian Evangelical Alliance. Thus the black-led churches will have a significant impact on the English ecumenical scene in the future.

The black churches have had a poor press as far as the ecumenical movement is concerned, despite the fact that many of them have become part of Churches Together in England. They have been accused by some badly informed white clergy of deliberately creating schism, despite the fact that the white churches' failure to be true to the body of Christ concept spawned many of the black churches. It has been argued too that separate denominations are due to the disunity which European Christians brought both to Africa and the Caribbean. It could be that the recognition of the black presence in the English churches in fact urges Christians to look for a deeper unity that transcends not only denominationalism but also the barriers between racial groups, so that Galatians 3.28 means in the last decade of the twentieth century in England that 'in Christ there is neither black nor white'. White churches have had to accept that black groups will want to share, let and even purchase church buildings. Some people would regard this as an opportunity where the older churches of England, the 'First' world as it were, can react positively with the newer churches, the 'Third' world represen-tatives. In that sense it could be a creative example of an alternative model of ecumenism, from the bottom up and not from the top down.

Black-led churches are no longer dividing the church but recognized as joint partners in the Christian mission. Ironically while some ministers were keen both before and after the arrival of the black-led churches on the wider ecumenical scene to get these groups using their halls and churches, the deeper Christian responsibility of recognizing the 'invisible' black people in the local situation was often forgotten. Black people are still vastly under represented in the ministry and in the leadership of the mainline churches. Movements to overcome this lack of representation exist now within the churches although the extent to which implicit racism has entered into those same churches is still clear. In 1978 the Centre for Black and White Christian Partnership was set up in Birmingham as a place where the needs of black pastors for accredited theological training could be met and where black Christianity could begin to make its voice heard. In 1981 the Association of Black Clergy was set up as a means of mutual support and in order to reflect theologically on social justice issues. Dr Sehan Goodridge in 1989 became the first principal of the Simon of Cyrene Theological Institute for the training of black lay students, the articulation of a British black theology which prepares black candidates for training at theological colleges and courses. An important role in all this belongs to Revd John Wilkinson who helped to create some vital initiatives during his time as Pastoral Studies tutor at The Queen's College, Birmingham. His reflection on the experience of a black ministerial student caused him in 1987 to begin three important pieces of work in the College. The first created racism awareness training for all students and members of staff; this has since become mandatory in many other theological colleges and courses. Staff agreed secondly to examine their courses in the light of the criticism that theology and related subjects were treated from a white perspective only. Some major corrections were made as a result of this in the teaching of the College courses. Lastly, a Black Christian Studies course was created to enable black theological students, and a few white ones, to understand the black theological method and to work towards an explicit black Christian theology for Britain. Black leadership for the course was provided in 1992 by the appointment of Robert Beckford, a member of a black Pentecostal group in Birmingham, as the first tutor in Black Theology in a British theological college. As this vital theme in English ecumenism develops it could be argued that the signs are that the 'sweet chariot' of black Christianity is coming to carry at least some black people home and help English Christianity to become the truly comprehensive thing that it could be.

18

The New Scene: The New Christians

In the history of the church there have been many instances of groups that have arisen in response to the perceived decline of the institutional churches. In the second century the Montanist movement emphasized the presence of the Holy Spirit as a sign that the last days had come; in the twelfth century Joachim da Fiore proclaimed that the age to come would be heralded by two new orders of spiritual men who would inaugurate the Age of the Spirit; in 1831 Edward Irving, a Church of Scotland minister in London, encouraged the reception of the gift of tongues and was expelled from his church, establishing the Catholic Apostolic Church.

By October Irving was permitting the exercise of tongues inspired by the Spirit in public worship. 'An awful stillness prevailed for about five minutes', wrote a critical visitor. 'Suddenly an appalling shriek seemed to rend the roof, which was repeated with heart-chilling effect. I grasped involuntarily the bookdesk before me; and then, suddenly, a torrent of unintelligible words, for about five minutes, followed by – 'When will ye repent? Why will ye not repent?' Prophecies in English and miraculous healings were also known. In one year forty-six spiritual cures were reported among the Irvingites of England alone. These unfamiliar proto-Pentecostal happenings soon became confined to Irving's Catholic Apostolic Church, which, despite erecting some magnificent places of worship, never became a power in the land.[1]

All these movements claimed the inspiration of the Holy Spirit long before classical Pentecostalism began.

The birth of Pentecostalism is usually dated from 1906 when William Seymour, a black pastor in Los Angeles, received baptism in the Holy Spirit and the gift of tongues. The experience spread in the congregation at Azusa Street and the themes of the new community showed that a spirituality of love could replace the hate which was the product of racism; the people were united across the barriers which divided black from white and rich from poor. Hollenweger in his book on Pentecostalism[2] suggests that the movement quickly lost its revolutionary thrust, particularly in the way that it broke down the barriers between black and white. In England classical Pentecostalism has created churches such as the Elim Pentecostal Church, the Assemblies of God and the Apostolic Church. Many of these groups of churches are black-led.

The more recent Charismatic Movement might also be called Neo-Pentecostalism. This arose in the 1950s in the United States of America and involved Baptists, Episcopalians, Lutherans, Methodists, Presbyterians and by 1967 Roman Catholics as well.

> Since 1972, the Vatican has held annual theological conversations with representatives of both the old and new Pentecostalism, from which a measure of mutual understanding has flowed. In 1975, Pope Paul VI received 10,000 charismatics in Rome, thanks largely to the good offices of the Belgian Cardinal Suenens, whose whole ministry has been reshaped by the charismatic renewal.
>
> Christians today have to rediscover the heart of the Christian message; they have been sufficiently 'sacramentalized'; they have not been sufficiently 'evangelized'. We are now faced with the task of rediscovering and explaining what really makes a Christian. We must help Christians to become more continually aware of their faith and to live it on a more personal level. Many must exchange a sociological or inherited Christianity for a full and active life of faith, based on a personal decision and embraced with full consciousness.[3]

The movement became important in England in the late 1960s and spread into all the major denominations. Later on a few schisms from some denominations occurred which resulted in the formation of house churches. Such groups are now the fastest growing parts of English Christianity and worshippers probably number about 200,000 at present and an estimated 250,000 by the end of the century. This rate of growth from about one hundred in 1970 is truly phenomenal and works out at about 13% per annum at a time when the major denominations are losing members at around 1% to 2% per annum. Numbers belonging to the newer movements worldwide are reckoned to be about four hundred million. Ian Cotton, in his popular presentation of the phenomenon, deliberately calls the groups Evangelical/Charismatic and reckons that they represent about one quarter of the world's Christians now and will total about one third by the end of the century. Cotton suggests that the quality which marks out this 'new' form of Christianity is the rediscovery of the supernatural. There is an expectation that God is an intervening God who is interested in the details of everyday; money will drop through the letterbox in answer to prayer; people will get jobs in a time of economic depression; God will heal the sick, even those given up by the medical profession. Such an expectation might be questioned in a sceptical world where evidence of a knockdown quality is needed which allows no room for doubt. The new Christians do not hesitate to proclaim that there is no doubt that the power of God can be proved time and again for whose who have faith.

The Hallelujah Revolution, Ian Cotton's book about the new Christians, shows that the period through which we have been moving has been a time of deep uncertainty. Just to catalogue the recent changes is to recognize the dislocating effects that they have produced: the break up of the Soviet Union and the diminution of the nuclear threat; the reunification of Germany; the certainty that workers in some industries would never work again; the decline of economic expectations for the middle classes; the increase in world population; the threat to the environment of massive pollution; the large increase in crime rates creating massive fears in many urban areas. The places where uncertainty has made its largest inroads would seem to be where steady incomes and the building up of family life, in houses bought on substantial mortgages, have been the expectation. The middle classes brought up on the work ethic have suddenly become vulnerable and the collapse of that which gave meaning to life as a 'this-wordly' attachment leaves the field open for the unfashionable 'religion' to take its place. Religion, for many years an optional activity in the West in its charismatic form, suddenly has ceased for many to be optional and has become of absolute value.

The Pentecostal movement may be seen as a reaction against the arid rationalism of the twentieth century. Others may view it as a movement which counters the prevailing secular and materialistic spirit of the age. It could be seen as an expression of man's longing for the 'otherness', the 'transcendent', some would say the 'supernatural'. Pentecostals see it as a gift from God to renew and restore his church.[4]

This can be seen for example in one of the more important and widespread manifestations of the house church movement, the Icthus fellowship which has one of its outlets in the Peckham area of South London. Icthus was set up in 1974 and grew to forty-two congregations mainly in London and the South East with some 2,100 adults at its meetings. Icthus takes its name from the Greek for 'fish', the early acronym for 'Jesus Christ, Son of God and Saviour' in the early church. It has had enormous effects on the social life of the areas in which its groups are set and has not proved to be interested only in those areas of life normally labelled 'religious'. For example, they run a launderette which has become something of a social centre, they have begun several nurseries and even a primary school, while an important project helps unemployed people to find work. Their positive successes are estimated at 75% for finding gainful employment, compared with 28% for comparable local schemes. An interesting difference from normal employment offices is that all employed in the Pecan project, as it is known, from the manager to the cleaners, earn the same yearly amount. An evangelical/charismatic group doing such charitable works and living in the community is somewhat rare but the motivation is partly to make disciples in the area and the charismatic input by means of worship and small groups is significant. Into this 'praise with tongues' environment they hope to draw others. The environment is 'holistic' and these new types of Christian are concerned to draw the body and soul together by means of their Christianity.

> Both New Age and New Christians are very big on making the body-and-mind (or soul) (or unconscious) re-connection apropos of healing. And in the case of New Christianity this process is unquestionably part of a broader promotion of the body from its traditional, lowly Christian status to something very much loftier. That hyper-physical hymn-singing, the new, more formal traditions of 'liturgical dance', the touchy-feely 'love hugs' at the Dawn

Conference, the young women in Gerald Coates' congregation, happily presenting their sexuality, visually, in church – all suggest a new balance of power between body and soul.[5]

The most famous representative of the house churches and a member of Icthus is the song writer Graham Kendrick. It would probably be true to say that in evangelical/charismatic circles he has become more famous than Isaac Watts or Charles Wesley. Kendrick has the advantage of being able to write lyrics which are Bible based which he then sets to tunes which are mainly of the catchy, ballad-like type that people hear on their television every day. The gift of doing this is not to be sneezed at; Charles Wesley would probably have envied it in his day and it is well known that he set some of his eighteenth-century hymns to popular tunes. A lot of Graham Kendrick's work is available in the popular song-book *Mission Praise*,[6] which is used not only by the groups described as 'house church/charismatic/evangelical' but by many mainline churches as well.

Here is one example of a song that manages to combine popular appeal in its tune with good theology:

From heaven You came, helpless babe,
entered our world, Your glory veiled,
not to be served but to serve,
and give Your life that we might live.
   This is our God, the Servant King,
   He calls us now to follow Him,
   to bring our lives as a daily offering
   of worship to the Servant King.

There in the garden of tears
my heavy load He chose to bear;
His heart with sorrow was torn,
'Yet not my will but yours,' He said.
   This is our God . . .

Come see His hands and His feet,
the scars that speak of sacrifice,
hands that flung stars into space
to cruel nail surrendered.
   This is our God . . .

So let us learn how to serve
and in our lives enthrone Him,
each other's needs to prefer,
for it is Christ we're serving.
    This is our God . . . [7]

Many other songs available in *Mission Praise* both in their theology
and in their musical settings fail to come near to the standard of
Kendrick. This is a pity if we think that theology cannot come into the
hymns that we sing and that when we sing we have to forget that we
have brains.

Evangelical/charismatics feel that attitudes to the supernatural went
wrong in the 1930s and a whole generation grew up which turned its
back on Christianity in all its forms. This generation became dedicated
to 'the classical scientism of the European Enlightenment'. In
shorthand, this meant that science became a sort of enthroned god;
'there is nothing science won't be able to do one day'. It also meant that
a purely rational view of the world would prevail and certainly the world
was not a place where one might look for the supernatural. Miracles did
not happen in the real world, as David Hume was said to have proved
many years before. That the supernatural would not lie down and die as
was shown when the post-war period proved to some extent to be 'an
age of faith', exemplified in the interest that was shown when the
evangelist Billy Graham came for the London mission at Harringay in
1957. Although books like *Honest to God* put a damper on supernatural
religion for some people in the early 1960s, and although 'That Was the
Week that Was' satirized everything from religion to the monarchy, it
was the same decade that the charismatic movement arrived in England
and people began to experience the power of the Spirit in new ways.
One of the ways was in the ministry of healing. Here was an area where
people could find real evidence of divine activity; a hopeless cancer
victim after laying-on of hands was able to live another twenty years; a
withered leg was made normal; a woman dying with deep resentments
was able to forgive not only her family but even life itself for not being
perfect. Critics of such 'healings' have often believed that wrong
diagnoses are at the heart of such 'miracles'.

In the UK, for instance, medicine's best-known miracle investig-
ator has long been Dr Peter May, a Southampton-based GP.

Dr May is himself a committed Christian, a member of the General Synod. He has been investigating claims of supernatural healing for twenty years . . .

Today he investigates such claims with the help of some five thousand colleagues worldwide, members of the Christian Medical Fellowship – and a profoundly rigorous, left-hemispherical affair it all is. In twenty years, in fact, Dr May believes he has not yet encountered one single medically-proven claim.[8]

However, to the eye of faith they have happened and have become huge pieces of evidence for the existence of a God who readily intervenes in human life. Perhaps critics do not believe in this same kind of God say the charismatic/evangelicals, though he is the God of the New Testament.

Other events in the lives of the groups are far stranger. The so-called 'Toronto Blessing' of being 'slain in the Spirit', has been rubbished by many. A few months past a group of students of a sceptical turn of mind (from a theological college) went to Holy Trinity in Brompton, London, where some of the group received the experience, in spite of themselves. Under the influence of prayer they collapsed backwards and felt a sense of peace and inward blessing. The Toronto church was a place of truly way-out charismatic experience which began in 1994 with the manifestation of 'slaying in the Spirit'. Over three thousand churches in England are said to have experienced it; uncontrollable laughter, moaning, barking like dogs, crashing to the floor after being slain in the Spirit. As somebody has said, we are all primal screamers now. Some theology approaches the bizarre and it is fair to say that most charismatic/evangelical groups are close to fundamentalist in their interpretation of the Bible. That would not be too bad if all the New Testament contained were the Sermon on the Mount. But there are passages which are milked for significance. Paul's expectation of the end is there in I Thessalonians and some groups expect to be caught up with the Lord in the air one day, leaving their empty cars motoring at 70 mph (not 80 mph, after all they are law-abiding) down the motorway, enabling them, perhaps, to get even with the lorries that hug the middle lane. Others look desperately for the sign of the beast whose mark is 666 in Revelation, and they find it in new technology and in numbers on credit cards, even in the effect on the ozone layer. Such 'lunatic fringes' exist more in the charismatic/evangelical groups than they do in the mainline churches. Perhaps there is something to be said for biblical criticism after all.

Ecumenically, the charismatic/evangelical groups are a mixed bag. In a local mission in South London a local house church joined in very happily and committed itself to the work and method of the mission in the way that the other churches did not. Their membership increased considerably and they showed the more conventional churches how to take spiritual risks in telling personal faith stories to their neighbours. The Pecan project in Peckham has been a classic example of inter-denominational co-operation. About 60% of the staff are Icthus members and the others include Baptists, Pentecostalists and Anglicans. Perhaps this is an example where doctrine divides and service unites. The doctrine which has in fact been able to unite the denominations and the house churches has been that of the priesthood of all believers. All Christian believers are equal and share the same priesthood, which takes away all sense of untoward reverence for priests and ministers. When groups march for Jesus, the denominational walls tumble. When they sing the same songs they are one in the Spirit.

> Jesus, stand among us
>   at the meeting of our lives,
> be our sweet agreement
>   at the meeting of our eyes;
> O Jesus, we love You,
>   so we gather here,
> join our hearts in unity
>   and take away our fear.
>
> So to You we're gathering
>   out of each and every land,
> Christ the love between us
>   at the joining of our hands;
> O Jesus, we love You,
>   so we gather here,
> join our hearts in unity
>   and take away our fear.[9]

The main thing noticed by North Americans about the English scene is the reconciliation between the denominations. The charismatic experience has enabled all types of people to lift up their hands in praise of God, in the power of the Spirit. Denominations are not needed if God is in the midst of us. Now where did we hear something like that before?

19

Finding the Perfect Church

It will be obvious from all that has gone before that the quest for the perfect church is at the moment futile. None of us has all that it takes to make us complete. While the Roman Catholics might claim completeness for their version of Christianity, many Protestants would argue that this completeness is illusory because they have raised 'pious opinions', for example about Mary, into dogmatic formulae that have to be believed. They might also argue that the Roman Catholic Church is like a warehouse where you can get almost anything. The problem is that some things on the shelves have not been taken down for years, perhaps for centuries. The Bible, for example, collected dust in the Catholic warehouse until Vatican II brought it off the shelves again and made it available.

Roman Catholics might well retort that the shelves of the Protestant warehouse are somewhat bare. Where, for example, is the shelf marked 'saints' and the shelf marked 'Blessed Virgin Mary'. These should surely be on any church's warehouse shelves. So the argument could go on about over abundance in one warehouse and only very basic stocks in the other warehouses.

But at the level where people are actually being attracted into church buildings and into church communities, doctrines do not at first create the major pull. Initially at least people look for things such as an acceptable welcome, a reasonable seat where the worship actions can be seen taking place and where the worship is comprehensible. Perhaps comfortable seats and a well-heated building are not absolutely necessary, but they do help when one has to stay in the place for an hour or even more than an hour.

It is fascinating to offer a couple of league tables in order to see how different groups come in the leagues when they are given marks out of five for their performance in each area of importance. Many other areas could be suggested but for the moment we shall divide them into the areas that are important on the human side of the life of the churches and those that emphasize the God-ward side of things. All this is necessarily over simple but it may serve to illustrate church differences.

On the 'human side' we ask questions as follows:

1. Is the church (or community) welcoming to those who come in from outside their community?

2. Does the church offer some kind of community life within its own boundaries, such as clubs and other organizations?

3. Are people drawn easily into worship and is the worship easy to understand?

4. Do the lay people of the church find it possible to make significant contributions in worship?

5. Is the church concerned about the political implications of Christianity and does it make a significant contribution to the social and political life of the area?

6. Are individuals able to grow in their Christian life and experience by being part of the church?

7. How committed is the church to ecumenical relationships to other local churches?

8. Is the church committed to the task of making disciples by evangelical endeavours?

On the 'divine' side we ask the following questions:

1. Does the worship of the church leave the impression that God is being encountered, i.e. is there a sense in worship of what has been called 'the numinous?'

2. Is there a clear feeling that this church forms a continuity with the earliest expressions of Christian faith, i.e. is there a sense of continuity with the doctrines of the apostles?

3. Is there continuity with the past in the sense of an appreciation of the communion of saints and the Blessed Virgin Mary?

4. Of what significance is the Bible in the worship of the church?

5. Do the classical creeds have a regular place in worship?

6. Are the sacraments celebrated regularly?

7. Does the Holy Spirit have a significant place in the worship of the church?

8. Does the church have a recognizable system of oversight for its

members so that they can grow in that holiness without which no one
will see the Lord (Heb. 12.14)?

Since we have chosen eight questions in each case, we will choose
eight sample English denominations and offer marks out of five for
each category. The denominations are:

1. The Baptists of the Baptist Union of Great Britain and Ireland
   (Bapts)
2. The Black Pentecostals such as the Shiloh United Church of
   Christ (BlPen)
3. The Church of England, at its high Anglo–Catholic end
   (CofEH)
4. The Church of England, at its lower Evangelical end (CofEL)
5. The Methodist Church in Great Britain (MethC)
6. The Roman Catholic Church in England and Wales (RoCth)
7. The Russian Orthodox Church (ROrth)
8. The United Reformed Church (UtdRC)

The marks offered only reflect my prejudices and my experience
of the churches involved. Others might give entirely different
numbers in all cases. The 'person-centred' church league table
looks like this:

	Baps	BlPen	CofEH	CofEL	MethC	RoCth	ROrth	UtdRC
1. Welcome	4	5	2	3	4	2	2	3
2. C'tty Life	4	2	2	3	4	2	1	4
3. W'ship Easy	4	5	2	3	4	1	1	4
4. Lay Contrbn	4	5	1	4	3	2	1	3
5. Polit imp	1	3	4	2	4	3	1	4
6. Indiv grow	5	3	2	4	3	3	2	4
7. Ecumenism	1	2	2	2	4	4	3	5
8. Evangelism	5	5	2	5	3	1	1	3
	28	30	17	26	29	18	12	29

Here the Black Pentecostal churches get the highest scores with the
United Reformed and Methodists coming a close second. Those
churches that stress a more 'objective' view of worship and church
life clearly are nearer the bottom of this league table.

When it comes to what are often regarded as the more 'God-centred' or objective aspects of church life, the table takes on a very different look and it seems as if those formerly last become first:

	Baps	BlPen	CofEH	CofEL	MethC	RoCth	ROrth	UtdRC
1. Numinous	1	3	4	2	2	4	5	2
2. Continuity	1	1	4	2	2	4	5	2
3. Saints, BVM	1	2	4	1	1	5	5	1
4. Signif Bible	5	4	3	5	4	3	3	4
5. Creeds	1	1	4	3	2	5	5	2
6. Sacraments	2	1	4	3	2	5	5	2
7. Holy Spirit	4	5	2	4	3	2	2	3
8. Oversight	4	4	2	3	3	4	2	2
	19	21	27	23	19	32	32	18

Here the winners are the Roman Catholics and the Russian Orthodox, as might have been expected.

When the two tables are taken together and the scores added up, the range between the eight church groups goes from 51 (the Black Pentecostals) to 44 (the Russian Orthodox). What is surprising here is not so much that the Black Pentecostals look to have won the overall race to be the best church to join, but that the range is so small. It seems as if all the church groups we have explored have scored significantly closely over the two ranges of activity. If people feel a little cheated by these results let them do the tables in the same way as has been done here, i.e. put down 'subjective' things and then 'objective' things. One dares to hope that the final answers might be nearly the same as above. What all this seems to show is that no one church can really claim to 'have it all' and to be the ideal church to which everyone ought to belong. All churches are high scoring in some areas and low scoring in others. It seems that on the evidence of the tables, we are all deficient in our ability to be complete and able to cater for all types of peoples and temperaments, to be 'catholic' in the sense of the creeds. May it not be that all the present churches in England have to say to each other, 'I need your faith to make mine whole.'

Bibliography

This bibliography is not an exhaustive one, but contains, in addition to the titles referred to in the textual notes, works which may be of interest to those who might like to take further any of the information provided in the previous chapters.

Anglican/Methodist International Commission, *Sharing in the Apostolic Communion*, Anglican Consultative Council/World Methodist Council 1993

Anglican–Methodist Unity. 2 The Scheme, SPCK/Epworth Press 1968

Anglican/Roman Catholic International Commission (ARCIC), *The Final Report*, CTS/SPCK 1982

ARCIC II, *Salvation and the Church*, CTS/CHP 1987

ARCIC II, *Church as Communion*, CTS/CHP 1991

ARCIC II, *Life in Christ*, CTS/CHP 1993

Bebbington, David, *Evangelicalism in Modern Britain*, Unwin Hyman 1989

Bede, *An Ecclesiastical History of the English People*, Penguin 1955

Bettenson, Henry (ed), *Documents of the Christian Church*, OUP 1967

Boff, Leonard, *The Maternal Face of God*, Harper & Row 1987

Bonhoeffer, Dietrich, *Letters and Papers from Prison*. The Enlarged Edition, SCM Press 1971

British Roman Catholic/Methodist Committee, *Mary, Mother of the Lord*, CTS/MPH 1995

Brogan, Denis, *The English People*, Hamish Hamilton 1943

Brox, Norbert, *A History of the Early Church*, SCM Press 1994

Campenhausen, Hans von, *The Fathers of the Greek Church*, A. & C. Black 1963

Carpenter, Edward (ed), *The Archbishop Speaks*, Evans Brothers 1958

Churches Together in England, *Churches Together in Marriage*, CTE 1994

Churches Together in England, *Called to be One*, CTE 1996

Conversations between the Church of England and the Methodist Church. A Report to the Archbishops of Canterbury and York and the Conference of the Methodist Church, CIO/Epworth Press 1963

Cotton, Ian, *The Hallelujah Revolution*, Little, Brown 1995

Davies, Horton, *The Worship of the English Puritans*, Dacre Press 1948

Dickens, A. G., *The English Reformation*, Batsford 1964

Drane, John, *Introducing the New Testament*, Lion 1986

Duffy, Eamon, *The Stripping of the Altars*, Yale University Press 1992

Dunn, James D. G., *Unity and Diversity in the New Testament*, SCM Press, 2nd edn 1990

Ellis, Christopher, *Together on the Way*, BCC 1990

Flannery, Austin (ed), *Vatican Council II: The Conciliar and Post Conciliar Documents*, Fowler Wright 1981

Hemphill, B., *The Early Vicars Apostolic of England*, Burns and Oates 1954

Hill, Christopher and Yarnold, Edward (eds), *Anglicans and Roman Catholics: The Search for Unity*, SPCK 1994

Hillerbrand, Hans J., *The Reformation in its Own Words*, SCM Press 1964

Houlden, J. L. (ed), *The Interpretation of the Bible in the Church*, SCM Press 1995

Inter-Church Process, *Observations*, BCC/CTS 1986

Inter-Church Process, *Reflections*, BCC/CTS 1986

Inter-Church Process, *Views from the Pews*, BCC/CTS 1986

Jackson, Michael and Butler, David, *Catholics and Methodists*, CTS/MPH 1988

Jeffery, R. M. C., *Case Studies in Unity*, SCM Press 1969

John Paul II, *Ut Unum Sint*, CTS 1995

Jones, Cunliffe, Wainwright, Geoffrey and Yarnold, Edward (eds), *The Study of Spirituality*, SPCK 1986

Käsemann, Ernst, 'The Canon of the New Testament and the Unity of the Church' in *Essays on New Testament Themes*, SCM Press 1964

Kerridge, Roy, *The Storm is Passing Over*, Thames and Hudson 1995

Kidd, B. J., *Documents Illustrative of the History of the Church*, 3 vols, SPCK 1920, 1932, 1941

Lewis, C. S., *Mere Christianity*, Bles 1952; Collins Fontana 1955

Luther, Martin, *Works*, 55 vols, 1958ff. First 30 vols by Concordia Publishing House, St Louis; others by Fortress Press, Minneapolis

McGrath, Alister, *Reformation Thought*, Blackwell 1988

MacLeod, George, *Only One Way Left*, Iona Community 1956

Matthews, John, *The Unity Scene*, BCC 1986

Meyer, Harding and Vischer, Lukas (eds), *Growth in Understanding*, Paulist Press/WCC 1984

Neill, Stephen, *The Church and Christian Unity*, OUP 1968

Newton, John, *Heart Speaks to Heart*, DLT 1994

Nunn, Roger, *This Growing Unity*, CTE 1995

Palmer, Derek, *Strangers No Longer*, Hodder 1990

Pickering, W. S. F., *Anglo–Catholicism*, Routledge 1989; new edn SPCK 1991

Pittenger, *Our Lady*, SCM Press 1996

Rouse, Ruth and Neill, Stephen, *A History of the Ecumenical Movement 1517–1948*, SPCK 1954

Rupp, Gordon, *Studies in the Making of the English Protestant Tradition*, CUP 1966

Rupp, Gordon, and Drewery, Benjamin (eds), *Martin Luther*, Open University 1970

Russell, Colin, *Crosscurrents*, IVP 1985

Stacpoole, Alberic (ed), *Mary's Place in Christian Dialogue*, St Paul Publications 1982

Staniforth, Maxwell (ed), *Early Christian Writings*, Penguin 1968

Steere, Douglas V., *Quaker Spirituality: Selected Writings*, SPCK 1984

Stevenson, J. (ed), *A New Eusebius: Documents illustrating the history of the Church to AD337*, SPCK 1957; new edn, revised by W. H. C. Frend, 1987 (page refs are to the original edition)

Stevenson, J. (ed), *Creeds, Councils and Controversies*, SPCK 1966; new edn, revised by W. H. C. Frend, 1989 (pages refs are to the original edition)

Sykes, N., *From Sheldon to Secker*, CUP 1959

Tabraham, Barrie, *The Making of Methodism*, Epworth Press 1995

Tavard, George, *Anglican Orders: The Problems and the Solution*, Collegeville 1990

Till, Barry, *The Churches Search for Unity*, Penguin 1972

Tillard, Jean, *The Bishop of Rome*, SPCK 1983

Towards Visible Unity: Proposals for a Covenant, Churches' Council for Covenanting 1980

Underwood, A. C., *A History of the English Baptists*, Carey Kingsgate Press 1947

Wakefield, Gordon S. (ed), *A Dictionary of Christian Spirituality*, SCM Press 1983

Ward, Neville, *Five for Sorrow, Ten for Joy*, Epworth Press 1972; reissued DLT 1993

Watts, Michael, *The Dissenters*, Vol 1, Clarendon Press 1978

Welch, Elizabeth and Winfield, Flora, *Travelling Together*, CTE 1995

Wesley, John, *Journal* ed. Nehemiah Curnock, 8 vols, new edn Epworth Press 1938

White, Gavin, *The Mother Church Your Mother Never Told You Of*, SCM Press 1993

Wilkinson, John, *Church in Black and White*, St Andrew 1993

World Methodist Council, *Towards a Statement on the Church* (Nairobi Report), 1986

World Methodist Council, *The Apostolic Tradition* (Singapore Report), 1991

Notes

Where publication details are given in the Bibliography, they are not repeated here

Introduction

1. Published by the World Methodist Council, 1991

1. *Was the Church United in New Testament Times?*

1. Kasemann, 'The Canon of the New Testament and the Unity of the Church', p. 103.

2. *What's Worth Keeping from the Early Church?*

1. *Confessing One Faith*, Faith & Order Paper No. 140, WCC, Geneva 1987.
2. Campenhausen, *The Fathers of the Greek Church*, p. 1.
3. John Calvin, *Institutes of the Christian Religion*, Bk 4, ch. III.
4. Ignatius of Antioch, *To the Smyrnaeans*, VIII; see Stevenson, *A New Eusebius*, p. 48.
5. From *The Constitutional Practice and Discipline of the Methodist Church*, Vol. 2, Methodist Publishing House 1994, p. 213.
6. *Dogmatic Constitution on the Church*, 29.
7. Justin, *Apology*, 65; see Stevenson, *A New Eusebius*, p. 66–67.
8. From the Council of Carthage, 251; see Stevenson, *A New Eusebius*, p. 238.
9. See Horton Davies, *The Worship of the English Puritans*, p. 234.

3. *A Theology of Ecumenism*

1. Stephen Neill, *The Church and Christian Unity*, p. 402.
2. Christopher Ellis, *Together on the Way*, p. 130.
3. Ibid., p. 93.
4. Ibid., p. 132.
5. Emmanuel Sullivan, 'Ecumenical Spirituality' in Wakefield (ed), *A Dictionary of Christian Spirituality*, p. 126.

6. Stephen Neill, quoted in Rouse and Neill (eds), *A History of the Ecumenical Movement 1517–1948*, p. 495.

7. Ellis, op.cit., p. 122.

4. *Past Problems in a Nutshell*

1. See Bettenson, *Documents of the Christian Church*, pp. 36, 37.

2. See Stevenson, *A New Eusebius*, pp. 97f.

3. Ibid., p. 113.

4. Ibid., p. 188.

5. Ibid., p. 115.

6. Ibid., pp. 97f.

7. See Kidd, *Documents Illustrative of the History of the Church II*, p. 69.

8. See Stevenson, *A New Eusebius*, pp. 97f.

9. See Stevenson, *Creeds, Councils and Controversies*, p. 291.

10. Ibid., p. 319.

11. See Trevor Jalland, *The Church and the Papacy*, pp. 256f.

12. See Bettenson, *Documents of the Christian Church*, p. 97.

5. *The Reformation Divides and Subdivides*

1. Martin Luther, Autobiographical Fragment 1545; quoted in Rupp and Drewery *Martin Luther*, pp. 5f.

2. Quoted in Rupp and Drewery, *Martin Luther*, p. 60.

3. See G. R. Potter (ed), *Huldrych Zwingli*, Edward Arnold 1978, pp. 108f.

4. Carpenter, *Cantuar*, p. 140.

5. Watts, *The Dissenters*, p. 30.

6. Underwood, *A History of the English Baptists*, p. 59.

7. The full text of the Declaration of Breda can be found in S. R. Gardiner, *The Constitutional Documents of the Puritan Revolution 1625–1660*, Oxford 1889, pp. 465–67.

8. Richard Baxter, *The Reformed Pastor* ed. Wilkinson, London 1939, pp. 84f.

9. George Fox, Epistle 149 (1657) in Steere (ed), *Quaker Spirituality*, p. 131.

10. *Reflections*, London 1986, p. 18.

11. Ibid., p. 18.

12. Ibid., p. 74.

13. Ibid., p. 79.

14. Ibid., p. 84.

15. Ibid., p. 53.

16. Quoted by G. Nuttall in *Richard Baxter*, Nelson 1965, p. 129.

6. Strange Ideas: Protestant

1. Quoted in Gordon Rupp, *Studies in the Making of the English Protestant Tradition*, p. 23.
2. *The Martyrdom of Polycarp* in Stevenson (ed), *A New Eusebius*, p. 21.
3. Heinrich Bullinger (Zurich Reformer) *Reformationsgeschichte*, I, pp. 237–39. Translated and quoted in Hillerbrand, *The Reformation in its Own Words*, p. 228.

7. Strange Ideas: Catholic

1. Maisie Ward, *The Wilfred Wards and the Transition*, Sheed and Ward 1934, p. 8.
2. Vatican II, *Dei Verbum* (Dogmatic Constitution on Divine Revelation), 8, 9.
3. *Lumen Gentium*, 6.
4. Leonardo Boff, *The Maternal Face of God*, p. 102.

8. Is there Convergence about the Bible?

1. *Dei Verbum*, 22.
2. Martin Luther, *Table Talk* (1540), *Works*, LIV, p. 406.
3. Colin A. Russell, *Crosscurrents*, pp. 128f.
4. The Pontifical Biblical Commission's document *The Interpretation of the Bible in the Church* was published in February in instalments in a journal with limited circulation, and was therefore not easily accessible. It was reissued, with a collection of responses and reviews, in *The Interpretation of the Bible in the Church* ed. J. L. Houlden, SCM Press 1995. Subsequent page references are to this edition.
5. *Interpretation*, p. 56.
6. *Interpretation*, p. 46.
7. *Interpretation*, p. 94.

9. The English Scene: Why are Protestants so Suspicious of Catholics?

1. Bede, *An Ecclesiastical History of the English People*, pp. 101f.
2. From Bettenson, *Documents of the Christian Church*, p. 164.
3. A. G. Dickens, *The English Reformation*, p. 132.
4. See Bettenson, *Documents of the Christian Church*, pp. 240–44.
5. Hemphill, *The Early Vicars Apostolic of England*, p. 16.
6. Cardinal Newman, 'Letter to His Grace the Duke of Norfolk' in A. Ryan (ed), *Newman and Gladstone: The Vatican Decrees*, Notre Dame Press 1962, p. 138.

7. W. S. F. Pickering, *Anglo-Catholicism*, p. 22.
8. John Paul II, *Ut Unum Sint*, 1995, para. 88.

10. Why Can't Anglicans and Methodists Make It?

1. University Sermon of Archbishop Geoffrey Fisher, 'A Step Forward in Church Relations', Great St Mary's University Sermon, 3 November 1946 in *The Archbishop Speaks*, pp. 64ff.
2. John Wesley, Preface to *The Sunday Service of the Methodists in North America*, London 1784.
3. John Wesley, *Journal*, 24 May 1938.
4. John Wesley, *Journal*, 20 January 1746.
5. A dissentient view in *Conversations*, pp. 58f.
6. From the Acts of Reconciliation as set out in *Anglican–Methodist Unity. 2 The Scheme*, pp. 159f.
7. Stephen Neill, *The Church and Christian Unity*, p. 402.
8. Fisher, 'A Step Forward in Church Relations', op.cit., p. 65.

11. What of Catholics and Anglicans?

1. Du Pin, *Commonitorium*, quoted in Sykes, *From Sheldon to Secker*, pp. 124f.
2. Cardinal Henry Vaughan in 1893 at the Catholic Conference in Preston. See J. Snead-Cox, *Life of Cardinal Vaughan*, II, London 1910, pp. 157f.
3. Anglican–Roman Catholic International Commission, *The Final Report*.
4. Ibid., pp. 13f.
5. Ibid., p. 21.
6. Ibid., p. 33.
7. Ibid., pp. 34f.
8. Ibid., p. 35.
9. Ibid., p. 44.
10. Ibid., p. 55.
11. Ibid., p. 58.
12. Ibid., p. 64.
13. *Salvation and the Church*, p. 13.
14. *Church as Communion*, p. 29.
15. *Life in Christ*, pp. 1, 3.
16. Meeting between Pope John II and Archbishop George Carey, 25 May 1992, recorded in Hill and Yarnold (eds), *Anglicans and Roman Catholics*, p. 185.
17. George Tavard, *Anglican Orders: The Problem and the Solution*, p. 137.
18. Priscilla Chadwick and Maria Gladwell, *Joint Schools*, English Anglican –Roman Catholic Committee, Norwich 1987.

19. Edward Yarnold in Stacpoole (ed), *Mary's Place in Christian Dialogue*, p. 130.

12. What of Methodists and Catholics?

1. Wesley, *Journal*, 27 August 1739.
2. The Reports from the Denver, Dublin and Honolulu Conferences are collected together in Meyer and Vischer (eds), *Growth in Agreement*. The Nairobi and Singapore Reports are published by the World Methodist Council.
3. Honolulu Report, paras 34, 35.
4. Nairobi Report, para 20.
5. Ibid., para 23.
6. Ibid., para 55.
7. Ibid., para 58.
8. Singapore Report, para 51.
9. Ibid., paras 13, 21.
10. Ibid., para 86.
11. English Roman Catholic/Methodist Committee: *Marriages with Roman Catholics*, MPH 1990; 'Justification: a Consensus Statement' in *One in Christ*, 1988–3, pp. 270ff.; *Can the Roman Catholic and Methodist Churches be Reconciled?*, MPH 1992. British Roman Catholic/Methodist Committee: *Mary, Mother of the Lord – Sign of Grace, Faith and Holiness*, CTS/MPH 1995.

13. We Are All Members One of Another

1. *The UK Christian Churches Handbook 1994/95*, Christian Research 1994.
2. Denis Brogan, *The English People*, p. 121.
3. See R. M. C. Jeffrey, *Case Studies in Unity*, p. 77. Jeffrey is quoting from *Unity Begins at Home*: A Report from the First British Conference on Faith and Order, Nottingham 1964, SCM Press 1964.
4. Gordon Wakefield in J. Champ (ed), *Oscott College 1838–1988*, Birmingham 1988, pp. 14f.
5. The Swanwick Declaration can be found in *Churches Together in Pilgrimage*, BCC/CTS 1989, pp. 7ff.
6. *Reflections*, London 1986, pp. 94f.
7. The Churches Unity Commission, *Ten Propositions*, BCC 1976.
8. From a 'Memorandum of Dissent' in *Towards Visible Unity*, p. 92.
9. Derek Palmer, *Strangers No Longer*, pp. 14f. Rupert Davies is being quoted from the *Church Times* of 6 October 1989.
10. *Pilgrim Post*, monthly newsheet of Churches Together in England, Issue no. 8.

14. The New Ecumenical Scene: Not Strangers But Pilgrims, *and After*

1. Contribution from the House Churches to the Inter-Church Process publication *Observations*, p. 38.
2. Inter-Church Process, *Reflections*, pp. v, vi.
3. East Midlands contribution to the Inter-Church process publication *Views from the Pews*, p. 33.
4. See Derek Palmer, *Strangers No Longer*, p. 64.
5. See ch. 13, no. 5.
6. Ruth Reardon, in the Interchurch Families Annual Report, 1994.
7. Neville Ward, *Five for Sorrow, Ten for Joy*, p. ix.

15. Do the Reformation Controversies Still Divide?

1. *Salvation and the Church*, p. 17.
2. Ibid.
3. For this Lutheran–Roman Catholic Dialogue (1980) see Meyer and Vischer (eds), *Growth in Agreement*, p. 243.
4. *The Final Report*, pp. 62f.
5. Authority in the Church I, *The Final Report*, p. 57.
6. Nairobi Report, para 58.
7. Authority in the Church II, *The Final Report*, p. 97.
8. Ibid., p. 98.
9. Luther, *Works*, XXXVII, p. 18f.
10. Lutheran–Roman Catholic Dialogue (1978); see Meyer and Vischer (eds), *Growth in Agreement*, p. 196, para 16.
11. Eucharistic Doctrine, *The Final Report*, p. 14.
12. From the Denver Report in *Growth in Agreement*, pp. 326f.
13. Luther, *Works*, XL, pp. 240f.
14. Mary Tanner, Moderator of the Faith and Order Commission of the WCC, from a lecture given at The Queen's College, Birmingham, 22 April 1992.
15. *Church as Communion*, para 43.
16. Nairobi Report, para 23.
17. Ibid., para 43.
18. Lutheran–Roman Catholic Dialogue (1980); see Meyer and Fischer (eds), *Growth in Agreement*, p. 221, para 33.
19. *Reflections*, pp. 37ff.

16. Ecumenical Convergence in Spirituality

1. In *The Church Quarterly*, October 1968, p. 151.

2. In his Preface to *A Dictionary of Christian Spirituality*, p. v.
3. John Paul II, *Ut Unum Sint*, 1995, 70.
4. *Lumen Gentium*, 40.
5. George MacLeod, *Only One Way Left*, pp. 151f.
6. Dietrich Bonhoeffer, *Letters and Papers from Prison*, p. 361.
7. John Townroe in James, Wainwright, Yarnold (eds), *The Study of Spirituality*, p. 580.

18. The New Scene: The New Christians

1. David Bebbington, *Evangelicalism in Modern Britain*, p. 91.
2. W. J. Hollenweger, *The Pentecostals*, SCM Press 1972.
3. Cardinal Suenens, in John Newton, *Heart Speaks to Heart*, pp. 109, 114.
4. W. R. Davies in Wakefield (ed), *A Dictionary of Christian Spirituality*, p. 297.
5. Ian Cotton, *The Hallelujah Revolution*, p. 69.
6. *Mission Praise*, Marshal Pickering 1986. This has been followed by a number of other volumes including *Mission Praise 2, Mission Praise Combined, Junior Praise 1 and 2* and *Children's Praise*.
7. Graham Kendrick, *Mission Praise Combined*, HarperCollins 1990, no. 162. Used by permission.
8. Ian Cotton, op.cit., pp. 139f.
9. Graham Kendrick, *Mission Praise Combined*, no. 381. Used by permission.

Index